K.

Roberto Calasso

*Translated from the
Italian by Geoffrey Brock*

Alfred A. Knopf
New York

2005

THIS IS A BORZOI BOOK
PUBLISHED BY ALFRED A. KNOPF

English translation copyright © 2005 by Geoffrey Brock

*All rights reserved under International and Pan-American Copyright
Conventions. Published in the United States by Alfred A. Knopf, a division
of Random House, Inc., New York, and simultaneously
in Canada by Random House of Canada Limited,
Toronto. Distributed by Random House, Inc.,
New York.*

www.aaknopf.com

Copyright © 2002 by Adelphi Edizioni S.P.A., Milano

*Knopf, Borzoi Books, and the colophon are registered
trademarks of Random House, Inc.*

*Originally published in Italy by Adelphi
Edizioni, Milan, in 2002.*

*Library of Congress Cataloging-in-Publication Data
Calasso, Roberto.
[K. English]
K. / Roberto Calasso ; translated from the Italian by Geoff Brock.
p.   cm.
Includes bibliographical references.
ISBN 1-4000-4189-9
1. Kafka, Franz, 1883–1924—Criticism and interpretation.
I. Brock, Geoffrey, 1964– II. Title.
PT2621.A26z564513 2005
833'.912—dc22   2004059622*

Book design by Anthea Lingeman

*Manufactured in the United States of America
Published January 21, 2005
Second Printing, December 2005*

for Katharina

Contents

K.

I. The Saturnine Sovereign

At the beginning there's a wooden bridge covered with snow. Thick snow. K. lifts his eyes "toward what seemed to be emptiness," *in die scheinbare Leere.* Literally: "toward the seeming emptiness." He knows there's something out in that emptiness: the Castle. He's never seen it before. He might never set foot in it.

Kafka sensed that by then only the minimum number of elements of the surrounding world ought to be named. He plunged the sharpest Ockham's razor into the substance of the novel. To name the bare minimum, and in its pure literality. And why so? Because the world was turning back into a primeval forest, too fraught with strange noises and apparitions. Everything had too much power. Thus it became necessary to limit oneself to what lay closest at hand, to circumscribe the zone of the nameable. Then all that power, otherwise diffuse, would be channeled there, and whatever was named—an inn, a file, an office, a room—would fill with unprecedented energy.

. . .

Kafka speaks of a world that precedes every division, every naming. It's not a sacred or divine world, nor a world abandoned by the sacred or the divine. It's a world that has yet to recognize such categories, to distinguish them from everything else. Or that no longer knows how to recognize them or distinguish them from everything else. All is a single unity, and it is simply power. Both the greatest good and the greatest evil are saturated with it. Kafka's subject is that mass of power, not yet differentiated, broken down into its elements. It is the shapeless body of Vritra, which contains the waters, before Indra runs it through with a thunderbolt.

The invisible has a mocking tendency to present itself as the visible, as if it might be distinguished from everything else, but only under certain circumstances, such as the clearing away of mist. Thus one is persuaded to treat it as the visible—and is immediately punished. But the illusion remains.

The Trial and *The Castle* are stories about attempts *to deal with a case:* to extricate oneself from prosecution, to have one's nomination confirmed. The point around which everything revolves is always *election*, the mystery of election, its impenetrable obscurity. In *The Castle*, K. desires election—and this thoroughly complicates every act. In *The Trial*, Josef K. wants to escape election—and this thoroughly complicates every act. To be chosen, to be condemned: two possible outcomes of the same process. Kafka's relationship to Judaism, every recess of which has been doggedly (often fruitlessly) examined, emerges most clearly on this point, which marks the essential difference between Judaism and what surrounded it. Much more so than monotheism or law or higher morality. For each of these, one can look to Egypt, Mesopotamia, or Greece for precedents and counterbalances. But the emphasis on election—that's unique, and founded on a theology of the unique.

The court has the power to punish, the Castle, to elect. These two powers are perilously close, at times identical. More than anyone else, Kafka, thanks to atavism and inclination, had antennae to recognize them. No one else was so aware of their proximity, their overlap. But this wasn't only a matter of Jewish heritage. It had to do with everyone, and all times.

The Trial and *The Castle* share a premise: that election and condemnation are *almost* indistinguishable. That *almost* is why we have two novels rather than one. The elect and the condemned are the chosen, those who are singled out among the many, among everyone. Their isolation lies at the root of the anguish that engulfs them, whatever their fate.

The main difference is this: condemnation is always certain, election always uncertain. Unknown persons show up in Josef K.'s bedroom, devour his breakfast, and inform him that he's being prosecuted on criminal charges. The prosecution is itself already the sentence. And nothing could be as undeniable as that intrusion in front of witnesses. For K., on the other hand, doubt remains: had he really been named land surveyor? Was K. called, or did he only wish to be called? Is he the legitimate holder of an office, however modest—or a braggart who claims a title that isn't his? On this point K., who is nimble and tenacious in his analyses, proves evasive. His history, prior to the "long, difficult voyage" that brought him to the Castle, remains murky. Had he received a summons—or did he set out on his voyage in order to obtain one? There's no way to know for certain. But there are many ways to aggravate and exacerbate the uncertainty.

The village superintendent tells K.: "You've been taken on as a land surveyor, as you say, but unfortunately we have no need for a surveyor." The cruelty is not in the final phrase but in the piercing "as you say." Nor do Castle authorities ever admit anything else, leaving open until the end the possibility that K.'s belief is delusory or simply feigned.

One fact only is certain, according to the superintendent, who likes to make clear that he is "not enough of an official"—and therefore not of sufficient stature to handle such questions—since he is "a peasant and nothing more." And the fact is this: one day long ago a decree was issued ordering the appointment of a land surveyor. But that remote decree, which the superintendent would no doubt have forgotten had his illness not offered him the chance to "think back on the silliest matters," couldn't have had anything at all to do with K. Like all decrees, it hovered above everyone and everything, without specifying when and to whom it would be applied. And it has languished ever since among the papers crammed in the cabinet in the superintendent's bedroom. Though buried in that intimate, unsuitable place, it has maintained its irradiant energy.

But uncertainty's torment never ends. On one hand the superintendent continues to converse with K., implying that K. has good reasons for questioning him. On the other, he never goes so far as to recognize the legitimacy of K.'s claim—and we've known at least since Hegel that the human animal requires *only* recognition. The superintendent continues: "Even your summoning was carefully considered; it was just a few incidental details that caused confusion." K.'s summoning, then, was in fact the object of reflection on the part of the authorities—but what of their conclusion? Was K. ever called? It's a question the superintendent is careful not to answer.

A further stage of torment emerges when the superintendent—while reconstructing the complex history of the decree to appoint a land surveyor and of the village's misdirected reply, issued by the superintendent himself, to that decree (a misdirected reply evidenced, according to the reconstruction, by an "empty envelope," now misplaced)—lets it be understood that sometimes, especially "when a matter has been considered at great length," it may resolve itself "with lightning speed," "as if the official apparatus could no longer tolerate the tension," the prolonged irritation of the unresolved question, and so proceeded to eliminate it by reaching a decision "without the help of the officials." Such a possibility, therefore, does exist, as the superintendent himself admits. But could this be what has happened in K.'s case? Here again the superintendent retreats, offering no guarantees: "I don't know whether such a decision was reached in your case—some elements speak for it, others against."

K. appeals to two other pieces of evidence to support his appointment: the letter from the official Klamm, addressed to him, and the phone call from the Castle the night he first arrived at the Bridge Inn, and these also— indeed these above all—are cast into doubt. The letter from Klamm is (as the salutation alone makes plain) a personal letter, and thus worthless as an official declaration, even if it might be invaluable for other reasons. And the telephone communication can't be anything other than misleading, since "there is no definite telephone connection to the Castle." The murmur, the song that issues audibly from the phone as soon as any receiver is lifted in the village, is the Castle's only acoustic manifestation. It is indistinct and, moreover, nonlinguistic, a music composed of words gone back to their source in pure sonic matter, prior to and stripped of all meaning. The Castle communicates with the outside world through a continuous, indecipherable sound. "All the rest is misleading," says the superintendent. Starting, then, with the clear and limpid word. At this point, like a great academic who ends a seminar by sending the students off to other places and classes to continue their debates, the superintendent tells K.: "You should know by now that the question of your being called here is too difficult for us to answer for you in the course of one little conversation." But all of life is no more than a "little conversation." And so the principle of the irrepressible uncertainty of election is once again affirmed.

The worlds of *The Trial* and *The Castle* run parallel to all other worlds but not to each other. Each is, rather, the extension of the other. Josef K. becomes K. Between them, a sentence and an execution. But the story is the same— and it keeps going. Now it's not someone else who comes looking for Josef K., but K. who goes looking for something. The terms are reversed. The climate changes but remains familiar. Women, officials, clothes. Long conversations, often terribly intimate, with strangers. A nagging feeling of estrangement. "I don't yet know a great deal about your legal system," says Josef K.—despite the fact that at that moment he's in a suburb of his own city, whose legal system he, as chief officer of a bank, is used to dealing with every day. It's as if two incompatible laws hold sway simultaneously. This is strange, but for Josef K. it will quickly cease to seem so, and not just for him, but for the reader too—which is stranger still. Nothing is further from *The Trial* than the sense of the fantastic, the visionary, the "extraordinary" that we might associate with Poe. Indeed for the reader the ever present suspicion is that it's a kind of verism. The reading catches the reader by surprise, just as the guard Franz, wearing his "travel clothes," catches Josef K. by surprise in the "riskiest moment of all": that of waking. The moment when one can be easily "dragged off," if one isn't prepared. And no one, on waking, is prepared. To be so, one would need to find oneself already in an office. As K. says to Mrs. Grubach,

"For example, in the bank I'm prepared; something like this could never happen to me there."

The Trial and *The Castle* take place within the same psychic life. After the execution of his sentence, Josef K. reappears under the name K. and distances himself from the large city. *The Castle* is Josef K.'s *bardo*.

The world of the *bardo*—that "intermediate state" that the Tibetan Book of the Dead teaches how to traverse—doesn't look drastically different from the world of the living. But it doesn't easily permit return. Frieda's fantasy of running away with K.—maybe "to the south of France or to Spain"—seems as far-fetched and unattainable as a longing to live in the Egypt of the pharaohs. Entering the *bardo*, like entering a dream, requires only a slight twist of what is, but it's irreversible and skews all relations. The procedures of the court in Josef K.'s city bear an obvious kinship to those of the Castle administration, but nothing assures us that their objectives coincide. The only sure things are certain differences of style: at the Castle there is no need to expel or to kill, practices that *The Trial*'s court, perhaps more primitive, still engages in. At the Castle, it's enough that life goes on. The simple passing of time is the judgment.

What distinguishes both *The Trial* and *The Castle* is that, from the first line to the last, they unfold on the threshold of a hidden world that one suspects is implicit in this world. Never had that threshold been such a thin line or so ubiquitous. Never had those two worlds been brought so terrifyingly close as to seem to touch. We can't say for sure whether that hidden world is good or evil, heavenly or hellish. The only evidence is something that overwhelms and envelops us. Like K., we alternate between flashes of lucidity and bouts of torpor, sometimes mistaking one for the other, with no one having the authority to correct us.

Compared with all other fictional characters, K. is potentiality itself. That's why his physical appearance can never be described, directly or indirectly. We don't even know whether he has "dark eyes" like his precursor, Josef K. And it isn't because K. undergoes, as Klamm does, continuous metamorphoses, but rather because K. is the shape of what happens.

December 1910—a barren, sullen time. Kafka uses his diary now mainly to record observations on his own inability to write. "With what can I justify the fact that so far today I've written nothing? With nothing," we read in a fragment. And immediately after: "I hear in my head a continuous incantation: 'O were you to come, invisible tribunal!'"

With these words, as if he'd resorted to a powerful left-handed spell, Kafka crosses the threshold into the enclosed space of *The Trial* and *The Castle*—and indeed of all the rest of his work. This is the site of his writing, where one awaits one's sentence, endures the delays of a never-ending case. It's an agonizing place, but the only one where Kafka knows he belongs. Newly arrived in the village beneath the Castle, having already been rebuffed and harassed, K. knows only that he has "come here to stay," as if any other kind of life were already closed to him. And he repeats: "I will stay here." Then, as if "talking to himself," he adds: "What could have drawn me to this wasteland, if not the desire to stay here." The "wasteland" is the Promised Land. And the Promised Land is the only land about which one can say, as K. does: "I cannot emigrate."

To be put on trial or to have dealings with the Castle is to enter into that hidden, dangerous, elusive life from which every other life issues—and of which every other life is only a poor counterfeit. The operation of a great bank, like the one where Josef K. works, with its bright offices, its spacious lobbies, and its corridors, imitates the sordid attic that houses the court offices—not the other way around. And one needs only to open the door to a junk room, in the bank's own offices, to find the court at work, as represented by a persecutor ("the flogger") and two victims. It is the court that encompasses daily life—not daily life that accommodates the court.

Writing begins when one enters into a relationship with the court or the Castle, a relationship that always will be, literally, a lost cause. Even Josef K.'s Uncle Karl said as much, when he arrived from the country to lend his nephew a hand: "A trial like this is always lost from the start." And proverbs, they say, are always true.

.   .   .

The articulation and the workings of the "invisible tribunal" can be seen on every page of Kafka, but only in *The Trial* and *The Castle* do they become the very substance of the narrative. The court of the big city, which must judge Josef K., is the invisible tribunal, as is the apparatus of Castle offices in the distant territories of Count Westwest. The "invisible tribunal" extends its reach over everything. The Castle offices, though administrative rather than judicial, use the same kind of language as the big-city court. For both the court and the Castle, the outside world, whatever that might be or represent, is in the legal sense a *party*, and they must constantly determine what relationships to allow with said party, if ever they must allow any. Their methods too are very similar, at times indistinguishable, and always exasperating, elusive, deceptive. Yet Kafka, when he in his despair dared to invoke an entity he named "invisible tribunal," was asking nothing other than to be delivered into the hands of the court and the Castle, despite knowing what lay in store for him there. For only within such torments, he suspected, lay the life he could never have reached in any other way.

The Trial and *The Castle* take place on the same plane of the *mundus imaginalis*. They stick out there, isolated. And there exists no easy or direct way to make contact between that plane and others. Connections between the two books, however, are innumerable. Kafka wrote *The Trial*, incomplete but with an ending, in a few months in

1914. He wrote *The Castle*, incomplete and without an ending, in a few months in 1922. There are no indications that, in the time between, he ever went back to work on *The Trial*, and in 1920 he gave the manuscript to Max Brod. When he began to write *The Castle*, without recording any comments on the undertaking, it was as if he had been hurled back into that land that he alone inhabited. There, he was to behave like an expert surveyor. He had only to move a short distance—and yet that journey would be "endless"—from the city of Josef K., with its offices and staircases and attics, to the village where K. comes to offer his services to the Castle.

The court that must judge Josef K. and the Castle administration by whom K. wants to be appointed are contiguous organizations that resonate, each in the other. Both are populated by scrupulous, peevish officials. "A nervous people," the Castle dwellers. "Irascible," those of the court. They share an easily wounded sensibility, quick to detect the slightest changes—and to suffer from them. Like space, *sensorium Dei*, they form a delicate spiderweb the extent of which they themselves are not in a position to judge. But in each of them, even the lowliest, one senses the breathing of a "great organism." In the court as in the Castle, the farther you go up the hierarchy toward the top, the easier it is to get lost. Common life always unfolds below, among secretaries and substitutes, if not among servants and waiters. But the divide between those who belong to the organism and the obscure *parties* who try to make contact with it is always unbridgeable. There's a

formless and perhaps meaningless life that is everyone's
life. And then there's another life through which forms
pass like a blade—like a flashing multiplicity of blades.
Whoever has dealings with the court or the Castle gets a
taste of it. This other life is overloaded with meanings that
tend to cancel one another out. Such is the throng of
meanings attributed, or attributable, to the *proceedings*—
a word used to designate the physiology of the "great
organism"—that these proceedings ultimately appear impenetrable. The imbalance between the two worlds is per-
manent and untreatable. Even those like Huld the lawyer,
who have long been used to the company of magistrates,
reach a point where "nothing seems certain anymore."
And then they may also ask themselves the more painful
question: perhaps some trials that "in their natural course
were proceeding well, later ended up on the wrong track,
thanks precisely to our assistance," that is, to the work
of the lawyers. The implication is that any intervention,
even when carried out with the best of intentions and a
thorough knowledge of the case (it's necessary to specify
this), would be injurious, worse than useless. Only a total
passivity, therefore, like that of a plant shaken by wind,
would have even the faintest chance of leading to a successful outcome.

Between the administration of the court and that of the
Castle there is also a difference of style, of manner. Corruption, for example, figures in both. But in the court it
can take on crude, unseemly aspects. The lawyers throng
around the "corruptible employees," always with the aim

of discovering "gaps" in the nearly airtight "rigorous isolation" of the court. On occasion—"in times past," of course—there were actually cases of stolen records.

With the Castle employees, on the other hand, it seems that corruption is tolerated for reasons of elegance, in order to "avoid pointless conversations." As if the employees know that, by allowing themselves to be corrupted, they are silencing the parties who continue to importune them, offering them the illusion of having taken a useful step, even if "nothing can be achieved that way." For the Castle administration, corruption is not unlike the traffic in indulgences. But it seems to be practiced not out of self-interest but rather to impart a certain linearity and neatness to the proceedings, avoiding what must inspire profound distaste: "pointless conversations."

From the start K.'s behavior seems "suspicious," and not without reason. Awakened at an inn where he's sleeping on a straw mattress, he says: "What village have I strayed into? Is there really a Castle here?" Yet moments later he admits that he knows perfectly well where he is and did not present himself at the Castle only because the hour was late. This behavior reminds us how Kafka's readers feel: displaced, disturbed, dismayed. And yet they know exactly where they are—and why.

Mizzi, the superintendent's inconspicuous wife and assistant, has sat down on the edge of her husband's bed (and how many other revelations will come, both to K. and to Josef K., from that position) in order to read him

Klamm's letter to K. "As soon as she had taken a look at the letter she clasped her hands softly—'from Klamm,' she said." That brief aside, like a sigh, suffices to evoke the reverential fear inspired by Klamm's name and the tremendous significance attached to it—but without having to specify any of it, almost as if even naming it might diminish it. Meanwhile, everything is concentrated in those two words, "from Klamm"—a whisper that floods the sentence, and in that gesture, barely signaled, of her clasped hands. At the end of the meeting, the superintendent recalls Mizzi's presence only when his leg starts hurting again, but she has been sitting there all the time: "playing, as if lost in a dream, with Klamm's letter, which she had made into a little boat." K., "frightened," grabs it from her hand. He fears his precious page will be damaged. But, more obscurely, he fears the childish, mocking vision of that little paper boat. Without admitting it to himself, he knows that this is one of many enigmas he will encounter on his way, enigmas that are always entrusted to feminine beings, that are very often not even noticed, that are never resolved.

K. desires only to be a "little land surveyor who worked quietly at his little drawing board." He doesn't ask for special aid or salvation. But his desire, precisely because of its modesty, has shattering potential. Above all because—as K. dares to tell the superintendent—he doesn't want "gracious handouts from the Castle, but his rights." His tone is that of the free man who intends to evade not only the oppression of the powers that be but their equally untrustworthy benevolence. And who makes, at the first opportunity, a pronouncement that is particularly insulting to the authorities. As soon as one enters the realm of one's desires, and especially when these desires begin mixing with rights, the powerful apparatus of the Castle, with its procedural minutiae and its ramifying regulations, becomes ultrasensitive, ferociously rejecting every claim made by the individual—or rather, as one would say in the officials' lexicon, by the *party*. Desire is the unknown—and one cannot lay claim to the unknown. It is the unknown that reigns, not he who, through the unknown, desires. This isn't how Castle officials would put it—they are more delicate and are obliged to follow the usual formulas. But sometimes they let the word get out.

K. quickly adopts the tone of one victimized by an abuse of power. If, however, he were really incontrovertibly within his rights, he ought at least to have in hand an official letter of appointment to the post of land surveyor. But it seems that he never received such a letter. A haze of mystification hovers around K., as around everything done or said by Castle officials. So if the village peasants have a grim, distrustful air, it's because they're always having to deal with suspicious behavior, about which many contrasting hypotheses are admissible, whether it involves officials come down from the Castle or a stranger such as K. who shows up at the village inn. And to the villagers it appears suspicious in the extreme that K. shows himself ignorant of the ways of the Castle. Yet K. also seems one of *them*, if by that word we mean anyone who doesn't belong to the village. Or rather, K. seems a parody of *them*, a cardboard cutout stripped of every whiff of power.

K. almost never speaks of his past; only with the superintendent does he indulge himself a little. He insists on the "long, difficult journey" that he had to undertake—having already, moments earlier, referred to his "endless journey." The power of the Castle, which had summoned him, must therefore have extended to very distant places—and through time too, perhaps, if the traveler who approached the Castle was like an ancient wanderer, a lone figure in the snow. It is probably in order to render his situation more pathetic—we can't say for sure, not knowing anything else about the matter—and certainly in order to make the superintendent understand how urgent it is that he obtain the land-surveyor appointment, that K. alludes to the "sacrifices [he] made in leaving home" and to the "reasonable hopes [he] had of being taken on down here." Up to this point, his words are no different from those of any worker who has left home in search of fortune. But now something else crops up: K. speaks of his "total lack of means and the impossibility of now finding suitable work back home." But why? In the village K. always tried to give the impression of being a capable, knowledgeable person who would have no trouble finding work elsewhere. One infers from this discrepancy that only for some reason that's left unsaid, but that must weigh heavily, K. *is no longer able* to go back. On the other hand, as the superintendent observes, the Castle is not in the habit of chasing people away: "No one is keeping you here, but that doesn't mean you're being chased away either." K. doesn't press the matter—perhaps he realizes he has said too much. Indeed he immediately wishes to muddy the waters, making reference, in order to explain the precariousness of his situation, to something close at hand: Frieda, his "fiancée who is from here." He doesn't mention that Frieda has been his fiancée for only a few hours. In any case, the argument is a pretext, as the superintendent observes with quiet irony: "Frieda would follow you anywhere." K. is exposed—and it's perhaps to avoid embarrassing him that the superintendent changes the subject. By hinting at his former life, K. has come close to revealing something that could harm him: his total dependence on the Castle. For him, no return is possible. The fifth of the Zürau aphorisms says: "Beyond a certain point there's no return. That's the point that must be reached." K.'s story begins one step beyond that point.

In Kafka's handwriting, the letter *K* plunged downward with a showy swoop the writer detested: "I find Ks ugly, almost repugnant, and yet I keep on writing them; they must be very characteristic of myself." Choosing the name K., Kafka obligated himself to trace hundreds of times in front of his own eyes a mark that vexed him and in which he recognized some part of himself. If he had narrated *The Castle* in the first person, as he started out doing, the story would have been less profoundly immersed in his physiology, in zones liberated from the empire of the will.

. . .

Did Kafka ever allude to his process of rigorous reduction to the prime elements, as if he sought to fix them in a periodic table? Perhaps in a notebook entry written in 1922, during a moment of stasis in the elaboration of *The Castle*—and of strong doubt about everything. "Writing denies itself to me" is the fragment's first sentence. Then he mentions a "project of autobiographical investigations." It's not clear what he's referring to—perhaps "Investigations of a Dog," which appears soon afterward in his notebook? Then he is more specific: "investigation and discovery of the smallest possible components." To what end? "Out of these [components], I then want to construct myself." Here he is no longer speaking of writing but of *self-construction*. And right after that we find the phosphorescent trail of a short story:

> Like a man who has an unsafe house and wants to build himself a safe one beside it, using the materials of the old one if possible. But it's a terrible business if, during construction, his strength wanes and now instead of an unsafe but whole house he has one that's half torn down and one that's half built, which is nothing. What follows is madness, a kind of Cossack dance between the two houses, during which the Cossack scrapes and hollows out the ground with the heels of his boots until his own grave takes shape beneath him.

A Cossack dance between Kafka and the literature that had preceded him.

.   .   .

Certainly it's not the case, as some continue to maintain, that the religious or the sacred or the divine has been shattered, dissolved, obviated, by some outside agent, by the light of the Enlightenment. That would have resulted in a world made of secular funerals, in all their awful bleakness. What happened instead is that such things as the religious or the sacred or the divine, by an obscure process of osmosis, were absorbed and hidden in something alien, which no longer has need of such names because it is self-sufficient and is content to be described as *society*. All the rest is, at best, its object of study, its guinea pig—even all of nature.

With Kafka a phenomenon bursts onto the scene: the *commixture*. There is no sordid corner that can't be treated as a vast abstraction, and no vast abstraction that can't be treated as a sordid corner. This phenomenon isn't a reflection of the writer's personal inclinations. It's a matter of fact. Svidrigailov, in *Crime and Punishment*, observes that for him eternity looks like a village bathhouse full of spiderwebs. It's a peculiarity of the period, a sign of the times.

When the secretary Bürgel speaks of the officials' "inconsiderate" behavior toward both the parties and themselves alike, he explains that their lack of consideration is also the supreme "consideration," because it consists of "the iron-clad execution and completion of their duty." But his words inevitably have a sinister resonance, even if

Bürgel is perhaps the most benevolent of the Castle officials and pronounces them after having stretched and yawned—behavior "which was in troubling contrast to the gravity of his words."

Commixture manifests itself above all in this: the social order is superimposed on the cosmic order, to the point of covering it and swallowing it. But the majesty and the articulations of the old order are retained even as the memory of it is erased. In the village no one of course speaks of the cosmos. Even nature might almost not exist at all. The only one who mentions it is Pepi, the servant girl. And the image is one of winter: "a long, terribly long monotonous winter." Color too has been revoked. But no one seems to need or remember it. Differences express themselves in gradations from *chiaro* to *scuro*. The lavish wardrobe of the landlady of the Gentlemen's Inn admits only shades of dark: "gray, brown, or black clothes," as ordered and compact as a phalanx. The mythic landscape has lost its pigmentation.

The cosmic order, as it presents itself in myths, could vanish with the myths themselves. Scientific knowledge could supplant it with an image that is ever more complex, ever changing, in which dimensions multiply to the point of pointlessness. But that's not how it happens. Camouflaged within the social order, the cosmic order continues to exist and operate. After all, it has dealt not only with stars and spheres but also with powers and archons. And those powers haven't gone away. Indeed now, in the absence of names to call them forth, they can operate more freely and wildly, even in plain view. K. puts this to the test every day during his harrowing residence in the village.

The gentlemen (*Herren*) of the Castle are the archons. It isn't that "archons" is an interpretation that accrues to or superimposes itself on *Herren* ("gentlemen," "lords," "rulers") but rather that *archon*, if only we give the word enough room to resonate, *means* "ruler." And this constantly happens in Kafka: behind the formulas of common speech a space suddenly opens where words reverberate and sprout meanings, acquiring an intensity that at times is paralyzing. The common speech par excellence is the language of the servants, hence of the servant girl Pepi. Accordingly, when it's her turn to speak to K., her words sound overloaded with meaning and seem to ask what we are always, secretly, wondering about him: "What does he want? What strange sort of man is he?" And indeed out of Pepi's mouth come what may be the most drastic words we'll hear: she goads K. to find "the strength to set fire to the entire Gentlemen's Inn and burn it to the ground, so that not a trace is left, to burn it like a piece of paper in a stove." To burn it like that sheet of paper torn from a notepad and left on the records cart, which K. (only hours earlier, during the scene of the "distribution of records") thought might be *his* record, that sheet on which would have been written his fate, because the *record* that concerns an individual can be nothing less than his fate.

· · ·

Kafka can't be understood if he isn't taken literally. But the literal must be grasped in all its power and in the vastness of its implications. One such implication is this: the *records* (*Akten*) with which the Castle gentlemen incessantly concern themselves must be the *acta*, that is to say the record of actions of every kind. The Castle maintains the archive of actions, the immense record of all actions that is *karma*. That's why the officials must always be on the job: actions never stop taking place. As Krishna explained to Arjuna on his war chariot, even when you think you're not acting, you're acting. That's why the secretary Momus is in such a hurry to fill in the last blanks of a report describing the events of the previous few minutes. Castle activity consists above all in taking down what already automatically happens: the accumulation of *karma*.

But one mustn't think that the records that pile up in columns in Sordini's room or those crammed into the superintendent's cabinets or those continually offered to Klamm and waved away by him pertain only to the villagers. Though poor and wretched, they nonetheless have been granted the dismal privilege of sharing a border with the Castle. And that's enough to mark their destiny. But the Castle records *all* actions, even those of foreigners, like K., who thinks he recognizes, in a little sheet of paper left on a records cart, his own file, the record of his own acts, as it is about to be distributed or dispersed in one of the officials' rooms. *Karma* is terrible even because of this: it exists independent of every faith and every cult. We may be irreverent or disbelieving, even in the extreme, but our actions accumulate and are filed, beyond our reach, just as with true believers. For *karma* not to exist, every action would have to dissolve immediately—as if without a trace. Were that the case, no premeditated, interrelated actions would be feasible. And if we observe village life, we can assert that such is not the case: it proceeds in a sensible way, like the dull, consequent lives everyone leads.

On one side, the progeny of the archons: the magistrates of the court that judges Josef K. and the officials of the Castle by whom K. wishes to be appointed. They are preoccupied by something known only to them, with respect to which every outside fact is a potential disturbance. And among those outside facts, on the opposite side, is the incessant, unstoppable swarm of defendants, or parties. Each day they swell toward the archons like a vast army, driven forward in a tidelike motion. Looking closely, we may discover that there exists also a counter-movement, more irregular and barely perceptible, like an undertow that flows from the archons back toward the parties (if we use that word as a generic term to indicate whoever waits to be processed and judged by a higher authority). The archons are subject to erotic obsession, which draws them outward. The court's obsession is crude, marked by the harshness of the penal code; the magistrates are a pack of "womanizers," and their reference books overflow with obscene images. Among Castle officials, who wait to be surprised and overwhelmed by the parties in the dead of night, the obsession is more lyrical and vague: they yearn to be forced to do something, they who spend their lives forcing others. Archons behave toward the world as the mind behaves toward what's external to it. They think themselves sovereign and self-sufficient, but they are continually drawn toward something foreign and refractory that resists them and that they want to dominate. They always fear, even if they never admit it, that a little grain of the outside world will penetrate their inaccessible regions, there where they gather only among themselves, and devastate them.

The celestial hierarchies—even the terrestrial or infernal ones, even hierarchies in general, even simply beings that occupy concentric circles—present themselves like this: "I was helpless in the face of that figure, who was sitting quietly at her table looking at the tabletop. I circled around her and felt as if I were being strangled by her. Around me circled a third who felt strangled by me. Around the third circled a fourth, who felt strangled by the third. And so it continued outward as far as the motions of the heavenly bodies and beyond. Everything felt that grip on the neck." That "grip on the neck" is the feeling through which beings communicate. As Canetti observes, "the Pythagorean harmony of the spheres has become a violence of the spheres." This is Kafka's cosmological tableau, implicit in his every word.

Everything is made of concentric circles. Each circle contains, next to something else, an exact reproduction of the preceding circle. For this reason it's easy to overlook the existence of the circles.

Each circle is self-sufficient. It offers a foundation and a justification to whatever belongs to it. The circles do not communicate, at least not officially. There is no constant or guaranteed means of access from one to another. In special circumstances—or, more commonly, by mistake—temporary passages open between them. Then they close again, leaving no trace.

Canetti observes: "Of all writers, Kafka is the greatest expert on power (*Macht*)." And here *power* must be understood in its fullest range of meaning, referring simultaneously to the *powers* whose applications are limited, and generally limited to society, as well as to the *Macht* that, as Kafka describes, invests all the celestial spheres and *beyond* ("as far as the motions of the heavenly bodies and beyond"). But what is there in that "beyond"? The "celestial ocean," the Vedic seers used to say: *samudrá*, which overflows with light.

Architectonic features of the Castle: it isn't a citadel, it doesn't belong to a feudal past, it isn't ostentatious. Nothing there is *new*, as in Alfred Kubin's city of Pearl. Everything is already pregnant with preexisting psychic life. A strip of low buildings, squatting on the slope of a hill. Paint long ago flaked off. It could be a military installation, a monastery, a hospital—or even the edge of a "small town" that is, in truth, "rather paltry." There's just one tower, which has something a bit "crazy" about it when its little windows glint in the sun. And it doesn't give the impression of a noble ascent toward the heights. It looks, rather, as though some "gloomy" inhabitant of the place had "smashed a hole in the roof"—perhaps to escape suffocation. A saturnine dwelling.

The saturnine sovereign, Count Westwest—who is concealed in the tower that rises up from among the Castle's dilapidated buildings and whom no one has ever seen, whom no one may ask to see—resembles no one so much as a character Kafka described in a fragment, a character who sat at his desk with his head in his hands. Outside, a crowd was waiting for him. And they all had "special requests." Perhaps they were phantasms. Or demons. Or simply random people one might meet in the street. The unknown character was prepared "to listen to them and then respond." But he didn't want to show himself on the balcony. In fact, "he couldn't, even if he wanted to. In winter the balcony door is locked and the key is nowhere to be found." And winter lasts forever.

If the inhabitant of the tower showed himself on the balcony or at the window, he would be nothing more than a medium. Life would be a flux of powers colliding like electrical discharges. But it wouldn't be able to *tell its story*. Everything would be reduced to a play of forces that clash, visibly and invisibly. Instead everything is much more opaque, uncertain, incalculable. The forces might even pretend to be unaware of one another. Each constructs a theater of its own, which one day will be annihilated by some random force among the forces it has ignored. But the fiction may well be maintained for a long time, long enough to be thought of as nature. Closed in his bare room, his elbows on the table, the unknown inhabitant of the tower is the guarantor of the world's opacity. He's the one to whom we're indebted if life at every turn is an adventure. He's the one from whom we await, at every moment, some kind of answer. And he's the one to whom we're grateful that it never comes.

Josef K. and K. fundamentally *await*, the one a verdict, the other an appointment. Whatever they do, their lives wear them down. They both belong to that vast crowd of those "who wait," who throng *outside*, in the world, in a "limitless mass that stretches into the darkness." *Inside*, in the tower or in the edifice of the "invisible tribunal," sit those whose job it is to respond. And perhaps they would like to respond. But something prevents their response from being direct. If the key to the balcony door reappeared, would anything be resolved? No, in fact the hidden intent of those who live *inside* would then reveal itself: to never show themselves at all and not to allow what's *outside* to be shown to them. Closed in a room that resembles a cell, elbows propped on the desk, the unknown character holds his head in his hands. That desk is the only indispensable object, the only contact he's permitted. He thinks: "I don't want to see anyone, I don't want to let any sight confuse me—my desk, that is my place." Like Calderón's Segismundo, he fantasizes about various figures and characters. Beyond the windows, the air teems with the tribes of the invisible.

II. From Pepi's Dreams

At the Gentlemen's Inn, the chambermaids stay shut in their room, which "is nothing more than a big closet with three shelves." The claustrophobia is heightened by the rule that bars them, for many hours of the day and night, from going out into the halls, where they would run the risk of disturbing the gentlemen, or even of simply seeing them. "In fact we don't know the gentlemen, we've hardly glimpsed them," Pepi remarks.

Every now and then the chambermaids hear someone knocking at their door and giving orders. But the terror begins when "no order comes at all" and the chambermaids hear someone (or something) *creeping* just outside the door. The girls "press their ears to the door, they kneel down, they hold one another in anguish." Then the terrifying sentence is sprung, which by now resembles Lautréamont: "And one constantly hears the creeper (*den Schleicher*) outside the door." In Lautréamont, so prone to sneering and mockery, the corresponding sentence would be: "But a shapeless mass pursues him relentlessly, on his trail, amid the dust." Kafka, as always, takes a more sober road. With a minimal expenditure of words he achieves maximum effect. Even the word *Schleicher* is both commonplace and alarming. *Schleicher* is the person (or entity) that creeps, but it has the additional meaning of "hypocrite," or someone who acts deceptively, furtively. Here, however, the word is returned to its most literal meaning—and the effect is all the more violent. We can understand that then, shut in their room, "the girls faint from fear and, when it's finally quiet again outside their door, they lean against the wall without the strength to climb back into their beds." This somber, rending scene, like something out of an Elizabethan play, is not, however, the climax of some crisis in a deadly adventure. It's merely the description of a day like any other day in the life of a chambermaid at the Gentlemen's Inn. And it is understood as such by the reader. It is plain daily life, recounted by Pepi to the stranger she's in love with.

Why are the chambermaids so worried? What is the danger that threatens them? That they might let themselves go. And why shouldn't they? They are prisoners. No one sees them—unless, fleetingly, the kitchen staff. Accordingly, to enter the gentlemen's rooms immaculately dressed is both "frivolous and a waste." Since the chambermaids are forced to work amid such filth, they might as well live in it all the time. Artificial light, stale air, excessive heat (the heat is always on). And tremendous, constant fatigue. The oppression of the chambermaids is vicious and subtle. Seen from the outside, however, their life is utterly common. They have a duty, they carry it out. They spend their free time waiting to return to duty. When they have the afternoon off, once a week, their favorite way to spend it is "sleeping soundly and fearlessly in some nook of the kitchen."

The barroom, where Frieda and Pepi roam and where the foreigner K. sometimes sits for a while, is a force field as lively and delicate and complex as any palace of government or strategic headquarters or imperial court. What goes on there is no easier to unravel or understand. In relations of power, the tension is not proportionate to the size of the elements in question. A room can be as charged as a continent. But in the room, the power relations will manifest themselves with maximum linearity, because potential distractions are minimal. Minimal, precious, and revelatory, like Pepi's bows or Frieda's rustling petticoat.

The reduction to prime elements doesn't by any means imply a reduction in the complexity of relations. On the contrary: Frieda is observed by many eyes when she works in the barroom, when the rumors of her relationship with Klamm begin to spread, and finally when everyone is certain about that relationship. Her every gesture gets carefully weighed, interpreted, connected to some other scene that isn't visible. She's like Madame de Maintenon, who methodically gains the affections of Louis XIV

even as she is being scrutinized by all of Versailles—
including Saint-Simon.

There is a physical intimacy between the gentlemen
and the barmaids who serve them. Pepi speaks of her
service as if it were a question of good manners, organiza-
tional efficiency, care in dressing. But it turns out that
"a word, a look, a shrug of the shoulders" isn't enough.
There is also physical contact. Every day Pepi's curly
locks are fingered, many times, by the gentlemen: "So
avidly did all those hands run through Pepi's curls that
she had to redo her hair ten times a day." And Pepi adds:
"No one can resist the allure of those curls and bows, not
even K., who is always so distracted." The barroom is a
simulacrum of a brothel, where certain gestures that are
appropriate to both places are repeated with one customer
after another. For this reason, a little later, in his reply to
Pepi, K. feels the need to observe: "The true barmaid
should be a barmaid, not every customer's lover" (this in
a crossed-out passage of the manuscript).

Pepi descends from the charming, sly servant girls of
the *opera buffa*. Like them, she has a sharp perception of
the world and of men. When she sees K. abandoned by
Frieda but still in love with her precisely because she has
run off ("it isn't hard to be in love with her now that she's
no longer around"), she makes him a proposition: "You
have neither a job nor a bed, come stay with us. You'll like
my friends, we'll make you comfortable, you can help us
with our work, which is really too burdensome for girls to

do alone. We wouldn't have to rely only on ourselves, and we'd no longer be afraid at night."

But how do Pepi and the other girls live? In a "warm, narrow" room. The other two girls are Henriette and Emilie, whose delicious French names, utterly anomalous in the village, lead us straight to the soft, abstract world of the music hall. Living in that closet-room is like living in a little dressing room backstage, where the air is stale and the light artificial. But "everything outside the room seems cold." In the end it's more entertaining to stay in the tiny room and tell one another stories about the world outside than it is to take part in that world: "In there one listens to such stories with disbelief, as if nothing could actually happen outside that room."

Pepi's invitation is chummy, almost as if K. were another girl who could be added to the group. There are no erotic overtones. But everything Pepi says is erotic, if only because, as K. observed, Pepi treats all her customers like lovers—and K. is the customer par excellence, the stranger. Let's examine the details: Where would K. stay? In one of the girls' beds. Perhaps he would take turns. In her magnanimity, Pepi even suggests to K. which of her two friends he might like better: Henriette. And her magnanimity goes further still: the three girls will also talk to K. about his absent lover, Frieda. They'll recount for his benefit complicated stories about her, which they know well. And they'll take out "portraits of Frieda" and show him those too. Three charming girls, actual or potential lovers of a young man, sitting together on the edge of a bed, all contemplating these portraits of another woman, also his lover—that life could last all winter. K. listens and asks himself two questions: Would such a thing be allowed? And then, more subtly: How much longer will winter last? Pepi is a great expert on timing. She knows how essential one day more or one day less might be. And her answer goes beyond meteorology: village life is, above all, winter—"long, terribly long, monotonous." After spring and summer have come and gone, they occupy in one's memory a period "so brief, it's as if they lasted no more than two days." The ominous sentence that follows is exemplary of Kafka's lyrical laconicism: "Even on those days, even on the most beautiful day, sometimes snow still falls."

The confraternity of girls, as Pepi tells it, is drastically opposed to everything that takes place outside. Founded on complete promiscuity and interchangeability, it is ready to receive K. as if he were a new girl, there to give a hand with the work, though exactly how is never clear. At the same time, K. would retain the ancient attributes of the male. Because of him, the three girls "would no longer be afraid at night." They would be "happy" to have "a man to help and protect them." And each—Pepi lets this be understood without saying it, since she always retains a certain shyness when speaking of sex—would offer herself in turn as his lover. But with K. it is enough that she, like a wise courtesan, drops the hint: "You'll like Emilie too, but you'll especially like Henriette." In that tiny room, charm and pleasure reign. The girls may know that theirs is a "miserable life," but they don't by any means want out. As Pepi says, "We make our life there as charming as possible," so that "even with just three of us we never get bored." And she sighs, thinking of K.'s arrival: "Oh, it will be fun."

The girls' complicity has a solid foundation: "That's precisely what kept us together, knowing that all three of us were equally denied a future." The maid's room must be enough in itself, because there will never be anything outside of it. Occasions for rancor or resentment don't ever arise. And even when Pepi gets promoted to barmaid and for four days leaves the room, the other girls do not feel betrayed. In fact they help her get her new clothes ready. One selflessly offers Pepi "some expensive fabric, her treasure," which so many times she had let the others admire and which so many times she had dreamed of someday wearing. Yet now, "since Pepi needed it, she offered it up." Then, sitting in their beds, one above the other, they begin to sew, while singing. At the same time, when Pepi returns, "they probably won't be astonished and, just to please her, they'll cry a little and lament her fate." So K. has nothing to worry about either: "You're not obligated in any way, you won't be tied forever to our room, as we are." Words of profound psychological insight. The maid's room is the only paradise where K. can come and go without incurring obligations or violating prohibitions. As long as he keeps their secret.

With the tone of a country girl who knows a thing or two about life and speaks plainly, Pepi at each turn suggests to K. the most radical and extreme solutions. A little earlier, she insinuated that the act that would make him her "chosen" would be the burning down of the

Gentlemen's Inn, "so that not a trace is left." Now she lets him glimpse another possibility: a tiny erotic paradise, stashed covertly within that same Gentlemen's Inn, and founded—in the way of the ancient Mysteries—on a secret. Like so many other hierodules of forbidden cults, the three girls are "enchanted by the fact that all this must remain a secret." As a result, they will be "bound together even more closely than before." K. need do nothing else but join them. And here Pepi's appeal to K. resounds in all its pathos: "Come, oh please, come stay with us!"

Should we believe Pepi? Certainly her immediacy, her enthusiasm, even her eloquence tempt us to go along with her. But on the other hand there are certain conflicting, confusing elements to her story. Pepi concludes her torrential outpouring to K., after she has abandoned her post as barmaid, by describing her life with Henriette and Emilie—and by inviting K. to join them. By the end of her peroration, the maid's room has emerged as a place of happiness, a caesura with respect to everything around it. But as we float in this mist, we might recall that Pepi has already spoken in a completely different way about that room—in the course of the same monologue. She has described it as a "tiny, dark room" where the girls work "as if in a mine," convinced that they will spend "years, or even worse their whole lives, without being noticed by anyone," often in the grip of terror, as when they hear something or someone creeping outside their room, which is continually ransacked by brutal "commissions" that rummage through their paltry things in search of lost or purloined records and subject them to "insults and threats." And no peace: "Racket for half the night and racket starting at dawn." How can they make room for K. in that slave's life? How can Pepi make him see that room as a place of hidden delight? And how can they keep their secret?

Which of the two versions is true? This time we cannot evade the question with the usual contrivances (different point of view, different mood). The point of view is the same: Pepi's. Her entire monologue has the same tonality—and the two opposing descriptions come a few minutes apart, one after the other.

Here we must look backward. As Kafka found his narrative substance in something that preceded even the division of gods and demons, indeed of the powers in general, so the narration itself seems to have gone back with him to the origin of the variants, to that most mysterious of points where every story begins to branch and proliferate, while still remaining the same story. Such branching is the lifeblood of every mythology. But Kafka had no rites or rhapsodists, which might have varied and recombined his gestures and meanings for him, at his disposal. He had to act with no help from the world. Alone before a sheet of paper—and using the latest form the times allowed stories to take, that of the novel—Kafka wove Pepi's monologue. After having listened quietly to it, K. says to her: "What a wild imagination you have, Pepi." And then: "These are nothing more than dreams born in your dark, narrow maid's room down below, which is the proper place for them, but here in the middle of the

barroom they sound very strange." These stories, like
Pepi's clothes and her hairstyle, are "the offspring of that
darkness and of those beds in your room."

K.'s reaction to Pepi's barroom monologue—he shakes
his head—isn't so different from the way the world would
react to Kafka's writings, which were also full of dreams
born in a dark subterranean room. Kafka in fact once
made this explicit: "We each have our own way of climb-
ing back out of the subterranean world; I do it by writing." That world that presented itself as a cellar is where
Kafka saw himself:

> It has already occurred to me many times that for
> me the best way to live would be to stay, with my
> writing materials and a lamp, in the innermost
> room of a vast, closed cellar. Food would be
> brought for me and would always be left far from
> my room, on the other side of the cellar's outer-
> most door. The journey to reach the food, in my
> dressing gown, beneath the cellar's vaulted ceil-
> ing, would be my one stroll. Then I would return
> to my table, I would eat slowly and carefully, and I
> would immediately begin writing again.

Kafka wrote that way about his cellar to Felice, to
frighten her. Pepi spoke that way to K. about her maid's
room, to attract him. The chambermaids' tiny room,
crowded with bows and petticoats, and the bare cellar
with the table and the writing materials are analogous
sites. Carved with difficulty into the solid surface of the
world, they are nooks that host hidden life, imperceptible

from without, life that can be both paradise and hell at once.

Pepi desperately loves K., loves him "as she has never loved anyone before," loves him like a little girl who reads romances and dreams of a foreigner who will carry her off: "a hero, a rescuer of maidens." Through her speaks a numberless female population: princesses and slaves, bourgeois ladies and peasant girls, office workers and waitresses. Whatever their social position, their words are the same, their devotion is the same—and their dreams are always "wild."

Klamm is an official of a certain age, a man of habits, always dressed in a "black frock-coat with long tails." He wanders about with an air somewhere between dreamy and sleepy, and sometimes "he'll go for hours apparently without uttering a single word and then suddenly say something so vulgar it makes you shudder." A flash of pure comedy. But do we think that with such details we've plumbed Klamm's depths? In the words of Olga, who does know something of the subject: "What can we know about the thoughts of gentlemen!"

Of all the gentlemen, only Klamm inspires exaltation and sacred awe. Not only in the landlady of the Bridge Inn and in Frieda, who are in charge of his cult, but also in Pepi, the incendiary servant. That Klamm doesn't make an appearance during the days when Pepi lends her services to the bar is the greatest blow to her. She waits,

expecting him "at any moment, even at night." Her disappointment exhausts her. She even dares wait for him in
a recess of the forbidden corridor, thinking: "Ah, if only
Klamm would come now, if only I could take the gentleman from his room and carry him in my arms down to the
public room. I wouldn't collapse beneath that weight, no
matter how great it was." Klamm, this gentleman similar
in appearance to other gentlemen who are "elderly and
attached to their habits," appears here helpless as a baby,
lovingly transported in the firm arms of the servant Pepi,
protected by that flighty, fervent Magdalene. After all, for
Klamm even this will merely be another of his many
metamorphoses.

During her vain wait for Klamm, Pepi becomes aware
of the quality of the silence that reigns in the gentlemen's
corridor. This silence is such "that you can't stand it there
for long"—it's a silence that "drives you away." Nevertheless Pepi doesn't give up. "Ten times she was driven away,
ten times she went back up." Why? Pepi, who has a gift
for direct expression, knows how to explain it: "It didn't
make sense, but if [Klamm] didn't come, then almost
everything was senseless." To wait for Klamm makes no
sense. But it is Klamm alone who imbues "almost everything" with sense. And so to wait for Klamm is practically
the only thing that does make sense. This is *Pepi's para-
dox*, which merits inclusion in logical treatises. One of its
applications is *The Castle*.

III. *"There's No Traffic Here"*

It's only the morning after his arrival when K. gives up the idea of presenting himself at the Castle. A sudden weariness descends upon him, such as he never felt during his long journey ("How he kept forging ahead for days, calmly, step after step!"). He starts out thinking that if he can "push himself to walk at least as far as the Castle entrance, he will have done more than enough." But he quickly realizes that he doesn't know which street leads to the Castle entrance. The village's main street, flanked with low, snow-covered houses, their doors all closed, a long street, an endless street, merely gives the illusion of leading to the Castle. Then it suddenly veers away— maintaining, from that point on, a constant distance from the Castle.

In these initial steps, in these initial observations, the whole of K.'s story is already prefigured. His movements seem to him casual, even capricious, like those of a traveler taking a look around in an unknown place. But that's not how it is. Every detail, every remark addressed to him, circles around him, cages him. To linger over some of these phrases is enough to become alarmed. K. always takes them as ordinary phrases, tossed off by people to whom he clearly attaches no importance: the landlord, the schoolteacher he meets on the street, the tanner whose house he enters. And yet their words are quite clear. "I don't think you have any power," the landlord says. "Strangers never like the Castle," says the schoolteacher, and then: "There is no difference between the peasants and the Castle." Finally: "Hospitality is not our custom here," says the tanner; "we have no need for guests." Frightening words. In the dark, smoky hovel where two bearded men soak in a huge washtub, where a young woman with "tired blue eyes" languishes on a "tall arm-chair," holding an infant to her breast, "inert," staring upward "toward some indefinite place" like a Madonna of melancholy, while from the one tiny window on the back wall a pale snow-light casts a "silky sheen" on her dress—in this archaic, torpid penumbra where the only recognized law might well be the law of hospitality, we encounter these brutal, resolute words: "Hospitality is not our custom here." And further: "We have no need for guests." These last words are the harshest K. will hear, but he quickly passes over them: "Of course not; why would you ever need guests?" His reply actually attempts to establish complicity, allowing K. to raise the point that he holds dearest: that he is the exception, the chosen one. He continues: "But every so often, you must have need of someone, of myself for instance, a land surveyor." And so K. rushes headlong past an opportunity to understand. A mist still surrounds him, protects him, mocks him.

The villagers know—for them it goes without saying—that their laws are different from those that hold sway in the rest of the world. First of all because the village is as close to the Castle as it's possible to be. But also for another reason: the village has a different constitution than the rest of the world, a different physiology. In the village, religion is reduced to a topographical reference: we infer that there is a church simply because a "church square" is mentioned, but other than that nothing religious is ever spoken of. And perhaps such talk would sound impious and incongruous, since the village is utterly absorbed in its proximity to the Castle. As for books, no one speaks of them. Only in the novel's last lines is reference made to a particular book: the old mother of the coachman Gerstäcker is hunched over it, reading, in a hut faintly illumined by firelight. But we won't learn anything more about that book, because that's where the novel breaks off, as the old woman reaches a trembling hand toward K. and whispers something incomprehensible to him. Books in the plural, on the other hand, appear only in the Castle, in a vast office. They are arranged on a wide, tall reading stand that divides the room in two. Only the officials consult them, only they know what is written in those books—and whether they're related in any way to the words those same officials dictate in a whisper to their copyists. As K. once obliquely remarks, with his usual mix of perspicacity and cheek: "A lot of writing goes on there." No act has been fully completed, as we can infer from the behavior of the secretary Momus, until it has been logged in the records. Thus, sitting at a table in the barroom, Momus zealously fills out his report on events that happened a few minutes earlier, crumbling his pretzel with caraway seeds onto the pages of the document as he does so. But apart from the *records*, with which the Castle officials are constantly occupied—either in compiling them or in consulting them or in preserving them or even in keeping them out of sight, as Klamm does—apart from these countless handwritten pages, sometimes underlined in blue, no other writings are mentioned. And above all: there's no trace of any sort of printed material. Perhaps none exists. It's hard to imagine shelves in the peasants' dark hovels. The barroom contains tables, chairs, and barrels. The servants' rooms, heaps of dirty clothes. The only gentleman's room in which K. will spend much time, Bürgel's room, is bare. The single example of represented reality is an unusual portrait at the Bridge Inn, which K. supposes to be a likeness of Count Westwest—his first and one of his worst gaffes, since it is instead a portrait of the Castle steward.

One therefore might suppose that, in the village, religion and culture subsist as mere backdrop, since life there must have some family resemblance with the rest of the world. But in essence they have been stripped away. And so, lacking any sort of mediation, the village proves to be the last outpost of the manifest, which *almost* yields to the unmanifest. This lack of mediation is the origin of the oppressive, suffocating, chronically distressing atmosphere that weighs on the village. It's behind the look one sees on the faces of its inhabitants, the look of creatures who are subject to something stronger than themselves, to an unbearable tension, out of proportion for a village in which so little apparently happens. It's also why K., like every foreigner, is considered abysmally "ignorant"—and as such is not only despised but also envied, secretly, because he's still enveloped in the blissful breath of unconsciousness. And when Frieda hints at the possibility of "going away" with K., of leaving that village where after all nothing is forcing her to stay, we detect in her voice an uncontrollable euphoria.

Were the villagers to see the exegetes of *The Castle* talking long-windedly of deities and of God and of how they interfere in their lives, they would probably act indignant. How simple it would be to have dealings with the deities or with God. It would be enough to study a little theology and to rely upon the heart's devotion—they would think. But the Castle officials are rather more complicated. No science or discipline can help in dealing with them. Only experience might help—the kind that's passed in whispers from house to house or from table to table in the barroom.

When it comes to reduction, no one has equaled the mastery of Yajnavalkya. Questioned by the cunning Sakalya, he was able to reduce the 3,306 deities to the one *brahman*. But the *brahman*, whatever that might be, must necessarily be divided into two parts: the "unmanifest" and the "manifest," *avyakta* and *vyakta*. The *one* is therefore always *two*. And among the two, its first part is always the largest. Three fourths of the *brahman* is unmanifest, one fourth is manifest. The *brahman* is the wild goose, the *hamsa* about which the texts say that "in rising from the water, it does not extract one foot. If it did, neither today nor tomorrow would exist." The water is the unmanifest *brahman*, the wild goose that emerges from it is the manifest *brahman*.

Kafka was born into a world where the unmanifest part—the greater part of what is—was increasingly being ignored or denied. The world was said to have been born out of nothingness, but the enormity and the blasphemy of these words were not yet understood. Blasphemy with respect not to a God but to the whole. At the same time, the world was being reduced to the visible, to the *vyakta*. This was said to be physics plus chemistry. Everything, then, was visible: either to the naked eye or to the eyes of cumbersome machines lurking in labs. This was the world in which Kafka was born and raised, as an affluent, assimilated Prague Jew who spoke German and would learn early that the world by then, in its normal course of operation, could do without every type of God, every type of deity. In that world, the distinction between *vyakta* and *avyakta* was not, to be sure, formulated in those terms, but accessible and immediate translations were at hand whenever the *visible* and the *invisible* were invoked. And these were after all the terms most familiar to the Christian liturgy. The wall of the barroom in the Gentlemen's Inn, in which Frieda has made a tiny hole that allows K. to gaze upon Klamm, immobile and perhaps dozing—that wall is the iconostasis.

.   .   .

To speak of deities, of God, and of the divine in regard to *The Castle* is a serious breach of decorum, because nothing of the sort is ever mentioned there, unless the whole of *The Castle* is taken as an Aesopian fable. But is that what it is really? The literary newness of *The Castle* consists first and foremost in its *not* being a fable, whereas many of Kafka's other stories—from "Investigations of a Dog" to "The Burrow" to "The Great Wall of China"— can (and perhaps must) be understood at least as apologues. Indeed they derive their force from that form. But the narrative force of *The Castle* lies elsewhere. *The Castle* is akin to the novels of Dickens or Dostoevsky, writers Kafka venerated. The difference lies in the *place* where this novel unfolds, which is the dividing line between *vyakta* and *avyakta*. No one had dared to write a novel about that boundary, which doesn't in the end manage to become a true boundary, since the village street never reaches the Castle, but rather veers away and proceeds parallel to it without getting closer than a certain distance. This is only one of the various oddities one encounters in these places.

The Castle, even more than *The Trial*, has provoked chronic vertigo in its exegetes. No novel is better suited for initiating its readers into the "torment of endless commentary," which, however, few can bear for long—the fiber of the Talmudist is rare. Most readers, unable to withstand that "torment," seek rest in an all-encompassing interpretation. Surely no novel is more scrupulously chaperoned, as if by sharp-eyed duennas, by its interpretations. For the most part these interpretations are tolerant and magnanimous, ready to admit of numerous others, even incompatible ones, provided that they be interpretations. And they are often eager to beat their breasts and declare their own inadequacy. Yet still they are voluble and intrusive.

At the beginning, K. is a land surveyor who arrives in a village to take up his post. By the end, he's the janitor at the village school. And the coachman Gerstäcker offers to let him take care of his horses, even though K. "doesn't know anything about horses." No matter, says Gerstäcker. Then why the offer? Because Gerstäcker is counting on K. to exert a certain influence on one of the Castle secretaries, Erlanger. From K.'s point of view, everything since his arrival has been a constant regression toward inadequacy, combined with escalating humiliations. Yet it's also true that influence is now for the first time attributed to him, as if by now he formed part of the Castle's web of relations, which extends over all the territory of the village. At the very beginning it was said that anyone who "lives or lodges here [in the village] is in some sense (*gewissermassen*) living or lodging in the Castle." That *gewissermassen* corresponds to the particle *iva* so often encountered in the Brahmanas, and it signals entry into the most secret realms of thought, where everything is understood as if preceded by that *iva:* "in some sense," "so to speak." Gerstäcker's offer is the last stage we are shown of K.'s peregrinations. At this point, as so often happens around the Castle, certain words that have long been buried in piles of irrelevant ones suddenly ring out again, rich with meaning and sarcasm. When K. and the coachman meet, that first day, before they even know each other's names, they exchange these lines:

> "Who are you waiting for?" "A sleigh that will take me," said K. "Sleighs don't come by here," said the man; "there's no traffic here." "But this is the road that leads to the Castle," objected K. "Just the same, just the same," said the man rather adamantly, "there's no traffic here."

K. prepares to visit the village superintendent. It's the fourth day since his arrival, and he hasn't had a single direct encounter with a representative of the Count's authority. Now he must begin—and clearly not at a high level. Nevertheless he feels "little concern." An unfounded intimacy has already been established between K. and the power of the Castle, thus far dormant. He *feels* that power, as a pianist feels the keys. His observations about the Castle's "service" are extremely acute; he has already perceived that it displays an "admirable unity," an operational continuity not found elsewhere. And even "in cases where that appeared lacking, one suspected that it achieved a special perfection." Is this a Taoist speaking? Not exactly, because Taoists don't struggle, whereas K. does, is even the "attacker" who assails those same "authorities," though they have "for the most part been obliging." If only in "trivial matters." But what other dealings has he had with them in those first hours?

Another, more urgent question is raised: Why is K. attacking? Why would he need to, since he has only to take possession of a post that, despite some misunderstanding, could—it seems—be granted him? But the struggle is on, and its peculiar nature immediately becomes clear: on one side the authorities, who must "defend remote, invisible things, always and only in the name of remote, invisible gentlemen." The crucial point of this stunning definition is the invisibility and distance not of the *gentlemen* but of the *things* that the authorities must defend. *Things* of what nature? And why is it that the first concern of these authorities is not to assert themselves, as one might expect, but rather to protect themselves from an obscure foreigner, from an aspiring "worker," with all that word's painful associations? With regard to the authorities—and to their exclusive relation with what is remote and invisible—K. is the extreme opposite: someone who "was struggling for something vitally close, for himself." To struggle *for oneself*: this must have appeared unseemly, maybe even repugnant, to authorities who are so accustomed to other spaces.

Nevertheless the authorities have from the beginning shown K. a generic benevolence, allowing him to "prowl around wherever he wanted," even if that language already betrays a certain deprecatory tone. But at the same time, in so doing, "they spoiled and weakened him." Perhaps that benevolence, then, is a higher form of malice, which serves to push K. ever further into a "non-official, completely uncontrollable, murky, strange life." And what sort of "life" is that, if not life itself, without qualifiers,

in its raw, amorphous, frayed state? Thus K., caught in
that amorphous life, might have been driven to self-
destruction. And then one might have been able to witness this spectacle: "The authorities, gentle and friendly
as ever, would have had to intervene, as if against their
will, yet in the name of some public ordinance unknown
to him, in order to haul him away." In these lines for the
first time the stakes are declared—and one realizes that
the game may be terrifying, that the authorities, while
maintaining their "gentle and friendly" manner, may
from one moment to the next, and perhaps reluctantly,
"haul him away" like a wreck that's blocking the road.
One would then conclude that theological subtlety and
police brutality do not belong to separate worlds. That
they can cohabitate. That each can even presuppose the
other. Perhaps only in this fashion, with just such a dis-
play of gentleness, would it be possible to "haul away"
someone who, after all, can be charged only with having
"proceeded recklessly" along a certain stretch, however
brief, of his "other life" (as opposed to his official life).
This would already be sufficient to sow terror. But there
isn't time to stop here. K. presses on, rightly asking himself: "What was it really, here, that other life?" And he
quickly hastens toward an ominous observation: "Nowhere else had K. seen one's professional service and one's
life so intertwined as here, so intertwined that at times it
seemed that service and life had switched places." Now
terror gives way to vertigo. Could the shabby life of the
village be the true service, concerned only with "remote,
invisible" things? And perhaps service is life itself, as

always "completely uncontrollable, murky, strange"? And finally, what does it mean, this intertwining of two extremes, so intimate that each apes the other's features? For example: till now authority has been for K. above all a name: Klamm. But where does Klamm's power manifest itself? In the signature at the bottom of the letter from the director of Bureau No. 10, a letter in which K. is addressed now with words of respect and recognition, now with imperiousness and veiled threats? Or is it in the air, much more solemnly, when Gardena, the landlady of the Bridge Inn, with her "gigantic figure that nearly darkened the room," sits beside K.'s bed in that maid's room that K. calls a "repugnant hole" and explains, "as if this explanation were not a last favor but rather the first of the punishments she would inflict," that K.'s proposed visit to Klamm is "impossible" ("What an idea!"—and then: "You're asking the impossible")? Yes, there in that sordid, suffocating place, where the maids' dirty laundry and the curled-up bodies of K.'s assistants blur together on the floor, it can be said that, for the first time since his arrival in the village, K. hears a speech of vast importance, which blends abstraction and gossip into a single amalgam—a speech furthermore rich with allusions to what could or could not be done, in accordance with rules unknown to K. And as for him, in those moments he sees himself for the first time imprisoned in a definition: "You are the most ignorant person here, and be careful," Gardena says. But perhaps it is this last thrust of hers that gives K. the chance to begin the game again, since after all "to the ignorant everything seems possible." This is the moment (a reckless one) when K., already opening the door to leave, says to Gardena: "But what is it you're afraid of? . . . Surely you're not afraid for Klamm's sake?"

K.'s audacious hypothesis, that "service" and "life" might actually swap "positions," implies consequences that only gradually become apparent. The first has to do with *modes of behavior*—a fundamental matter, crucial to K.'s story. And regarding precisely this matter a reversal is proposed that will be rather difficult to put into practice, as it runs counter to common sense: "here"—K. reflects, meaning the area surrounding the Castle, and this adverb is as pregnant as Plato's "down here"—perhaps it would be "appropriate" (*am Platze*, "in its place") to maintain "a rather carefree attitude, a certain ease of manner only when dealing directly with the authorities, while everything else always called for great caution, looking in all directions before taking a step." Nothing is more dangerous—we must understand—than everyday life. There, even when performing the most casual, inconsequential acts, we must remember we are continuously under surveillance. We must watch our every step, looking in all directions, as if under siege. As soon as we come before the authorities, on the other hand, where the usual response is to stiffen for fear of doing something wrong, of committing some infraction prejudicial to our cause, we are advised to adopt instead a casual attitude, a certain recklessness we would ordinarily rule out on the grounds that it might easily appear careless, disrespectful, frivolous. In a single sentence, K. has outlined nothing less than a Copernican revolution in behavior, a revolution he glimpses even before he has managed to meet with his first authority, the village superintendent. It is in this very meeting that K. is able to confirm just how far the promiscuity between "service" and "life" goes: the superintendent keeps the official records, those pages that are the very embodiment of service, crammed in a cabinet in his bedroom. When those great sheaves spill onto the floor "tied together in bundles like kindling," the superintendent's wife, Mizzi, jumps aside "with fright." Apparently Mizzi knows that these pages are irradiant and corrosive, even at a distance of years.

K.'s primary characteristic is a certain insolence. The insolence of the ignorant, some will suggest, until Gardena puts it to him as bluntly as possible. But K. can't help himself. When the superintendent explains the story of his file, in which the word *surveyor* is underlined in blue, a file that was held up for a long time by a variety of circumstances and the occasional mistake, K. finds the story "amusing"—and elaborates: "It amuses me only because it allows me some insight into the ridiculous muddle that at times can determine a man's life." This is certainly not the kind of language with which one would generally address an official. But the superintendent forges on, implacable and "serious." He objects at once that if K. supposes he has gained any "insight" from his story he is mistaken, because the story has just begun—and K. doesn't know that yet.

K., no less tenacious and implacable than the superintendent, lets him keep talking, lets him describe in ever greater detail the error—though "who can ever say for sure that it's an error?"—that concerns K. But then K. immediately returns to his distinction. On the one hand, he says, there are the services, the offices and what happens within them: a self-sufficient world that can be understood only in "official" terms. On the other, there is a being who exists "outside those offices" and is an "actual person" and is "threatened by those offices"—and what's more, the threat is "so senseless" that K. finds it hard to "believe in the gravity of the danger." Once again, K.'s remarks are pointed and terse, in sharp contrast with the undulating, winding course of the superintendent's arguments. But K.'s brusqueness doesn't prevent him from following—perhaps even ironically—a certain protocol of compliments and praise, for he is quick to extol the "amazing, extraordinary knowledge of these matters" that the superintendent has just displayed. This prelude renders all the more effective the zinger that follows: "However at this point I would also like to hear a word or two about me."

The superintendent loves, more than anything else, to talk about Sordini. K.'s presence at his bedside gives him a good excuse for returning again and again to the subject of that Italian, "famous for his conscientiousness," who works in Department B as a relator—"virtually the lowest position of all," observes the superintendent thoughtfully.

Even to an "insider" like him, it seems "inconceivable" that "a man of [Sordini's] abilities" is being made use of in that way. Nonetheless, despite his lowly position there's something intimidating about him, as those who've had the experience of being attacked by him know all too well. He then becomes "terrifying for the person under attack, but splendid for that person's enemies." Something feral infuses his high capacity for "attention, energy, presence of mind," as if some spring inside him is always about to pop. Of course, the superintendent himself has two cabinets, in addition to a barn, full of papers. But he remains a peasant who sometimes acts as an official, knowing full well that he isn't up to the task. While Sordini . . . The superintendent recalls, dreamily, the descriptions he's heard of Sordini's office. He's never seen this office—just as he's never seen Sordini, who never comes down, being always "overburdened with work." Thus: "all the walls are lined with columns made from stacks of bundled files," and those are only the records Sordini is working on at that moment. It's often necessary, therefore, to extract documents and reinsert them. Since this happens "in a great hurry," muffled thuds are constantly emanating from Sordini's office: the sounds of columns of documents giving way, collapsing one after another. This sound is considered characteristic of Sordini's office. Having arrived at this point in his story, the superintendent, enthralled, adds a general observation: "Yes, Sordini is a worker and devotes the same care to the smallest cases as to the biggest ones."

Even in the face of this majestic vision, which seems to call for silence, K. doesn't abandon his impudence. And like a good adversary, he quickly latches onto the use of *small* and *big* in order to suggest to the superintendent that his own case, though originally "one of the smallest," as he has been told on more than one occasion, perhaps in part to keep him at bay, "has now become, thanks to the zeal of officials like Mr. Sordini, a big case." Already in these words we recognize a certain lack of respect, but those that follow are obviously provocative. He isn't at all happy about becoming a "big case," says K., "since my ambition is not to have great columns of records concerning me rise up and then collapse, but rather to work in peace, a little land surveyor at his little drawing table." Nothing could be simpler, and nothing further from the somber frenzy of Sordini's office. Nor could anything be more unrenounceable, if we recall what Kafka wrote in a letter, during the time he was drafting *The Castle*, about the relationship between writers and their desks: "The writer's existence truly depends on his desk, if he wants to avoid madness he can never really stray from his desk, he must hold fast to it with his teeth." Holding fast with his teeth to something—the *possibility* of a desk—is also an apt description of K.'s behavior.

The tension is evident. But even an official who is "not enough of an official" like the superintendent knows how to dodge such a provocation. Almost reassuringly, he emphasizes: "No, [yours] is not a big case, on this score you have no cause to complain, it's one of the smallest of the small. It isn't the volume of work that determines the rank of the case." This sentence sounds like a general rule about how the offices work—and also serves, once again, to knock K., the attacker, back on his heels. The official's most powerful weapon against the foreigner is implicit humiliation.

At the beginning of *The Castle*, when official "recognition" of K.'s surveyor title is at issue, the text describes that recognition as "certainly spiritually superior." But Kafka's deletions reveal a wavering: before coming to that "spiritually superior," he had written: "like everything that is spiritually superior, it's also a little oppressive." He vacillated here too, between "oppressive" and "mysterious." And this wavering between something crushing and something secret, with each understood as a prime characteristic of that which is "spiritually superior," points to the very substance of the "struggle" that K. has taken up. Why must the "spiritually superior" also be a weight that oppresses whoever approaches it? Why must its modus operandi be so similar to persecution, even—and perhaps above all—when it comes to the highest of its prerogatives: recognition? K.'s most disconcerting thought takes shape immediately after he learns, indirectly as usual and via the telephone, that he has been "named land surveyor." Instead of cheering up and calming down, K. thinks: "And if they believed that with their recognition of his surveyor title, recognition that in itself was certainly spiritually superior, they could keep him in constant fear, they were deceiving themselves; he felt a slight shudder, but that was all." It's easy to pass over this early sentence on our first reading of the novel, as if it were a normal claim. But if we pause to examine it, it's like a lunar land-scape pocked with craters.

To the villagers, K. is a nuisance. He has the air of one who doesn't know how life works. But he is also a romantic figure, shrouded in the breath of another world. At least he is for women, for Frieda and Pepi and Olga; they all respond to him immediately, as if with an ancient familiarity. And K. is always confident and direct when he speaks to them. The first positive confirmation of this romantic aura, however, comes from a child, Hans. When Frieda asks him what he wants to become, Hans tells her: "A man like K." But what is K. in this moment? A janitor who's just been fired. Sitting at the teacher's desk, he's finishing his breakfast in a freezing room that is at once a gym with some gymnastic equipment, a classroom with a few desks, and a makeshift bedroom, signaled by a straw mattress on the floor and "two stiff, scratchy blankets." The remains of dinner too are scattered on the floor, along with sardine oil, shards of a coffeepot, and clothes. Hans, an observant child, has seen this wretchedness, but K. remains his ideal. Why? Hans has grasped that K. is not a person but rather potentiality itself. He is the kingdom of the possible, encroaching upon the compulsory automatism of the Castle. Thus Hans could "believe that, though K. found himself in a low, despicable condition now, he would eventually, albeit in the almost inconceivably distant future, surpass everyone else." Little Hans, with his tone of "dark gravity," shows himself to be highly astute. He's the first to recognize that K., despite the meanness of his present state, is in some way "vaster" and even younger than anyone else in the village. For it's a place where babies are born old—or at least they're immediately forced to adopt, like Hans himself, an "*altklug*" tone—the tone of sententious old men.

The Castle is woven through with conversations—exciting ones, exhausting ones. Sometimes they read like the arguments of sophists. Often they lead us into areas that bear little relation to the conversation's point of departure. And then abandon us there, perplexed. But such is the subtlety and the specificity of these dialogues that we always forge ahead with the impression that something essential has been said—and has escaped us. Exasperation grows, in the reader as in K. But there is some relief: the comic. Like tears in the fabric of the dialogues, lively scenes intrude. K.'s first night as janitor-custodian in the school's freezing gym, for example, is a grand pantomime, where the word gets stripped of its power and the gesture triumphs. As in a Busby Berkeley musical, the characters—K., Frieda, the assistants—take their turns at center stage, before a silent audience of gymnastic equipment, a few student desks, and the teacher's desk on its platform. The secret, demonic director is a fat, old cat that jumps on Frieda in her sleep, terrifying her. And the wild, abstract scene of the distribution of records—toward the end of the novel—is equally evocative of the most penetrating spirit of the musical. In that scene Kafka seems to quote himself, returning to the root of every musical, which is the scene in *The Missing Person* (a.k.a.

Amerika) of the changing of the underporters at the Hotel Occidental, with its inexorable nexus of centrifugal and centripetal motions.

Comedy is in the details, that's the rule. Kafka formulated it but then crossed out the passage in which it appeared. (We find it now in the critical apparatus to *The Castle*: "The truly comic is of course in the details.") As for its applications, they are scattered through all his writings. In *whatever* he writes it's enough for him to be meticulous and exacting in his description of developments and rigorous in observing their phases—and the comic erupts, invincible, sovereign.

In everyday life, K. discovers at a certain point, it's wise to "look in all directions before taking a step." That's how people behave when they know they're being watched from on high. But when Klamm, the prime and exemplary emanation from on high, is himself seen on the move, witnesses agree that "after coming outside, he looked around repeatedly." And one reports that he did so with a very "uneasy" air. "Perhaps he was looking for me," K. remarks—and his words spark general hilarity in the barroom. But then what was Klamm afraid of? Who did he fear was watching him? The secretary Momus suggests that, indeed, it was K.: "Once you quit standing guard, Klamm was able to leave."

The low and the high mirror each other, according to the *Tabula Smaragdina*. But this doesn't mean they must touch. Or that they could touch with impunity. The whole of *The Castle* is the story of an obstructed meeting, a meeting that, for reasons that are undeclared but vastly important, *must not* happen. For K., everything conspires to prevent him from introducing himself to Klamm. And nothing makes Gardena, guardian of secrets, as nervous as the idea that K. might pursue the matter "on his own." As for Klamm himself, he *must not* even consider the possibility of meeting K. Indeed care is taken that Klamm's gaze not light on any discernible trace of K.'s presence. Thus K.'s footprints in the snow-covered courtyard of the Gentlemen's Inn are immediately erased. Such care should reassure Klamm, allow him to remain unaware of K. Or else—and this is the most daring hypothesis—someone wants to prevent Klamm from having any excuse for thinking that he might be able to meet K. The high and the low must not touch; this rule governs the course of the world. Yet Klamm and K. will continue to stand in relation to each other, even if never face-to-face. Minutes after Klamm's exit from the Gentlemen's Inn, K. receives a letter from him, delivered by Barnabas, that concludes with these words: "I won't lose sight of you."

More than a person, Klamm is an emanation, an element, like nitrogen. "There is already too much Klamm here," says Frieda—and she seems to be speaking of the composition of the air. "You see Klamm everywhere," K. tells her a little later, one theologian to another.

In the village below the Castle, much is imagined about power, but K. yearns to witness an epiphany of it. Only once is he granted his wish—and then by surprise. He skulks about in the snow-covered courtyard of the Gentlemen's Inn, waiting for Klamm. He has the audacity to wait for Klamm. A coachman wrapped in fur is sitting up on the driver's seat facing two horses. Behind him, like a dark, squatting animal: Klamm's sleigh. With an unwarranted familiarity, the cold-numbed coachman invites K. to take a flask of cognac from an inside pocket of the sleigh and to share it with him. K. doesn't even wonder at the coachman's nerve. He's drawn irresistibly to the sleigh. It's the coffer of power, its portable tabernacle. When he sticks his head inside, he feels a warmth unlike any other—a warmth undiminished by the outside chill. In the sleigh, one doesn't sit, one sinks—among blankets, cushions, furs: "no matter how one turned or stretched, one always sank down into softness and warmth." Power is an engulfing element, like the warmth of Klamm's sleigh. Something that allows one to sink into it, that makes every thought of returning to the outside world seem unimportant. The air that K. breathes inside Klamm's sleigh is its aura.

K. begins to feel a little foggy. The obvious thought that it wouldn't be a good idea for him to be surprised in that position no longer seems so obvious; it enters "his awareness only indistinctly, as a slight disturbance." And then the cognac . . . Finally K. extracts a little flask from a pocket in the sleigh door. "Without meaning to, he had to smile, so sweet was its perfume, like a caress, like hearing praise and kind words from someone very dear to you, and you don't even know exactly what's being talked

about and don't even want to know and are just happy in
the knowledge that that particular person is speaking in
that way." So profoundly enchanting is that perfume that
K. wonders if it's really cognac in the flask. And he dares
to taste it. "Yes, it was cognac, strangely enough, and it
burned and warmed him." But "as he drank, it transformed from something that seemed merely the vehicle
for a sweet perfume into a drink fit for coachmen." K.
doesn't know it, but this is the last time he'll be allowed to
breathe the essence of power. Suddenly the courtyard is
flooded, every corner of it, with harsh electric light. It
turns out that the calm country inn is studded with lamps,
"on the stairs, in the corridor, in the entryway, outside
above the door," making the courtyard look like a police
barracks. With that shrill signal the vision ends.

IV. The Way of Women

Frieda, Pepi, Olga, Leni: female, disyllabic, subordinate, erotic—they are the only interlocutors with whom K. and Josef K. speak as if they were speaking with themselves. The sexual intimacy is merely a consequence of a prior psychic intimacy, as if each of these beings has always inhabited some niche in the minds of K. and Josef K., caryatids over whom the eye passes without lingering, with just a nod—and now they breathe and move like living flesh. Not only that: they speak and offer themselves as advisors, even if it isn't clear just where their advice might lead.

Like Talleyrand, K. thinks that in order to get results, one must *"faire marcher les femmes."* But this isn't merely one of K.'s proclivities. It's also the only way that appears open to him. In the village, the men's activities have an uncertain contour. We know there is a cobbler, a tanner, a coachman, a schoolteacher. But we don't see them on the job, and their work is never discussed. The first men K. encounters live—we quickly learn—in a state of

subjection to the women beside them: the landlord dominated by Gardena, Schwarzer crouched at the foot of
Gisa's desk, "content to live in the proximity, in the air, in
the heat of Gisa."

The women are presented quite differently. What we
quickly come to know about them converges toward a
single point: sex. Gardena lives in the memory of her three
amorous encounters with Klamm. Frieda is first of all
Klamm's lover *en titre* and then becomes K.'s lover a few
minutes after meeting him. Pepi flirts with the customers
at the Gentlemen's Inn. Olga regularly gives herself for
money to the gentlemen's servants. Amalia's life is entirely
the consequence of having refused the outrageous erotic
propositions of one of the Castle gentlemen, tearing up
the letter that contained them. To speak of these women is
to speak of their sexual vicissitudes. And theirs are the
stories that energize village life, which is otherwise amorphous and inert, and expose the exacerbated tension between the village and the Castle. K., then, must inevitably
become intimate with these women if he wants to gain
any degree of familiarity with those places. Sex for him is
the only lingua franca.

The effectiveness of *the way of women*, K.'s chosen
path, is confirmed when at last the Castle, in the person of
secretary Erlanger, must ask a favor of K. And the favor
in question regards Frieda. The Castle wants her to return
to her post in the barroom, since even an insignificant alteration in Klamm's routine might in some way disturb
him. Or more precisely: the possibility that Klamm might
be disturbed might itself disturb the other officials who

"watch over Klamm's well-being." Erlanger likens the favor asked of K. to reversing the "slightest alteration of a desk, the removal of a stain that had been there forever"—in this comparison the "stain" corresponds to Frieda herself. And the more he insists on the favor's smallness, even its irrelevance, the more suspect it seems, as if Erlanger wanted to conceal the fact that its importance is actually enormous, so enormous that "peace" among the officials, and therefore within the entire apparatus of the Castle, hangs in the balance. Erlanger lowers himself to the point of telling K.: "If you acquit yourself well in this little matter, it might turn out to be useful for you sometime down the road." Here, for a moment, K. witnesses the humiliation of the Castle, which is normally the source of every humiliation. As in a dialogue between diplomats or merchants or criminals, Erlanger hints that K.'s friendly little gesture might be answered one day, in turn, by another friendly gesture, maybe even a more substantial one.

But K. has by now developed too fine an ear for Castle-speak not to detect Erlanger's undertone of "derision." In fact, even if K. wanted to prove himself eager to bring about Erlanger's desired result, he couldn't, simply because that result has already been achieved. Frieda has already reached an agreement with the landlord to resume her service behind the bar. They merely agreed to postpone her return by twenty-four hours so as not to inflict on Pepi "the shame of having to leave the barroom right away." K. was informed of all this only after it was a done deal. And where is Frieda in that moment? A few steps away, in bed with the assistant Jeremias. How could Frieda have resisted her "childhood playmate"? And besides, she's taking care of him, since he's a bit of a wreck after the hardships of the preceding days.

Thus even the one instance when K. is called on to intervene confirms the rule of the place: that, whatever the Castle's orders might be—and they could be "unfavorable or favorable, and even the favorable ones always had a final unfavorable core"—they always, for K., "passed over his head." Why? Evidently, reflects K., because "his position was too lowly for him to be able to intervene or even to silence them so that his own voice would be heard."

Is Erlanger, then, simply making fun of him, asking his help in resolving a matter that has already been resolved? One can't be sure. Perhaps Erlanger, with the unerring perspicacity typical of Castle officials, is using Frieda's return to the barroom as a simple pretext, when all he really wants is for K. to agree to behave in a certain way toward her: to declare his own willingness to make her return *to her place* in the village order. Leading her back to the barroom would be the same as handing her back over to Klamm.

It's true that, minutes earlier, Frieda told K.: "I'll never, ever come back to you, I shudder to think of such a thing." But she was referring to a life with K. in the village. And just before that, Frieda had admitted that she still daydreamed about what would have happened had they "gone away at once that very night," the first night. By now they would be "safe somewhere." But "safe" from what? The threat that underlies each moment of life around the Castle is on the verge of surfacing. Is that, perhaps, what Erlanger feared? And perhaps he also feared the sentiment that Frieda now confesses to K.: "To be close to you is, believe me, the only dream I dream; there is no other." If this is the case, then the favor Erlanger asked of K. is to smother his fiancée's only dream. Such a deed would certainly redound to K.'s credit. It is the only deed for which the Castle seems willing to reward him.

When K. reaches the village beneath the Castle, he repeats with the women whom he encounters the gestures and reactions of Josef K. at the beginning of his trial. Josef K., like K., is made to feel like "the first foreigner to come along," as soon as a woman lays eyes on him. In his case it's the washerwoman, the wife of the court usher, and Josef K. immediately wonders whether she's looking at him that way because she's "had her fill of court officials." It's the same sort of disenchantment with a high-level official that K. attributes to Frieda. As for Josef K., he immediately begins to investigate the possible "relationships" between the washerwoman and the high-level officials, in order to use them to his advantage—just as K., according to Pepi, has become engaged to Frieda only because he's attracted to her "connections that no one else knows about" with Castle officials.

Josef K. elicits the same kind of reactions from women that K. does. The washerwoman, Frieda, Pepi: these women who seem at times to be at the disposition of the officials, as in a garrison brothel, all dream immediately of being carried off by the ignorant stranger—Josef K. or K. They want to emigrate, run away forever. At the end of their first conversation, the washerwoman, already moving off toward another man, whispers to Josef K.: "If you take me with you, I'll go wherever you like, you can do with me as you like, I'll be happy just to be far away from here for as long as possible, even better forever."

Of course, there's a big difference between Frieda's lover and the washerwoman's. Klamm is a high-level official, whose name suffices to inspire reverence in servants and gentlemen alike. Many doubt that K. will ever succeed in speaking a single word to him. But Bertold is merely a student: small, bowlegged, with a short, reddish beard. He summons the washerwoman, his erotic slave, "with just a finger." The washerwoman considers him "a repellent person" and in his presence calls him a "little monster." It's said of him, however, that he "would in all likelihood one day attain a high-level official position." This looming future is what enables him to exert his "tyranny" over the washerwoman. As soon as he sees her, he touches her, kisses her, strips her, and throws her to the ground, regardless of who might be present, whether it's the entire crowd gathered in the hearing room or Josef K. alone. Her body, to Josef K., looks "luxuriant, supple, and warm in her dark dress of coarse, heavy material," and the student presses against it wherever he can: up against a wall or window, on the floor. The washerwoman seems to detest the student, but Josef K. suspects she loves him, and he is therefore jealous of him—as he is of the examining magistrate who merely saw the washerwoman asleep and told her that "he'd never forget that vision." Later he sent her, "via the student, whom he trusts a great deal and with whom he collaborates," a pair of silk stockings that the washerwoman finds "beautiful but really too nice and not suitable" for her.

The world of *The Trial* is more brutal and crude than that of *The Castle*. The transitions are more vexing and jarring, more jagged. But the erotic mechanisms are identical—and they repeat themselves precisely.

Women are attracted to Josef K. the way "the court is attracted to guilt." From the moment of his arrest, he is enveloped, wherever he goes, in an erotic halo. His every relation with the court and its representatives, official or not, is counterpointed by sex. During his first deposition, he becomes aware of a certain commotion in the back of the room. Through a "dazzling whitish" light, he is able to make out a woman who is being pressed against the wall by an unknown man. It's the washerwoman, who shortly before had opened the door to the hearing room for him, the guardian of the threshold of the court. In fact, as we will learn, she's the wife of the court usher, and these places are their apartment. Every time there's a hearing, they have to clear their things out of the adjacent room. Josef K. sensed at once, without any reason and "from the moment she first appeared," that this woman would cause "a serious disturbance." Now even amid the throng, breaking off his deposition, he finds a way to fix his gaze on "her unbuttoned blouse," which "hung down around her waist" as the unknown man forced himself on her (crossed out passage).

We will soon come to know this: the washerwoman entered the room because she was attracted to Josef K., particularly to his "beautiful dark eyes." She has never before risked such a thing, because the hearing room is for her "more or less off limits." Perhaps that's why Josef K., like an old sailor who sees a woman striding across the deck of his boat, immediately recognized her presence as a sign of a "serious disturbance."

The woman enters the room while the defendant is being deposed. Josef K.'s words are vehement—they cannot be taken as anything less than an accusation against the court itself. Just then the woman gets pushed up against the wall by a student who has pursued her for some time. Then the two of them fall to the floor together. When the woman sees Josef K. again, a week later, she regrets that she had to miss part of his speech, which she otherwise "liked very much," because "during the last part she was lying on the floor with the student."

Hard to imagine a more unspeakable and unseemly commingling than that between the life of the court and the private lives of those who are linked to it. In the spaces used for offices one often finds "laundry hung out to dry," which renders even more "unbreathable" the air of those attic rooms, already overheated by the sun and overcrowded by the "heavy traffic of the parties." On Sunday morning, when court is not officially in session, the usher is sent off to deliver a "message that's useless anyway" simply in order to get him away from home for a few minutes, so that the student Bertold, who collaborates with the examining magistrate in the offices one floor up, can carry off the usher's wife, maybe on his back. And maybe he won't subject her to his lust—but will offer her to the examining magistrate instead.

The usher knows perfectly well that his errand is a pretext, and so he sprints off hoping to return in time to catch the student. But the student is always too quick, because he needs only to "come down the stairs from the attic." It's like a scene out of Feydeau, with a single difference: here the seducer hides not behind a screen but behind the door to a court office. Meanwhile the usher's futile rage grows. He has already imagined the student squashed into the wall, with his bandy legs and his blood spattered around him. "But up to now it's only been a dream," he confesses to Josef K., shortly after shaking his hand for the first time. If no one dares lift a finger against the student, it's because "everyone fears his power." No one can do anything—no one except, paradoxically, someone like Josef K., a defendant. The usher is one subordinate among many; his life is squeezed, almost crushed, between the hearing room, adjacent to his apartment, and the court offices, a few steps above. He isn't eloquent, but one gets the feeling he knows what he's talking about. Like Pepi, the servant girl who goads K. "to set fire" to the Gentlemen's Inn, the usher too makes it clear to Josef K. that he would be happy to see him intervene violently, even if he isn't counting on it. And he adds: "People are always rebelling." Nobody else, not even K., will say anything as abrupt and radical as this.

The erotic nature of the women in *The Trial* and *The Castle* generates some unruly psychic turmoil in Benjamin and Adorno. It's as if these characters forced them to reveal their own closeted sexual fantasies. For Benjamin, Kafka's women emerge from the "world of dust, fluff, and mustiness, as if from some primeval landscape." Their psychopomp is Bachofen, inventor and singer of a hetaeric swamp stage at the threshold of which we'll find Leni with her webbed fingers. But in other passages, Benjamin is less dreamy and more angry, speaking of "whorish women" who correspond to the "shamelessness of the swamp world," with their *luteae voluptates*—and who can't therefore attain "beauty," as if because of some moral shortcoming. And as for Adorno, he's the only exegete who seems to have been deeply affected by Gisa, the schoolmistress, a minor figure who appears in a single scene of *The Castle*, retaking possession of the classroom where K. and Frieda have camped out with the assistants. Kafka describes her as "a tall, blonde, beautiful, rather stiff girl." Nothing more. This is how Adorno describes her: "Gisa, the blonde schoolmistress, cruel and fond of animals—perhaps the only beautiful girl he [Kafka] depicts as unscathed, as though her hardness scorned the Kafka maelstrom—belongs to the pre-Adamite race of Hitler Jungfrauen, who hated Jews long before there were any."

Implications of that sentence: doesn't Gisa, the blond schoolmistress, with her "full, luxuriant body," her wide hips—doesn't she represent, as a member of a "pre-Adamite race," those Hyperborean ur-Indo-Europeans evoked by Herman Wirth? The ones who seem ready to hate the Jews who don't exist yet, because they are too modern? Perhaps they are impatiently awaiting the creation of the first Jew so they can hurl themselves on him. His name will be Adam.

All those girls who will introduce themselves one after the other, under the names of Leni, Pepi, Frieda, and Olga, are prefigured by Fini, who emerges from the charred rubble of the Hotel Kingston in Istanbul, in an enchanting story left suspended by Kafka. The man she is supposed to lead astray and drag into a "dubious affair" is named Liman. He has just arrived in Istanbul on a business trip and has been driven to his usual hotel. The coachman is careful not to tell him that in Istanbul's last fire the Hotel Kingston was destroyed, and so Liman finds himself faced with a heap of ruins. These turn out, however, to be inhabited by some of the hotel staff, now jobless. By this point we're already in a state of happy anticipation, as with any of those films from the 1930s that are set in Macao—or even in Istanbul. But the hallmark that confirms we've entered an authentic Kafka situation is the appearance of a gentleman "in a frock-coat and a bright red necktie," who begins recounting in great detail the story of the fire while twisting "the tip of his long, thin beard around his finger." We already know by this point that Liman will soon be embroiled in a story that will lead him off in some direction he would never choose. But for now he's just a traveler who has had some bad luck and would like to get settled in a hotel as soon as possible. "Hotel Royal," Liman tells the coachman. In vain. The man with the frock coat has already offered to lodge him in a private residence, in rooms arranged for by the hotel management, which doesn't want to abandon its old guests. On top of that, the man in the frock coat has called for Fini's assistance—which is enough to send a shiver through the rubble. "Everyone was looking for Fini," like some new Figaro. And she appears: laughing, holding her hands over her brand-new hairdo, running toward the coach. She introduces herself at once: "I'm Fini," she tells Liman "in a low voice," as "she runs her hands over his shoulders, caressing them." Then one of those comic scuffles erupts that Kafka never tires of describing in all their variations, as in *The Missing Person*. Fini wants to force her way into the coach; Liman wants to block her entry—a sign of unpleasant complications to come. With the help of the man in the frock coat, who pushes her from behind, Fini prevails and secures a seat in the coach, adjusting immediately and "hastily her blouse, and then, more carefully, her hair." Liman falls back into his seat, facing Fini. "This is unheard of," we hear him exclaim—as if those were his last words before sinking into a soft, ambiguous fog, where only the hand of Ernst Lubitsch could guide him. And here the story breaks off, trailing a wake of Turkish perfume.

·   ·   ·

At the beginning, Leni is "two large black eyes" looking through a peephole in a door. The door doesn't open. A little while later the two eyes reappear, and "now they might almost have seemed sad." Finally Leni shows herself; she's wearing a long white apron, well suited to her role as nurse, and she holds in her hand a candle that casts a weak light through the apartment of Huld, the lawyer. From the first moment, Leni stares at Josef K.— and he stares back, examining her doll face, its every part round or rounded, even her hairline and her hair, which is "thick, dark, tightly gathered." When Leni speaks, a hint of mockery enters her voice, as if she can't help it. In order to lure Josef K. out of the lawyer's bedroom, she breaks a plate against the wall. When he opens the door to see what has happened, she quickly scolds him for having made her wait. Meanwhile her little hand is already resting on his, even before he has let go of the doorknob. Leni wants to become his lover as soon as possible. She asks him questions about his so-called lover, Elsa, disregards his defense of her, then examines a snapshot of her dancing and immediately zeroes in on her physical defects. Moments later she kisses him, bites his neck and hair— and gloats: "You see, now you've already traded for me!" Meaning: Josef K. has already traded Elsa for me, and now I've taken the place of Elsa, who is "clumsy and rough," as well as a bit fat. And who, above all, wouldn't be able, according to Leni, to sacrifice herself for Josef K. It all gets wildly jumbled, as inevitably happens when Josef K. meets a woman: instant sexual intimacy, discussions of his trial. All in stark contrast to the "chatter of the old gentlemen" in the next room. Leni is sober, blunt, precise—we can't rule out the possibility that she alone knows how to "escape" the court. She hints at a decisive intervention, at mysterious undercurrents, between bouts of frivolity and flirtation that include the game in which she reveals her "physical defect": the webbing between the middle and ring fingers of her right hand. "What a pretty claw," Josef K. says, quickly placing a gallant kiss on that "prank of nature." It's the first kiss between them, and in that moment a pact is sealed between Josef K. and a nature that hasn't yet entirely emerged from the waters. It's then that Leni takes his head in her hands and kisses and bites his neck and "even his hair." Meanwhile "hurriedly, mouth open, she climb[s] with her knees onto his belly," giving off as she does an "exciting, bitter, peppery odor." Then the two tangled bodies slide down onto the carpet, a primordial swamp glazed with moonlight. "Here are my keys, come whenever you like" are Leni's last words, punctuated by a "stray kiss." For pure erotic intensity, libertine literature offers little to rival this scene, steeped in that "peppery odor."

When K. meets Pepi for the first time, in the Gentlemen's Inn, a descriptive machine seems to come suddenly to life, meticulously recording, like a police report, the details of her physical appearance and her wardrobe: "small, rosy, healthy." It observes her "head of luxuriant reddish-blond hair, knotted into a thick braid." Neither her "almost childlike" air nor her carnality escapes notice. And we also learn that she's dressed in a misguided, inappropriate way, "corresponding to her exaggerated notion of a barmaid's importance." All this in a few seconds, while Pepi speaks to K. in that tone of instant intimacy that all the village women seem to adopt with him, while for his part he seems to know her well enough already to say what inconsistent notions she has about her job.

It's clear during all this what's on K.'s mind: everything that happened with Frieda could also happen with Pepi, "if only he had reason to feel that Pepi had some kind of relationship with the Castle." This according to a few lines crossed out of the manuscript, lines that even add a violent stroke: "He would have tried to wrench her secret from her with the same embraces he'd had to use with Frieda." The final version, on the other hand, says only that K. rejects this thought and tells himself: "Oh yes, it was different with Frieda."

K.'s sexual rapacity is now pushed to one side with a denial, which in the end only highlights the evidence of it: "K. would never have touched Pepi. Still, he now had to cover his eyes for a moment, so greedy was his gaze." The crossed-out passage is what the reader glimpses between the lines, or rather, *sees*. But the reader alone must come to that blunt, drastic realization. Must see that wire. The writer must obscure it, with rags, dirt, leaves, twigs— or whatever else happens to be at hand.

Frieda, Pepi, Olga, Amalia, Hans's mother, Gardena, Leni, the washerwoman: everything feminine is preyed on by the court magistrates and the Castle officials. After all, the women belong to the court and to the Castle. No one would dare assert that they might not be at the disposition of any official or magistrate at any time. And yet it would be misguided to lump them with the sort of prostitute whose clients are all members of the same club. They should be seen, rather, as hierodules, no less knowledgeable than priests when it comes to the cult's secrets—but more willing to expose and explore them. Gardena exemplifies the older hierodule, who has already trained a younger one to take her place: Frieda. The little girls on Titorelli's stairs, the newest pupils, are still playing games before assuming their role. With the exception of Gardena, who is the strict custodian of the cult and defends the Castle as strenuously as the prison chaplain defends the court, one sentiment unites them all: they dream of a lover, foreign to their world and already for this reason guilty. Just as K. is attracted to Frieda and Josef K. to the washerwoman because they imagine that those girls, whom they already plan to use to their own ends, have "relationships" or "connections" with the Castle or the court, so for Frieda and the washerwoman K. and Josef K. exude first and foremost the lure of the foreigner, of one who has come from a place where the air is less dense and suffocating than their own. This doesn't imply, however, that they seriously oppose the Castle or the court. The only radical opponent—mute and rejected—is Amalia. The others have mixed, complex feelings. Frieda in the end chooses her old erotic games with the assistants over K. and reclaims her post at the Gentlemen's Inn, as if she had left it only so that she might be acutely missed. And it's hard to tell to what degree the washerwoman is tor-

mented and to what degree she's complicit with her sexual pursuers. It's true that, as the student was carrying
her off like a sack, the washerwoman waved at Josef K.,
"shrugging her shoulders" in an effort "to show him that
the abduction wasn't her fault." But it's also true that
"her gesture didn't express a great deal of regret," as if
Josef K. were witnessing not an instance of coercion but
the repetition of a rite, mechanical and ineluctable, one
that prompted him to shout: "And you don't want to be
freed."

That's a sentence that strikes deep. One might suspect
that all of them—Josef K., K., the women—want above
all else to enter ever more deeply into the Castle and the
court, despite sometimes yearning to destroy them. Meanwhile, however, they act in such a way as to bring about
their own destruction.

The "Barnabas women": that's what the villagers, with
sneering sarcasm, call the two sisters of Barnabas. One,
Amalia (the "extraordinarily reserved," the "accursed
Barnabas woman"), is the local untouchable. No one
speaks a word to her, nor would they get a reply. Olga is
the family breadwinner, by virtue of her official status as
prostitute—it is her duty to satisfy the stable hands. Just
as the assistants, even the sounds of their names, are "repugnant" to K., so are the Barnabas women to the rest of
the village. They are the pet targets of perfidy, especially
for other women. And above all for Frieda. In her last
exchange with K.—the breakup conversation—Frieda
makes it clear that the truly irremediable difference be-

tween them, which reveals that they come from "completely different worlds," is represented by the tension between the assistants and the Barnabas women. You can choose one side or the other but never both. They are hopelessly incompatible. When this subject comes up, alarms go off. There is no longer any room to argue or "refute," activities to which Frieda and K. are fervently dedicated. The only valid response on this subject is an instant, physical repulsion. Just after saying that being near K. is her "only dream," Frieda mocks K.'s peroration in defense of his relations with the Barnabas women and retires to her room with the assistant Jeremias, to take care of him. She attends to him as one would a sick child or an old lover. Jeremias has won—and K. begins to suspect that in "any other struggle" Jeremias would triumph as well. Not long after having come to the village determined to be the "attacker," K. now reaches the conclusion that, in any conflict, he would be defeated even by the Castle's lowliest creature. At last he is coming close to removing what has up until now been his most serious obstacle. At last he understands that Klamm's omnipotence is reflected even in the two assistants. Which explains why Jeremias, occupying Klamm's place in Frieda's bed, can claim that he feels like "a little Klamm." And why Frieda herself might find in the assistants, even "in their filth and in their lechery, traces of Klamm."

Only when together do the assistants go around with a loose, "electrified," nimble gait. If we happen to encounter them on their own, as we do Jeremias, they appear "older, wearier, more wrinkled." Jeremias even "limps a little" and seems "elegantly infirm." K. has trouble recognizing him. Why? "Because I'm alone," says Jeremias, perfectly aware of the change. He knows that, by himself, he's no longer animated by the disturbing force of the double.

Other writers, a German Romantic for instance, would have presented K.'s assistants as demonic offspring, creatures "as alike as snakes," with a primordial nature not easily reconciled with civilized order. Not Kafka. Artur and Jeremias are fake youths, with their "reddened cheeks that seemed made of slack flesh." They are "seemingly good-natured, childish, funny, irresponsible," and they would be merely irritating but for a few details that give rise to graver suspicions. When the village superintendent smiles, K. discovers that his smile is "indistinguishable" from those of the assistants. As children, the assistants played with Frieda in the shadow of the Castle. Erotic games, no doubt, which they are now ready to resume, in order to wrest her away from K. To the villagers, Artur and Jeremias are "old acquaintances"—the landlord even respects them—and everyone's familiarity with them confirms for K. his own irredeemable foreignness. If there is any radical change in K.'s understanding of the Castle, it can be seen in his attitude toward the assistants. In the beginning, he treats them like gadflies that have been assigned to him in a "thoughtless" manner and need to be squashed. But the superintendent, patient and calm, explains: "Nothing here happens in a thoughtless manner." In the end, K. realizes with frustration that he has always neglected the importance of the assistants. "I keep underestimating them, I'm afraid," he whispers to Frieda, whom he has now lost. An unforeseen conclusion suggests itself: "Perhaps it would have been even shrewder to have kept them as his assistants, letting them torment him, rather than have them wandering about so recklessly, freely plotting their intrigues, for which they seemed to have a special knack." To be tormented by some official or by Artur and Jeremias ultimately amounts to the same thing. Even those two mocking creatures have been "inspired from above, from the Castle."

The story of Barnabas's family takes up six of the twenty-five chapters, 115 pages of the German edition—a novel within the novel. In *The Trial*, no episode focusing on secondary characters expands to such an extent. Furthermore, direct connections between the story of Barnabas's family and K.'s vicissitudes (connections that include the message Barnabas delivers and Frieda's rancor toward the Barnabas women) are scarce. Taken together, it's a story that stands alone—and on a slightly different level than the rest of the village stories.

If K. senses right away that there was "something special" about this family, that it is composed of "people for whom, at least on the surface, things were going much as they were going for himself, so that he could ally himself with them, and could agree with them about many things," if K. notices *a family resemblance* in that family, it's because their implicit hopes and relentless fears are much the same as those of Hermann Kafka's family. The primary difference lay in the father figure, who in Barnabas's family has lost every trace of imperiousness, becoming utterly pathetic and helpless. Aside from that, whether the head of the household manufactures excellent boots or sells wholesale fancy goods, the profile of the two little family groups, above all in their manners, their feelings, their fears, and their hopes, is extraordinarily similar. And K. is never so cruel, never so deeply involved, as in his relationships with Barnabas's family. He is torn between a certain repugnance, which he feels most strongly toward the corner of the table where the parents sit moaning and incapable of moving, and an irresistible inclination to feel at home, like one who finds himself *among his own.* The idea of spending the night at their house thus seems to K. both "distressing" and "the most natural thing in the whole village."

Even before anyone tells him that Barnabas's family is condemned and execrated by the village community, K. seems to know it. As soon as he enters their house, he gets an "unpleasant impression." And this only because he's seen Amalia's gaze, which "wasn't unpleasant in itself, but rather proud." If K. were to go a step further, he would realize that the house seems unpleasant to him because there's something *too* familiar about it. With everyone else, he makes an effort to present himself in the best light, because he anticipates that any of them might turn out to be useful to him, and yet "with these people he didn't bother at all." Indeed, "where they were concerned he felt, as it were, no shame." To Amalia, whom he barely knows, he has no qualms about saying: "You're always so sad, Amalia. Is something tormenting you? Can't you say what it is?" Yes, the torment exists—and no, she can't name it.

In Olga's house, K. senses and recognizes that feeling of familiarity that the assimilated Jew feels in the home of other assimilated Jews. Indeed the intimacy is greater still: like K. himself, this entire family is among those who are simultaneously assimilated and cast out. And they aren't foreigners, but locals. The excessive ease and directness of his relationships with them, that disagreeable *instant understanding* that he feels in Olga's house, repels him—as if he has been plunged into an element that is too familiar, that holds him back and draws him in, instead of giving him the support and energy to move forward. Whereas that is precisely what he expects women to provide.

Psychology is sharpened, honed to an exaggerated fineness—sometimes so painful as to seem unpresentable—when the Jewish family leaves the shtetl or some other remote place in central Europe and takes up residence in a bourgeois apartment in the big city. The transition spans roughly two generations, Freud's to Joseph Roth's: extreme, reckless perceptiveness, never again regained.

Kafka, with ill-concealed impatience, was drenched in it—to the point of loathing it. When he wrote: "For the last time psychology!" perhaps he meant that one had to go through psychology before it could be left behind. He could have made his way through its marshy wastes with an animal-like dexterity and expertise. Comparable perhaps only to that shown, in the same years, by another assimilated Jew: Marcel Proust.

K. isn't merely brazen and defiant. At times he can be honey-tongued and eager to ingratiate himself with his interlocutor however he can. We see this twice in one night. First with Frieda, who rebukes him for the hours spent with the Barnabas women. Then with the landlord and landlady of the Gentlemen's Inn, who are disgusted by his inexcusable nighttime wanderings through the hallways onto which the officials' rooms open.

With Frieda, K. wants to show that he fundamentally shares her loathing of the Barnabas women, the two outcasts with whom he feels rather too *at home*—a feeling otherwise unknown to him in that village. As for Amalia, K. doesn't have the courage even to speak her name. Regarding Olga, he's quick to state that she isn't "seductive," in an attempt to deflect Frieda's jealousy. Thus he sets her up for this retort: "The stable hands think differently," seeing that they have spent the night with her "at least twice a week for more than two years." But above all K. wants to make clear that he too, like the village as a whole, condemns the family: "I understand your aversion to that family and I can share it." If he has had anything to do with them, it has been only to protect his interests, since he has been expecting news from Barnabas and is counting on using the messenger to his advantage. He's like a man who says that sure, he's had dealings with Jews, but only out of professional necessity.

With the landlord and landlady of the Gentlemen's Inn, K. defends himself in no less dubious a fashion. He attributes his errors to weariness and to the fact of "not yet being used to the strain of the interrogations." He neglects to mention that he barely said a word to either Bürgel or Erlanger. He merely listened—or slept. It is then, at best, an exaggeration to say that he "had to face two interrogations in a row." As for the distribution of records, K. denies having "been in a position to see anything." In this case, the opposite is true. His excuses may seem simpleminded, but they touch pressure points. And they succeed above all because of his obsequious tone. In fact, "the respect with which he spoke of the gentlemen left the landlord favorably disposed toward him." As for the landlady's reaction, nothing is said. She is much harder to fool.

The Firemen's Festival is celebrated on the third of July—Kafka's birthday. Just as the day of the *comices agricoles* sealed Emma Bovary's fate, so will this day seal Amalia's. Festivities sniff out disgrace. They unite communion and wound, marriage and immolation. They are the heirs of sacrifice.

Amalia is decked out like a bride and accompanied by her father's unlucky words: "Today, mark my words, Amalia will find a husband." Wearing the necklace of

Bohemian garnets that Gardena (in those days a family
friend) once loaned Olga, who in turn has offered it to her,
and wearing also her white, lace-covered blouse, Amalia
advances toward the festival. Her gaze always has something "gloomy" about it, but more than anything else it is
regal: people "nearly bowed down, without meaning to,
before her." Even then, in the midst of the crowd, "her
gaze was cold, clear, fixed as ever; it wasn't aimed directly
at what she was observing, but rather—and this was disturbing—slightly to one side, in a way that was barely noticeable but undeniable." This slant is due not to any
shyness or "embarrassment," but rather to a calling that
she felt even before becoming the village outcast, a "desire for solitude that overpowered every other feeling," as
though she were trying to rid herself of all attachment to
the world. Amalia is the only person who simply doesn't
want to accept the rules of the village and therefore of the
Castle. K., on the other hand, wants first to understand
them—and then to use them to clear his way.

Perhaps it is precisely this aloofness that strikes Sortini,
the "tiny, weak, brooding" official, as he leans against the
fire truck. And he knits his brow in his usual manner, so
that "all his wrinkles etched a fan-like pattern into his
forehead, converging toward the bridge of his nose."

Amalia isn't spectacularly beautiful. She has "the age-
less look of women who don't grow old but were never
truly young." What is unique about her is that gaze,
which an official like Sortini can't fail to notice as soon as
he lifts (since "she was much taller than he was") his eyes
toward her. It isn't merely attraction that grips him but

also a certain sense of danger, as if he has for the first time brushed up against something utterly foreign. This may perhaps help us understand why an official as reserved as Sortini would resort to such brutish manners when inviting Amalia to meet him. He acts both as suitor and as guardian of the Castle rules. His message to her is a challenge that will force her to expose herself.

Olga, confident and severe in her telling of the story, depicts Sortini as an arrogant abuser of power. But aside from her portrayal, all we know about him is his reputation as a thoughtful and retiring official. To this is added Amalia's violent reaction to a message that no one but she and her sister see. And thus a doubt creeps in, not about Amalia but about Sortini. Perhaps their relationship isn't as simple and crude as it seems. Perhaps Sortini is above all an official distinguished by his great, almost pathological acumen, which allows him to recognize in Amalia, with commendable foresight, and perhaps only because of the singularity of her gaze, traces of a wicked, wholesale rejection of the Castle. And perhaps Amalia too realizes that she has been unmasked. Her despair may stem from that unmasking more than from a sexual insult, which would be in stark contrast to Sortini's manners and nature. After all, we don't know for sure what his message said. Maybe it told Amalia just this: "You're caught." Maybe it was a blackmail note or even a proposed pact of silence. Or maybe it was simply a notice informing her that someone has seen through her little game. Now that's something Amalia could never reveal, for such a notice would in itself be tantamount to expulsion from the village community—it would expose her apostasy, and thus her guilt, leading to the ruin of her entire family.

Amalia is an Antigone who doesn't appeal to natural law but rather simply refuses to "let herself be initiated" into that unnameable amalgam of community and cult that is the Castle. Her rejection of the rules is much more radical than is implied by her gesture of shredding an official's abrupt, coarse, and threatening invitation. The message couldn't, after all, have been an unheard-of outrage, since, as her sister explains to K., relations between village women and officials have a singular characteristic: "We know that women can't help but love the officials if the officials ever approach them, indeed they love them even beforehand, no matter how much they try to deny it." Olga, a shrewd, lucid woman, in whom K. has "complete trust," never speaks imprecisely. And here she uses the word *love* twice. She doesn't say that sometimes, out of self-interest, the women of the village yield to the powerful officials who approach them. Rather she asserts that all the village women *love* the officials, even before they are approached by them. Amalia's gesture is therefore something that profoundly unhinges the order of things, something that denies the very foundation of village life: the irresistible attraction to anything that emanates from the Castle—and above all to its officials.

Before Amalia's gesture, her family was among the most prominent in the village. Her father had plenty of customers who ordered their boots from him. Amalia herself sewed "very beautiful clothes" for the most distinguished villagers. They had kind, influential friends, like Gardena. The father had hopes of an imminent promotion in the Firemen's Association. They lived in a bourgeois house. That fateful third of July, the Firemen's Festival was to have marked the culmination of a slow but sure social ascent. The festival's success might have persuaded the authorities to select Amalia's father as instructor to the Castle firemen. Amid all this, with "the wildest sounds" of the festival trumpets still echoing in their ears, Amalia performs her gesture—and destroys everything. There's no punishment. It's enough that the world withdraws from the family, little by little. All sap ceases to flow. Soon they will find themselves "sitting together with the windows closed in the heat of July and August. Nothing was happening. No summons, no news, no visitors, nothing."

No image of humiliation is more piercing than that of Amalia's father pestering the Castle copyists to let him know his crime so that he might then attempt to obtain a pardon. But no one answers him, because the cobbler has committed no crime—and then he imagines that "they are concealing his crime from him because he isn't paying enough." He has no idea that Castle officials "accept bribes, but only for simplicity's sake, in order to avoid pointless conversations, and in any case you can't get anywhere that way."

To bribe someone for the favor of being accused. Only Block, in *The Trial*, reaches such heights of humiliation.

In his case, however, he must complement it with physical degradation dispensed by Leni, his erotic jailer. Amalia's father punishes himself on his own, with his silent, tortured brooding.

Between Amalia's gesture of shredding Sortini's letter and her father's grueling attempts to make his petitions heard sprawls the gamut of situations that accompanied the persecution of central Europe's Jews. What happened later, in the Hitler years, was first and foremost a literalization of this process, as Karl Kraus warned when he wrote that "to pour salt in open wounds" had ceased to be a metaphor, for the metaphor had been "reabsorbed by its reality." Now the word was etched directly into the flesh, as with the machine in "In the Penal Colony."

The story of Barnabas's family shows what can happen when individuals take themselves out of the game of customs and unspoken precepts. The punishment is archaic and ferocious; it strikes not only the ones who have acted, but all their relatives as well. The Castle doesn't require specific acts of devotion. But it presupposes unquestioning assent to its order. And it avenges itself like nature when one of its equations is questioned.

In addition to her gaze, Amalia has another peculiarity, which K. observes immediately—and it alarms him: she is so "imperious that not only did she appropriate everything said in her presence, but it was all spontaneously conceded to her." It's as if Amalia knows how to take possession of other people's words and turn them inside out until she reaches an ulterior meaning, the only one that matters. Whoever spoke the words meant them in just that way but doesn't dare admit it, even to himself. Thus to converse with Amalia implies offering up one's own hidden thoughts.

In her brief exchanges with K., this happens twice. First, K. says to her, giving his words their most common meaning: "Perhaps you are not initiated into Barnabas's affairs, in which case all's well and I'll drop the matter, but perhaps you are initiated—and this, rather, is my impression—and in that case it's an ugly business, because it would mean your brother is deceiving me." K. seems to focus only on his captious and insinuating distinctions. But for Amalia, it's as if K. has said one word only: "initiated." She responds: "Calm down, I'm not initiated, nothing could induce me to allow myself to be initiated, nothing, not even my regard for you, though I would do many things for you, since we are, as you said, good-natured." With these words, Amalia allows K. to glimpse her secret: she doesn't want to be initiated, at any cost. She's the only person in the village who doesn't want to know what even K. longs to know. One might think that's because she already knows it—and refuses to accept it. There's something stony in her, something impervious to the emanations of the Castle, to its power to ensnare. Perhaps Amalia is mistaken in what she thinks she knows, and yet she's the only person, among all those K. encounters, who is capable of remaining "face to face with the truth." There's no doubt that she clearly understands the

causes of the horrible events that, because of her, have be-
fallen her family. And it's easy to imagine her standing
"quietly in the background, observing the devastation."

The second instance is less obvious. K. begins: "'You
are'—K. was searching for the right word, didn't immediately find it, and made do with a vaguer one—'perhaps
the most good-natured (*gutmütig*) people I've met so
far in the village.'" In his clumsy attempt to maintain
distances, K. chooses the most inappropriate word. Especially as regards Amalia. As Olga informs him a few
moments later, "Amalia was many things, but 'good-
natured' wasn't one of them." Amalia herself is very careful not to say this. Instead she immediately subjects K.'s
word to her process of appropriation, pretending to accept
it ("since we are, as you said, good-natured"). Here we
are witnessing a superior and severe *marivaudage*. First
of all, Amalia uses the inappropriate word, which K. has
chosen, as a pretext for telling him that she will do "many
things" for him. For someone like Amalia, who doesn't
waste words, this is like a fiery confession of love. At the
same time, with her perennial irony, Amalia makes it
clear to K. that his discordant "good-natured" ought to be
replaced by another adjective. Perhaps *good*, a term not
apparently in common use in the village.

The verbal exchanges between Amalia and K. are
scanty; they get straight to the bottom of things—and
then stop there. Olga, on the other hand, speaks continuously. At times one gets the feeling she could go on

forever. But Amalia suddenly enters and interrupts her: "Telling Castle stories? Still sitting here together? And you, K., who wanted to take your leave at once—and now it's nearly ten. So these stories worry you, do they? There are people here who feed on such stories, they sit around together, like you two, and take turns tormenting each other, but you don't strike me as one of those people." Amalia's every word is charged with meaning, but—as Olga will explain later—"it's not easy to understand exactly what she means, since often you can't tell if she's speaking ironically or seriously, mostly she's serious, but sounds ironic." That's the case here with K.: irony is attending her last, profoundly serious, almost desperate attempt to wrest K. away from what Amalia calls "the Castle's influence." But K. doesn't follow her, and instead goes on the offensive with hard words directed at Amalia herself: "I am indeed one of those people, whereas those who don't concern themselves with these stories, leaving them for others to worry about, do not greatly impress me." Words spoken to wound, and well aimed. But Amalia is quick on her feet and replies with a fable in which, if only he wanted to, K. might recognize his own story, held up to the light and sketched with cruel, wise, sarcastic strokes. Amalia says: "I once heard of a young man who devoted his days and nights to contemplating the Castle, neglecting everything else. People feared he might lose his mind because he always kept it up at the Castle, but in the end it turned out that he hadn't really been eyeing the Castle at all, just the daughter of a woman who washed floors in the offices. When he managed to get her, everything went back to normal." Those words are coded. Only K. can know how close they are to the mark—and how full of scorn.

The last completed scene from the incomplete *Castle* features K. and the landlady of the Gentlemen's Inn in the office next to the barroom. The landlady is annoyed by K.'s impertinence—a few hours earlier he dared to comment on her clothes. She reminds him of that, and he pretends not to remember. But his remark was undeniably cheeky: "I'm not looking at you, I'm looking at your dress." Their conversation becomes heated, with K. on the defensive and the landlady on the attack. But what do the landlady's dresses have to do with the complex, ramifying adventure of a land surveyor who has now been reduced to the rank of janitor? We don't know and we aren't told. But we hear in this conversation, as in other episodes, the flutter of something that might be vitally important—and that continues to elude us. The reader's uncertainty here is shared by K., who is sure of only one thing, which he dares to assert: "You're not merely a landlady, as you claim." And a little later he affirms again: "You're not merely a landlady, you have other goals." But what disguised power might the landlady represent? And why the disguise? And to what heights might that power reach?

But all this would remain pointless and abstract, were it not for the landlady's dresses. Put on the spot like a child caught in the act, K. defines them thus: "Made of good material, expensive, but outmoded, overdone, often mended, and threadbare." Furthermore, he tells the landlady, "they're not suitable for a woman of your age, figure, or position." Insolent janitor. But, once again, perceptive.

When the landlord and landlady, the night before, rushed in to reproach K. for having remained in the hallway during the distribution of records, K. noticed at once that the landlady was strangely attired, in a "dark dress, with a full skirt that rustled like silk, poorly buttoned and laced." And he wondered: "Where could she have possibly found it in the rush?" Now the landlady shows him. Right there in the office, next to the iron strongbox, she slides open the doors of a vast, deep wardrobe. Like a satrap, she unveils her treasure: numberless dresses, these too in a range of dark shades, pressed one against the other. And then she adds: "Upstairs I have two more wardrobes full of dresses, two wardrobes, each nearly as large as this one." After this revelation, the dialogue becomes clenched. K. has the nerve to say: "I expected something like this, it's as I said, you're not merely a landlady, you have other goals." And the landlady replies: "My only goal is to dress well." Here the expression "to dress well" seems to belong to the figurative language of the *arcana imperii.* One can imagine Plato and the tyrant Dionysius, in Syracuse, exchanging similar words. Each remark could be said by either of them. And maybe Plato was told at some point what the landlady now tells K.: "You're either a fool or a child, or else a very malicious and dangerous man. Get out of here, now!"

. . .

The role of landlady—whether played by Gardena, who oversees the more modest Bridge Inn, or by the landlady of the Gentlemen's Inn—presupposes a hidden relationship with the Castle. And K. immediately feels its pull. Thus the astute Pepi can hint that K. is less interested in Frieda than in Gardena, since "when one speaks of Frieda one is really speaking of the landlady, whose creature Frieda is."

Gardena is the chief hierodule of Klamm's cult. Frieda is in line to succeed her, but she is ready to abjure. The dresses that the landlady of the Gentlemen's Inn keeps shut away in her vast wardrobe are the temple vestments. Just as Io's brief visits from Zeus gave way to a long life of wandering, remembrance, and despair, so Gardena survives by contemplating the little mementos she was able to pilfer from Klamm. And her devotion has grown in the absence of her beloved. She's now the guardian of the inviolable space that surrounds him wherever he goes. That explains why Gardena has become K.'s most tenacious, most "powerful enemy." She spotted him immediately, just as the high-level agents of the Ochrana could spot a young terrorist in a shapeless mass of students.

Massive and solemn, the only bearer of gravitas in the dense air of the inn she rules over, Gardena is heir to countless generations who, even before being devoted to the *brahman* or to Yahweh, were devoted to certain sharp-eyed Brahmins or sons of Aaron who concerned themselves above all with keeping the locus and liturgy of authority as separate as possible from that surging, shapeless, impure expanse that was the rest of the world. For Gardena, K. is the grain of sand in the gears. She is his great, unrelenting adversary; she clashes with him more than anyone else—and understands him better than anyone else. Or understands, at least, how dangerous he can be.

The landlady of the Gentlemen's Inn is profoundly akin to Gardena, but on a level of higher formality: she is a devotee of an office, which by its nature she doesn't consider to be in the service of anything else. Indeed, the office is the goal toward which all else converges. The true officials are those who protect the officials. Such is the landlady.

K.'s stay in the village rests upon two pillars: his conversations with the two landladies. Both instruct him, rebuke him, and restrain him. Gardena, the landlady of the Bridge Inn, is lower in rank and more exposed to contact with ordinary villagers. Also more vulnerable and pathetic. The other, the landlady of the Gentlemen's Inn, is occupied exclusively with the worship and service of the officials. She is harsher and crueler than Gardena. But they share the same knowledge. What K. at one point thinks about Gardena could be said about either: "An intriguing nature, which seems to operate like the wind, senselessly, following strange remote orders that could never be fathomed."

. . .

The higher circle, to which K. would like to gain access, where indeed he would like to take up residence, since he has "come here to stay," is certainly not the home of good, as benevolent interpreters say, nor is it the home of evil, as malevolent interpreters say; rather it is the site where good and evil arrange themselves into shapes that can't be recognized or distinguished by those who have encountered them only in other circles. The ancient Chinese would not be surprised by this; they would say that they are the two elements united in the Holy Place. But who nowadays is able to reason like the ancient Chinese? The landlady of the Gentlemen's Inn is the only one capable of adoring and venerating the Holy Place *as such*, without requiring any further explanations. Everyone else—not just the foreigner K., but the villagers too—seems divided between memories of blessings enjoyed and curses suffered. They agree on one point only: they would rather remain silent, like the survivors of a patrol that has escaped an ambush. They don't feel like talking and absentmindedly run their fingers over their scars.

The landlady of the Gentlemen's Inn is the true guardian of the orthodoxy. For her the distances separating the parties—that is, everyone—and the Castle are never large enough. Her argument is first of all an aesthetic one, and derives from her "pathological striving for refinement." Simply put, it wasn't pretty when the parties thronged the same spaces frequented by officials. "If it's really necessary and they actually must come," she would

say, "at least, for heaven's sake, let them come single file."
For the landlady the parties, whoever they are and whatever they want to discuss, are merely varieties of postu-
lants, and scarcely more dignified. Essentially, they are all
weak-natured, incapable of getting by on their own—hin-
drances, some worse than others, to the running of the
Castle. That's why the landlady, little by little, drove the
parties out: first into a hallway, then onto the stairs, then
onto the landing, then into the barroom—and finally out
into the street. "But even that wasn't enough for her. She
found it unbearable to be constantly 'under siege,' that's
how she put it, in her own house." How pretty it would all
be, if only it weren't for the traffic of parties. Ultimately,
she can't see what the point of it is. "To get the front steps
dirty," an official once told her, in an angry tone. But
the landlady was careful not to ask herself whether his
sarcasm might have been directed at the question she
had asked. Indeed, "she took pleasure in quoting that
phrase." Her latest idea is to have a building constructed,
facing the Gentlemen's Inn, expressly for the waiting parties. She speaks of it often. But even that project would
be nothing but a stopgap. The ideal solution would be
to prohibit the parties from ever setting foot in the Gentlemen's Inn. Unfortunately, the officials themselves are
against that.

The Castle gentlemen—at least those officials who occasionally make appearances in the village—often behave
more like artists or eccentrics than employees of a vast
administration. They always regard themselves as just

passing through. Something impels them, makes them appear to be thinking about something other than what's in front of them. Even at the lowest level, that of the secretaries, they are easily irritated, because they lead "an uneasy life, not fit for everyone." But even if it's true that "the job is hard on the nerves," they won't give it up for anything, for they can "no longer do without this kind of work." Any other job "would seem insipid" to them. Like all artists, they don't know the "difference between ordinary time and work time." Even when sleeping, they keep a notebook under the covers. They deal with business-related matters seated in the barroom or in bed, letting it be understood that these are the best, most fitting moments for doing so. At times, they take those matters up just before falling asleep, as if they can't disengage from them and want to carry them even into slumber. Some— like Bürgel—admit that they slip directly from office conversations into sleep, and vice versa. They are loath to move "with all their papers" to another location, as if a swirling wake of words adheres to them, has by now become part of their bodies. Some obscure, unending toil seems to be taking place within them. And it must be exhaustion that sometimes leads them—in order to distract themselves, redirect their energies, exercise their limbs, and above all "recover from the constant intellectual exertion"—to take up "carpentry, fine mechanics, and the like." In this they are much like Kafka, who at various times sought refuge from the obsessive nature of his thoughts in carpentry and gardening. Certainly the Castle characters are more persistent, since even at night hammering can be heard coming from their windowless rooms in the Gentlemen's Inn.

The landlady of the Gentlemen's Inn, who knows the Castle officials well, bows to their will, and is able to appreciate the reasons behind it, when they let her know that they won't be accepting her proposal to transfer the interviews and interrogations of the parties to a new building, separated by only a few meters from the Gentlemen's Inn and conceived expressly in order to prevent the parties from setting foot in the Gentlemen's Inn. Every deviation is bothersome, every change a rupture in the delicate sequence of their acts.

Like the two heads of opposed secret-service agencies, K. and the landlady of the Gentlemen's Inn are each capable of anything except believing the other. The game is encoded by both parties. To the landlady, K. isn't a land surveyor or even an aspiring land surveyor (not that she knows anything about that trade; it "made her yawn"). To K., the landlady isn't "merely a landlady." Her clothes alone prove it: ill suited to her position, embellished "with frills and pleats," as overdone as a Byzantine dignitary's. If the two principal adversaries are not what they claim— and at the same time can't say what else they are ("What are you really?" the landlady asks K.)—then doubt hangs over everything. Even the village might be an improvisation, like a Potemkin village. Even the Castle.

Of course, one might be tempted to consider K.'s vicissitudes as the frantic and fruitless attempts of an aspiring land surveyor, on finding himself in the position of school janitor, to assert himself. That is, in short, as a fairly inconsequential series of events. But the landlady of the Gentlemen's Inn, who knows how the world works, thinks differently. She has "had to deal with unruly people of various sorts" and considers K. the worst case she has encountered. With his irresponsible and disrespectful behavior, which leaves her "trembling with indignation," K. has succeeded in making happen "that which had never happened before." If the danger that K. poses is so frightening, if the gentlemen are reduced to wanting to be "finally free of K.," that implies that what has happened around him up to then—the pathetic skirmishes, the mocking equivocations, the long, meandering conversations—must have touched in some obscure way the nerve centers of the Castle's admirable organization, as "gap-free" as Hilbert had wanted the axiomatization of mathematics to be. The landlady and landlord, like true police, are quick to point out that K. will "certainly have to answer" for all this. And his punishment might be as simple as the protraction of his torturous life in that village. But the fact remains, and it is as troubling as ever, that by retracing step by step K.'s course of action, others too might find a way to discover the Castle's various delicate, arcane points. And perhaps to make happen again "that which had never happened before."

Some part of what is, a sizable part, must not be accessible as knowledge. It isn't clear whether that's the case because the knowledge would lead to breakdowns or simply because it would, at a certain point, become inconvenient. In any case, knowledge is the first enemy. This is the premise of the landlady of the Gentlemen's Inn. This is the sanctuary she wants to protect. To her, K. is the interloper, he who—out of thoughtlessness, curiosity, self-interest, arrogance, defiance—wants access to everything. And so must be excluded from everything. In the clash between the landlady and K., every word has a double resonance. From the start, with the complicity of monomaniacs, they address one question only—as they well know. But they address it by speaking incessantly of other things. Even clothes.

V. Powers

I have the privilege, as it were, not only of seeing the night's phantasms during the helpless and blissful abandon of sleep, but also of meeting them in reality, when I have all the force of wakefulness and a calm capacity for judgment.

—from "The Burrow"

In the same octavo notebook, a few lines apart, Kafka drafted two untitled apologues, the first twelve lines long, the second around fifty, which take as their protagonists respectively Sancho Panza and Odysseus. They constitute Kafka's highest tribute to Western literature as well as to Western survival skills. Like all stories about essential matters, these have to do with demons.

Sancho Panza and Odysseus have this in common: both saved themselves using "inadequate, even childish means." Don Quixote, however, was lost. But we will discover through Kafka's story that Don Quixote was a puppet. It wasn't he who spent years reading chivalric romances and losing himself in feverish daydreams. It was Sancho Panza, who quickly grasped that those stories, with all the demons they roused, would soon have killed him. So he concocted the figure of Don Quixote. That's what he chose to call the "devil" that dwelt within him and whose destructive rage he wanted "to divert from himself." Once he had found a name and it had become a character, it could be observed from a certain distance rather than simply endured. And above all he'd get a chance to think about other things. Sancho Panza knew perfectly well that nothing in life was as gripping as one's relations with demons. Demons, however, soon caused one to undertake "the craziest exploits," as indeed would one day happen with Don Quixote. Better then, for Sancho Panza, to redirect the actions of his demons onto another being. He could then resume his own life of modest interest while still following Don Quixote on his expeditions, mainly because he felt a certain "sense of responsibility," since, after all, the knight was his creature. But also because Don Quixote was forever dealing with demons, and Sancho Panza recognized at once that such a situation would provide him "great and useful entertainment." Thus Sancho Panza survived and, among other things, told us the story of Don Quixote.

In more ancient times, when people could still appear beautiful and bold, before it became obligatory to take on a clumsy, scruffy appearance, we find a precursor to Sancho Panza in Odysseus. In those days, it was common knowledge—and not just the domain of the few who went off by themselves to read adventure stories and daydream about them—that life consisted above all in waiting to be possessed by other voices, which brought with them every happiness and every grief. It had been passed down that the most irresistible of these voices, which offered supreme happiness followed at once by certain ruin, were those of the Sirens. Everyone knew that living meant being exposed—someday—to the Sirens' song. Men employed a wide range of stratagems in their attempts to pass by the Sirens and survive. A few succeeded. They sailed by the Sirens' rocks and saw them pass before their eyes. In the air, a perfect silence. They concluded that the Siren song had been only a superstition. But this discovery provoked in them such "arrogance" that they quickly committed some rash act and perished. Thus humanity never learned that the Sirens' song simply didn't exist, and people persisted in their erroneous belief that it was fatal.

Then Odysseus appeared. Common knowledge had it that no expedient, such as stopping the ears with wax or lashing oneself to the mast, was effective against the Sirens. But Odysseus placed his faith in those "poor tricks" alone. (And here Kafka's version departs from Homer's, according to which Odysseus was the only one among his crew *not* to stop his ears with wax.) When his ship passed before them, the Sirens—knowing full well that they were dealing with a powerful adversary—resorted to the weapon that was "even more terrible than their song, namely their silence." And so Odysseus passed unscathed before them, believing that the Sirens' song had failed to penetrate the wax in his ears. The weapon of silence couldn't do its work, because Odysseus was convinced that the Sirens had been singing. He remembered their chests heaving, "their eyes brimming with tears, their mouths half-opened," and believed those signals to be the accompaniments of "arias that were ringing out, unheard, around him." If the Sirens let him pass unharmed, it was probably out of admiration for the man who had endured their silence while lashed to a mast with wax in his ears.

A childish image, certainly, perhaps ridiculous. And yet Odysseus was the only one who, having passed before the Sirens, didn't go off on a rampage pretending to have conquered powers that no one by this time could have overcome. Not just that: of all those who passed before the Sirens and survived, Odysseus was also the only one who didn't doubt the power of their song. Perhaps the Sirens cast a benevolent eye on that tribute. And finally the last, most daring hypothesis, seemingly blasphemous but in truth the most devout: Odysseus "actually realized that the Sirens were silent and held up the fictitious version described above simply, so to speak, as a kind of shield, against both them and the gods." If this hypothesis is true, it doesn't conflict with the previous version of events: Odysseus would have been so complicit with the gods and the Sirens that their benevolence would seem to go without saying. In fact, Odysseus would appear to have collaborated with them to elaborate the legend of the Sirens' song, an extreme metamorphosis of the song itself.

Don Quixote is only a puppet, charged with enduring Sancho Panza's phantasms, who furiously attack and batter him. Sancho Panza sits quietly and reflects. He gazes tenderly on that shaky, feverish creature, whom he's thrown into the world and into literature simply so that he himself—Sancho Panza—can stand back and catch his breath. Don Quixote can speak with impunity about theology—or chivalry—and can let himself be devoured by them. Sancho Panza observes it all quietly. And he "never boasted about it." According to some, all he made of it was a novel.

In June 1913 Kafka noted in his *Diaries:* "The immense world I have in my head. But how to free myself and it without tearing. And a thousand times better to tear than to hold it back or bury it in me. It's the reason I'm here, that's entirely clear to me." To tear, but what? His head, or the phantasms? Or both? Judicious action was called for, so that the phantasms, on being uprooted, wouldn't injure his head—or disfigure themselves. In any case, the liberation was always a double one: of the phantasms and from the phantasms. That's why Sancho Panza invented Don Quixote.

For Kafka, as for Sancho Panza, relations with the powers were so rooted in physiology, perceptible even in the act of breathing, that the first thought, and the rashest, was to liberate oneself from them. But Kafka knew that such a liberation would be illusory.

The greatest accomplishment consisted in establishing a certain distance. In sitting at a table and observing the powers—such as those apparitions of Don Quixote's unbridled delirium—with relief, but also with something at stake. Following their transformations, but always standing off to one side, like an extra. That's all one can ask. It's the highest wisdom. Sancho Panza is the only person Kafka ever characterized as "a free man."

.   .   .

There's a point where all the powers get sucked into the same well. The closest approximation of that point was Kafka's writing table. That's why, as he would write one day to Oskar Baum, "the moving of a table in my own room" seemed no less terrible than the prospect of a trip to Georgental. And then he explained why the prospect of that trip frightened him so much: "In the last or next-to-last analysis, it's only fear of death. In part also the fear of attracting the gods' attention; if I continue to live here in my room, if every day passes as usual like the one before, it's obvious that someone will have to attend to me, but the thing is already in motion, the gods hold the reins only mechanically, it's so lovely, so lovely not to be noticed, if there was a fairy by my cradle it must have been the 'Retirement' fairy."

The next day, in a letter to Brod, Kafka spoke again of this "fear of attracting the gods' attention." But this time the expression is the opening chord of a *Leçon de Ténèbres* on writing. What follows is the closest thing to a demonology of writing that has come down to us. Even if the writer restricts his field of vision to one room, and within that room to a desk, his condition is still not secure. What he's missing is the floor, "fragile or positively non-existent" beneath his feet. And that floor covers "a darkness, whose obscure power surfaces of its own accord, and heedless of my stammering destroys my life." What, then, does writing consist of?

> Writing is a sweet, marvelous reward, but for what? In the night it became clear to me, as clear

as a lesson for children, that it's the reward for
having served the devil. This descent toward the
dark powers, this unchaining of spirits that are
naturally kept bound, the dubious embraces and
everything else that can happen down below, and
of which you don't recall anything when you're
up above, writing stories in the light of day. Perhaps some other kind of writing exists, but I know
only this. At night, when fear won't let me sleep, I
know only this. And its diabolical element seems
absolutely clear. It's the vanity and the sensuality,
they circle continuously around our own figure,
or someone else's—in which case the movement
multiplies, becomes a solar system of vanity—and
feast on it. What the ingenuous man sometimes
desires ("I would like to die and see how they
mourn me"), is played out constantly by a writer
of this kind, he dies (or doesn't live) and constantly mourns himself. This is the origin of his
terrifying fear of death, which can't present itself
as fear of death, but might appear instead as fear
of change, fear of Georgental.

The vortex swirls fiercely. But the most difficult and
esoteric part isn't that involving the "descent toward the
dark powers," in which the highest Romantic tradition
and the distilled spirit of *décadence* seem to converge.
The part that's most coded, and most unexpected, is
where Kafka speaks of "the vanity and the sensuality"
that belong to a certain practice of writing, the only one
he claims to know. What sensuality, what vanity, does
he mean? And what is the "dark power" that assails the

writer's life in order to destroy it? Kafka pointed to it a little later in the same letter:

> I'm sitting here in the comfortable posture of the writer, ready for all things beautiful, and I must observe without intervening—because what else can I do but write?—as my poor, defenseless real self (the existence of the writer is an argument against the soul, because the soul has plainly abandoned the real self, but only to become a writer, unable to go beyond that; could the separation from the self possibly weaken the soul that much?) is stung, cudgeled, nearly ground to bits by the devil, on a random pretext, a little excursion to Georgental.

When these lines are placed alongside certain shamanistic confessions, phrases that seemed obscure and thorny become piercingly clear. That abandoned body, that living corpse, that "forever corpse" whose "strange burial" the writer is quick to observe, is the shaman's body, inanimate and motionless as his spirit travels widely, among the branches of the tree of the world, in the company of animals and other supernatural assistants. One can't, however, take much pleasure in the journey (as "vanity" might wish): breaking away from the "real self," the soul is left weakened, capable only of becoming "a writer, unable to go beyond that" (acme of sarcasm). And his activity will consist above all in "enjoying with all [his] senses or, which is the same thing, wanting to tell the story of" what happens with the writer's "old corpse." But this can succeed only in a state of "utter self-forgetfulness—the first prerequisite of being a writer isn't wakefulness but self-forgetfulness." Twice, in this phrase and in the parenthesis on the soul and its split from the "real self," Kafka has gone quite far in his description of the *prima materia* of literature. This is his Kamchatka. For those who wanted to follow him, he left, at the end of the letter, the most concise definition of the kind of writer he felt himself to be: "The definition of a writer, of this kind of writer, and the explanation of the effects he has, if he ever has any: he is humanity's scapegoat, he allows others to enjoy sin without guilt, almost without guilt." Painful, abysmal irony in that "almost without guilt": a nod to the illusory innocence of the pleasure that binds every reader to literature.

There was a graphologist in Sylt, in the pension where Felice was staying during a vacation. Felice asked him to examine Kafka's handwriting and later sent Kafka the results. These seemed to him false and rather ridiculous. But "the falsest assertion among all the falsehoods" was this: according to the graphologist, the subject showed "artistic interests." No—that was an insult. Kafka replied sharply: "I don't have literary interests, I'm made of literature, I'm nothing else and can be nothing else."

A few days later, and still as part of his attempt to explain to Felice why he considered himself unsuited to spending his life with another person, Kafka described himself as a creature who "is bound by invisible chains to an invisible literature and who screams when approached, thinking someone is touching that chain."

. . .

It's awkward to speak of symbols in Kafka, because Kafka experienced everything as symbol. It wasn't a choice—if anything, it was a sentence. Symbols belonged to everything he perceived, just as fluidity belongs to our perception of water. He didn't call them *Symbole*, but rather *Sinnbilder*, "emblems," at least in the beginning. That noun is composed of *Sinn*, "sense" or "meaning," and *Bild*, "image." *Images that have meaning:* Kafka felt himself compelled to live perennially among them. At times he wanted to escape them.

When his tuberculosis manifested he wrote Brod: "In any case, there remains the wound, of which my wounded lungs are merely the emblem (*Sinnbild*)." And in his *Diaries*, two days later, he wrote the same words: "If the wound to my lungs is merely an emblem, as you maintain, an emblem of the wound whose inflammation is called Felice and whose depth is called justification, if that's how it is, then even the doctor's advice (light air sun quiet) is an emblem. Seize it."

But how does one move from symbols to the story? Kafka gave his illness a theatrical shape: first, subtly, in his letter to Brod where he spoke of his "wound"; then again, more crudely, in one of his first letters to Milena:

> It happened that my brain could no longer bear the anguish and suffering it was burdened with. It said: "I surrender. But if there are any others here who care about preserving the whole, they're welcome to take some of my load so that we can keep going a while longer." At that point my lungs

came forward, having little to lose. Those negotiations between my brain and lungs, which took place without my knowledge, must have been frightening.

The scene is already set. The characters enter. The dialogue might be like certain exchanges that are sprinkled through his *Diaries*—disjointed, meandering. Something like this: "You kill him, I can't do it." "Okay, but I'll need a little time." "Fine, but don't forget."

Kafka's intolerance for big words. If uttered by a young woman, breathlessly, he had the impression that they emerged "like fat mice from her little mouth."

"The bystanders stiffen when the train goes past." It's the first sentence of his *Diaries*, set apart. The train is time, which doesn't permit us to grasp its shape. Only a sudden wind, jumbled outlines. But we can tell it's passing. And it's impossible not to stiffen as we watch it: one last gesture of resistance. This is an example of what Kafka wasn't able to avoid perceiving: reflexes, fixed gestures, involuntary gestures, dead metaphors that brood over their secrets like insects trapped in amber.

For Kafka, the metaphorical and the literal had the same weight. The passage from one to the other was smooth. The metaphorical could take the place of the literal and transform the literal into metaphor. That life may be a trial punctuated by punishments could give rise to the metaphor of an entire life as a judicial trial.

But that judicial trial could then become literal, its articulation so ramified and subtle as to evoke as metaphor the proceedings of life itself. The back-and-forth between the two planes was continual and imperceptible. And the presence of the metaphorical plane also worked to distance the literal from its proximity to the ground of things, rendering it dense and muffled, lacking that breath that comes only with the capacity to split in two.

Like Wittgenstein in the margins of Frazer's *Golden Bough*, Kafka revealed his "primitive gaze" only in passing or between parentheses. An exemplary instance can be found in a letter to Robert Klopstock from March 1922 (as *The Castle* was being written):

> You need only keep in mind that you're writing to a poor little man who is possessed by every possible evil spirit, of every type (one of medicine's undeniable merits is having introduced, in place of the notion of possession, the consoling concept of neurasthenia, which has however rendered recovery more difficult and furthermore has left open the question of whether it is weakness and sickness that lead to possession or whether, on the other hand, weakness and sickness are themselves a stage of possession, preparing the man to become a bed of rest and pleasure for the impure spirits), a man who feels tormented if this condition of his isn't recognized, but apart from that it's possible to get along decently with him.

From Psellus's treatise on demons to Judge Schreber and Freud, a long, jagged stretch of psychic history is covered with cool irony in those parenthetical lines, which seem written by a Desert Father, wise in the ways of spirits.

Kafka once recounted to Milena an episode that settled in advance a vast part of the literature that would accumulate around him: "Recently a *Tribuna* reader told me that I must have done great research in a madhouse. 'Just in my own,' I told him. And then he tried to compliment me again on 'my madhouse.'"

Peremptorily, unexpectedly, Kafka one day wrote in his *Diaries* that "all such literature" (meaning first of all his own) was an "attack on the frontier" and could even "have developed into a new secret doctrine, into a Kabbalah" (adding, in a clarification that goes to the heart of his thought on modern Judaism: "had Zionism not intervened"). In the fragment that precedes this, "the attack on the frontier" is more explicitly an "attack on the last earthly frontier." But how did Kafka arrive at that expression? The fragment appears in the context of an account of an extremely severe, overwhelming crisis experienced in January 1922, shortly before he began the draft of *The Castle:* "In the past week I suffered something like a breakdown, worse than any except perhaps that one night two years ago; I haven't experienced other examples. Everything seemed over, and still today nothing seems much different." What had happened? "First of all: breakdown, impossible to sleep, impossible to stay awake, impossible to endure life, or more precisely the course of life." The cause of the breakdown is a tear in the fabric of time. External time and internal time now proceed at different rates: "The clocks don't agree, the internal one chases along in a diabolical or demoniacal or in any case inhuman fashion, the external one limps along at its usual pace." They differ not only in speed but in direction: thus "the two different worlds divide and keep dividing or at least tear themselves horribly." The decisive word here has already sounded: "chases." The internal process resembles a mad chase, a chase that "takes the path that leads away from humanity." Its "wild nature" can't be described in other terms—and in fact the word *chase* returns six times in the next few lines. In the end, however, Kafka recognizes that the chase is "only an image." But what can take the place of an image? Only another image. Such as this one: the chase could be called an "attack on the last earthly frontier." Thus the image is developed— and even more coded. Enigmas can be resolved only by further enigmas. And as if to prove that, Kafka immediately takes the image of the attack on the frontier and splits it in two. Because *two* types of attack can be made: an "attack launched from below by mankind," which can be "replaced, since this too is only an image, with the image of an attack directed at me from above." If there is one passage that distills Kafka's peculiar process, it's this one. Knowledge leads to the evocation of an image. And that image is immediately recognized as "only an image."

To move beyond it, it will have to be replaced—with another image. The process is never-ending. No image exists about which it can't be said that it's "only an image." But neither does any knowledge exist that isn't an image. This vicious circle offers no exit and perhaps approximates a definition of literature. Through image.

Here the passage breaks off. The next begins: "All such literature is an attack on the frontier." On the heels of that comes the reference to "a Kabbalah"—a further image. The chase and the Kabbalah: each unleashes the other.

But what feeds that chase its endless, unruly energy? Kafka knows that the frenetic "internal pace" may have "various causes," but certainly "the most obvious is self-observation, which never allows an image to rest quietly, but rather keeps chasing it farther and farther, only to become an image itself and be chased in turn by a new self-observation." The demoniacal, provocative, hounding element is, therefore, self-observation. Which in Kafka was extreme. But precisely because he was so adept at it, he always regarded it with suspicion, rather the way Homer's characters regarded the gods—for they had occasionally encountered them and bore the scars to prove it. To Kafka, the avoidance of self-observation thus seemed, at times, felicitous, yet just two months before his chasing crisis, in November 1921, he called self-observation an "unavoidable obligation." His reasoning behind that declaration is in itself suggestive of the movements of his stories: "If someone else is observing me, then naturally I ought to observe myself as well; if no one is observing me, then I must observe myself all the more closely."

Self-observation appeared, therefore, inevitable, like breath. On the other hand, it was self-observation that instigated and aggravated the wild chase that later rendered his life intolerable, because of the enormous split it created between internal time—the time of the observing conscience—and the time of the outside world. Such a declaration did not allow any way out, except, perhaps, as Kafka suggested once (but only once and even then he quickly backtracked), a way out through writing: "Strange, mysterious, perhaps dangerous, perhaps liberating consolation of writing: a leap out of the murderer's row of action-observation, action-observation, creating a higher type of observation, higher, not sharper, and the higher it is, the farther from the reach of the 'row,' the more independent it becomes, the more it follows its own laws of motion, the more incalculable, joyous, ascendant its course." *Trostlos*, "unconsoling," is a word Kafka often used at crucial points. "The good is, in a certain sense, unconsoling," according to the thirtieth Zürau aphorism. And in *The Castle*, when Bürgel reveals to K. how the world keeps its equilibrium, he describes the "system" as wonderful but "in some ways unconsoling." So it's all the more surprising that Kafka attributes a certain amount of "consolation" to "writing." Only here does writing appear as the one way to free oneself from (*hinausspringen*, "to leap out of," is Kafka's strongly dynamic verb) the murderous chain of action and reaction, forged from matter and mind, that otherwise constricts and coerces our lives.

The only chance for salvation lies in *splitting one's gaze in two*. And the second gaze needn't be "sharper"—it's enough that it operate from a certain height (in order to observe the proceedings below in their entirety). The wound produced by the original split in the self-observing gaze can, therefore, be healed only by a *further* split. Thus every ingenious vision of a salvation reachable through a recovered unity of the subject is denied. Such a unity has never existed, except as a mirage inspired by the fear of disintegration. Kafka said nothing more on this theme in this entry, which is from January 1922. And he never took it up again. But his only expressible *promesse de bonheur* related to writing appeared in those lines.

Just after the words about the "strange, mysterious, perhaps dangerous, perhaps liberating consolation of writing," Kafka noted: "Although I wrote my name clearly at the hotel, and although they themselves have written it correctly twice already, they still have Josef K. written in the register. Should I explain the situation to them, or should I have them explain it to me?"

"It's as if spiritual combat were taking place somewhere in a forest clearing." Like some Father Scupoli restored to life, and without any modern mitigation, Kafka maintains that everything revolves around that combat. What else could it be about? But how to approach it? At this point the scene quickly becomes muddled and snarled, becomes a story without an ending: "I enter the forest, find nothing and quickly, out of weakness, hurry back out; often, as

I'm leaving the forest, I hear or think I hear the clanging of weapons from that battle. Perhaps the combatants are gazing through the forest darkness, looking for me, but I know so little about them, and that little is deceptive." If the forest, the *aranya*, is the place of esoteric knowledge, then the combatants are like the *rishis*, the sages who observe the world through the dark tangle of branches rather than from on high among the stars of Ursa Major. Whoever ventures into the forest feels stalked by their gaze but can't manage to see them. And what has been passed down about them is by now very unreliable. Memory of names, of characters, is lost. What remains is the sound of metal clashing in the dark.

In the first weeks of 1922, when internal time breaks away from external time to run its mad race, wakefulness is constant, tormenting. Distance from the world grows. Demons throng—or phantasms. Whom else would Kafka mean when he writes: "Escaped them"? *Them:* the pronoun of the possessed and the obsessed. An invisible struggle is under way, a game of stratagems, a protracted duel: "Escaped them. Some kind of nimble jump. At home by the lamp in the silent room. Unwise to say this. It calls them out of their forests, as if one had lit the lamp to help them find their way." Demoniacal shorthand. Only the writer and the phantasms know exactly what is being said. The rest of us might notice, at most, a certain violent tremor in the still air, amid the snow, the woods, the squatting houses—the landscape of *The Castle*.

The last entry in the *Diaries* seems to imply that by now "the spirits" had *taken Kafka's hand*. Once again: literally. Thus the writer is afraid to make marks on paper: "Every word, twisted in the hands of the spirits—this spring of the hand is their characteristic motion—becomes a spear pointing back at the speaker. Particularly an observation like this." Writing itself has become the weapon the spirits use to run the writer through. And the process repeats itself "ad infinitum" for the man who sees himself now as "incapable of everything, except suffering."

Appropriate precautions when approaching Kafka, according to Canetti: "There are certain writers—very few, in fact—who are so utterly themselves that any statement one might presume to make about them might seem barbarous. One such writer was Franz Kafka; accordingly, one must, even at the risk of seeming slavish, adhere as closely as possible to his own statements."

Entry in the *Diaries:* "I don't believe there are people whose inner state resembles mine, though I can at least imagine such people. But that the secret raven flies constantly around their heads, as it does around mine, this I can't even imagine." Approaching Kafka, the air is lightly stirred by those black wings.

VI. On the Waters of the Dead

The hunter Gracchus is covered by a "large, flowery silk shawl with fringe," like a woman from the South. No signs of rigor mortis are visible, though he lies "without moving and, apparently, without breathing." On the contrary, his sunburned face, his bushy, disheveled hair and beard, radiate the vitality and virility of a hunter. Or an old salt. One day—in the fourth century after Christ—this young hunter of the Black Forest, while stalking a chamois, fell off a cliff and died. Since then he has wandered on a boat, utterly adrift. Osiris had shown how to cross the night sky on the boat of the dead. Had described the route, the currents, the necessary magic words. But little was said about what might happen if one got lost because of an inadvertent turn of the rudder, "a momentary lapse of the pilot's attention." There seems to be no remedy for that. As Gracchus says, "the desire to help me is a sickness that can be cured only by bed rest."

Was he a pagan, Gracchus? Was he a Christian? We don't know. He was a hunter. Like a sailor in a tavern, and with the single-mindedness of a loner, Gracchus continues to repeat: "I was a hunter, is that some kind of crime?" He doesn't know that his existence is like a trap-door through which one tumbles down the walls of time. And the farther one falls, the clearer it seems that his question has an answer: "Yes, it's a crime. Indeed, it's *the* crime." If there's one thing humans have always felt as such, at every latitude, it's that unprecedented transition, after having been torn to pieces for thousands of years by invincible predators, to becoming predators themselves, by inventing a prosthesis, the arrowhead, to rival the fangs of the great cats. The other animals never forgave humans for this leap. They kept on faithfully being what they had always been. They killed and let themselves be killed according to the ancient rules. Only humans dared expand their repertoire of gestures. Gracchus was the latest witness to that transition, the latest manifestation of the hunter in his pure state. The most modern, even if he is fifteen centuries old. His life—now so remote—appeared to him as the natural order itself: "It was my lot to be a hunter in the Black Forest, where wolves still roamed in those days. I would lie in wait, shoot at my mark, hit it, skin it—is that a crime? My labors were blessed. The great hunter of the Black Forest, they called me. Is that a crime?" Yet a nagging doubt persisted, unreasonably. Unless perhaps because, in the long hours he spent lying on his bier, covered by the flowery shawl with the fringe, Gracchus was forced to look at "a small image on the facing wall, clearly a bushman, who is aiming a spear at me and taking cover as best he can behind a magnificently painted shield." That image, "one of the stupidest" of the many incongruous, haphazard images that one encountered on all kinds of boats, taken from some kind of *Magasin pittoresque*, annoyed the hunter Gracchus because its absurdity reminded him of something. It reminded him of history, the history that gets lost in the shadows of time, that history in which his own part was negligible at best—and yet still excessive, if one sought to understand it, follow it. Too many things had happened in fifteen hundred years. And now, who knows why, Gracchus has ended up in that port on an Italian lake, and a stranger is asking him, with a grave and inquisitive air, to explain the "connections." The connections! What did he expect to learn from them? Here Gracchus's sarcasm, his painful sarcasm, erupts. "The ancient, ancient stories. All the books are full of them," the hunter replies—and if we listen closely, we'll notice that he's about to be overcome by an unusual form of aphasia: the aphasia born of history. "So much time has passed. How can I keep it all in this overstuffed brain," says Gracchus, as if to himself. For such a man, who lives amid an overpopulation of stories that can no longer be understood, nothing remains but to pour more wine for the ignorant stranger who continues to pester him with questions—he's company, after all, someone to talk to. Such a companion might be found in any port and is always comforting, because he offers the chance to repeat certain phrases, phrases others before him have heard in countless other ports: "And here I am, dead, dead, dead. And I don't know why I'm here." Words to repeat yet one more time before the story breaks off and Gracchus turns his gaze back toward the bushman whose spear is pointing toward him.

Many are the hardships that the hunter Gracchus must endure. Like the legendary mariner, he has a story to tell that no one will hear to its end. Or that no one will be able to grasp. Because Gracchus is *made* of time. His body has accumulated the impatience of centuries. Gracchus knows what it means to approach, dozens and dozens of times, the celestial waters only to be turned back each time. Not violently, but as if by a trick of the currents. And yet those waters looked so similar. The transition looked easy. And it had been for countless dead. But not for Gracchus. On an immense stairway of waters, his boat sometimes rose, sometimes fell, "sometimes to the right, sometimes to the left, always in motion." But he never succeeded in reaching the liberating, celestial waters.

At the same time, this aberrant, lonely condition, in which Gracchus is completely alive and at the same time "dead, dead, dead," isn't even an object of people's curiosity. "You are *not* the talk of the town," his anonymous and cruel interlocutor, who belongs to the land, informs him. For those who live on the land, it isn't news that Gracchus is wandering all the earthly waters without ever reaching the celestial waters. By now figures such as "the great hunter of the Black Forest" are found only in the occasional children's book or an ethnographic encyclopedia. When people stop to talk with Gracchus, they may demand that his story's "connections" be made clear to them, but nothing in their experience bears any relation to that time when wolves still roamed the Black Forest. How, then, to explain, how to tell that story? People think it's enough to have historiographers who sit "in their studies gaping at the distant past and describing it incessantly." They describe, sure. But do they know? Have they ever felt that terror, that awe? This is what the hunter Gracchus wonders, as his brain churns with stories that will never find an outlet, a listener who can understand them, just as the boat that carries him will never plow through celestial waters.

VII. A Photograph

*I came into this world with a fine wound; I wasn't provided
with anything else.*

—from "A Country Doctor"

During the night of September 22, 1912, Kafka experienced his birth as a writer. It was a delivery: "The Judgment," he would one day write, "came out" of its author
"covered with filth and mucus." The labor lasted eight
hours, from ten in the evening till six in the morning. A
new structure, a previously untested chemical compound,
was introduced to the world in a perfect, self-contained,
compact form. The drastic, ceremonial nature of the event
brought the writer's greatest strengths to bear on that
story. Reading "The Judgment," we see parading past us
the traits that will later appear everywhere in Kafka, and
first among them an irrepressible tendency to play with
disproportion. On one hand, we observe the steady pace
of the narration, its calm, considered, diligent tone. And
on the other the enormity, even the horror, of what is
being narrated.

The plot is an insolent absurdity. One Sunday morning,
a young businessman (Georg Bendemann) looks out the
window of his house by the river. He has just finished

writing a letter to a friend who years before moved to Russia—without achieving notable success there. The young businessman, meanwhile, has seen his business flourish. Now, he feels embarrassed as he writes to his friend, thinking that any reference to his own successes might seem an allusion to the other's failures. Thus he has always avoided discussing the details of his life. But now there's a new fact: the young businessman has become engaged. Should he reveal this to his friend? He decides to do so in the letter he writes that Sunday morning.

Later he stops by his father's room and tells him that he has written to his friend, announcing his engagement. The father, after a brief exchange, asks his son whether the St. Petersburg friend really exists. A little later, he asserts that the St. Petersburg friend doesn't exist. The son insists that, three years earlier, the father even met the friend. Then he lifts his father in his arms and lays him down in bed. After further remarks, the father stands up in his bed and begins to rage. He says he knows the son's friend. He asks his son why he has deceived him. Then he starts in on the fiancée and declares that his son chose her "because she lifted her skirts." Father and son continue to argue. And the father concludes: "I sentence you now to death by drowning!" The son feels "driven from the room" and makes a dash for the bridge. He throws himself nimbly into the river, yelling: "Dear parents, still I've always loved you."

"The Judgment" is a spare story. If the plot is reduced to its threads, its strangeness becomes even more arresting.

Nothing in the course of the telling gets explained, but one feels the pressure of enormous forces. Is this psychology? Or an astral storm? If it is psychology, how can its elements be named, isolated? This once, Kafka himself shows how it's done, like an obstetrician: only he has "the hand that can reach the body itself and the will to do so." Thus he explains that the name Georg Bendemann is a transformation of Franz Kafka, obtained through a few easy operations on the letters, of the kind many writers practice almost automatically, without needing to resort, as some have zealously supposed, to the Kabbalah. Similarly, the name of Georg's fiancée, Frieda Brandenfeld, corresponds to that of Kafka's future fiancée, Felice Bauer, to whom the story is dedicated. It would be difficult to demonstrate more plainly the relationship between the short story and certain facts of the author's life. And not only of his past and present but of his future. Just as the story elsewhere exposes Georg's friend, in 1912, to "Russian revolutions" that didn't reach their climax until 1917, one passage anticipates a scene that will take place in Kafka's life seven years later. In the story, as the father is raging against Georg, the fiancée suddenly becomes his target: "Because she lifted her skirts," the father began to whisper in a flutelike voice, "because she lifted her skirts like this, that disgusting goose," and to demonstrate, he lifted his nightshirt up high enough that the scar on his thigh from the war was visible, "because she lifted her skirts like this, and like this and this, you thrust yourself forward and, in order to have your way with her in peace, you disgraced our mother's memory, betrayed your friend, and chased your father into bed so that he can't get out." Ferocious, grotesque words. At this point the story, which had begun as the chronicle of an ordinary daily event in a bourgeois interior, worthy of being told only for a certain play of nuance, bursts open onto a horrible intimacy, so excessive that it seems to distance itself from any possible autobiographical pretext. Wrong impression.

One day in 1919 Kafka revealed to his father his intention to marry Julie Wohryzek, and he received in reply the following words, which can now be read between quotation marks in his *Letter to His Father:* "She probably put on a fancy blouse, something these Prague Jewesses know how to do, and so you, of course, immediately decided to marry her. And what's more, as soon as possible, in a week, tomorrow, today. I don't understand you, you're a grown-up, you live in a city, but you can't find any solution other than marrying the first girl who comes along." The lifted skirts of the short story have become the "fancy blouse" of the dramatic dialogue between father and son. The story, however, lacks the dialogue's conclusion: "Aren't there other options? If they scare you, I'll come with you myself." In order to divert his thirty-six-year-old son from his intention to get married, Hermann Kafka offered to accompany him to a brothel, if he was scared of going alone. As his father spoke, his mother entered and left the room, removing objects from the table with an expression that indicated tacit accord with her husband. It was her silent motions that Kafka focused on.

His father, meanwhile, kept on amassing words that were even "more detailed and more direct."

On a page of his *Diaries*, written when he was correcting the proofs of "The Judgment," Kafka decided to describe "all the relationships" that had "become clear to [him] in the story." The result was something almost unbearably psychological, which doesn't, however, resemble anything called by that name before or since. Let's observe. First of all, what or who is the distant friend? "The friend is the link between father and son, he is their greatest commonality." Sitting at the window, having just finished the letter to the friend, "Georg wallows pleasurably in this commonality, he believes he has his father within him and feels at peace with everything, except for a fleeting sadness in his thoughts." For a moment the son feels as if he has incorporated his father into himself, thus dominating him. But "the story's development" will show that this feeling is an illusion: like a demon from a bottle, the father "emerges from their commonality, from the friend," and pits himself against Georg, taking over, also, the other elements that link them, such as the dead mother and "the clientele, originally won over to the store by the father." The father, therefore, has everything, "Georg has nothing." Not even the fiancée remains: "she can't enter the ring of blood that encircles father and son" and so is "easily driven away by the father." This, then, is the father-son "relationship": a "ring of blood" that expels every foreign element, a magic circle that surrounds them. Georg passes from the delirious belief that "he has his father within him" to the certainty that the "ring of blood" excludes his own existence. Indeed his place is occupied by another Georg, the friend, a puppet who was "never sufficiently protected, exposed to Russian revolutions," and who in any case has now become "foreign, become autonomous." What is left, then, for Georg? "The gaze toward the father." That's how Kafka defines the eye that observes the scene that his hand is writing down in "The Judgment." And if the story's ending, with the sentence and the suicide, seems at first monstrously irrational, it now seems the final, consequent, and almost self-evident step in the working out of an equation.

As long as Bendemann remains brooding in his room, the episode appears to promise what might be called psychological chiaroscuro, in the end of little interest. The prose in this section, however, stands out immediately for an incisiveness and clarity that seem almost excessive with respect to the episode's slightness. Something changes when the young Bendemann moves from his room to his father's, "where he hadn't been in months." And we notice at once, even if we can't say why, a change in the tone. The room is dark, the father is sitting beside the window. On the table, the remains of a breakfast. Then the father gets up and walks. His heavy dressing gown falls open, and the son thinks: "My father is still a giant." This sentence introduces us to a new register, which belongs under the heading *disproportion*. But it's a disproportion that is never signaled. Everything proceeds as before, as if the father were an actual giant, confined to a little room, while both the reader and the son consider him such only metaphorically.

An imperceptible line of demarcation separates the events in the son's room—which are dull, calm, and reasonable—from the events in the father's room—which are obscure, violent, and extreme. The great nineteenth-century writers shared a worshipful—or at least respectful—attitude toward that line. Some placed themselves in the son's room, others in the father's room. And occasionally they passed from one to the other. But they always took the necessary precautions—and each time they gave warning that they were passing to *the other side.* With Kafka there's no warning. The shift is smooth and nothing foreshadows it. A current takes the narrative, the current Kafka referred to when describing the eight consecutive hours he spent one night writing "The Judgment," from start to finish: "The frightening strain and the joy, the way the story unfurled before me, while I moved forward inside a wave." And at the same time he felt overwhelmed by the feeling that "anything could be dared," because "for all ideas, even the strangest, there awaits a great fire in which they dissolve and are reborn."

The father is a toothless giant. As soon as he begins to speak with his son, the intensity rises. The tone becomes allusive, laden with pathos. We hear him speak of "certain unpleasant things that have happened since the death of our dear mother." And then suddenly a question that is also a provocation: "Do you really have this friend in St. Petersburg?" One of the two is crazy, the reader immediately thinks. Either the son, who concocts with all

manner of trickery a letter to a nonexistent person. Or
the father, who is convinced that his son is talking to
him about a nonexistent friend. By this point, the narrative ground has already begun to give way beneath the
reader's feet. But not beneath the narrator's, who continues on, unflappable.

The son now declares that he's worried about his father's health. Perhaps he thinks his father is crazy, but he
limits himself to suggesting a few changes in his father's
"way of life." And in the meantime he should get more
light (as if the father usually remained in the dark). Open
a window. Maybe change rooms. But the son's attentions
go further: he wants to put the giant to bed, to help him
undress. One suspects that each of them considers the
other crazy. The torturous dialogue resumes: "You don't
have any friend in St. Petersburg. You've always been a
prankster and you've never spared even me," the father
says. Now the son looks more like a mocking deceiver
than a madman. Meanwhile he is undressing the father.
He lifts him from his chair, as he might a child or an in-
valid. And he patiently explains that the father himself
met the friend three years earlier. He reminds the father
that on that occasion the friend had told "amazing stories
about the Russian revolution" (of 1905). The undressing
continues: now the son removes the father's long, woolen
underwear and his socks. He observes moreover that the
undergarments are not "particularly clean" and wonders
whether he shouldn't take it upon himself to change them.
This question leads to another, much more important one:
where will the father live when the son marries? The son

planned to have him "remain in the old apartment alone." But now, suddenly, as he's undressing him, the son decides to bring his father with him to his new home. At this point he takes his father in his arms and lays him down on the bed. In the space of a few lines the giant shrinks. He's helpless and light, and yet his son feels a "frightening sensation" as he approaches the bed with his father in his arms. The father is playing raptly with his son's watch chain. He's tenacious, doesn't want to let go. Perhaps that implies something terrible already. Then the father stretches out and covers himself up to his shoulders. This scene of filial attention seems about to end—and we still don't know whether it's the father or the son who's delirious, or the pair of them.

And here, abruptly, we enter the story's third phase: pure violence. The father throws off the cover. He rises up on the bed, placing "one hand lightly on the ceiling." (Has he turned back into a giant? Or is the room unusually small?) His words reveal a new scenario. The St. Petersburg friend exists, of course he does, indeed the father says he would have been "my kind of son." And the father adds: "That's why you've deceived him all these years." The son is once again accused of being a deceiver: not of the father now but of the friend. But the father, "fortunately," can see through the son, who can't escape his gaze. Now the father appears to the son as a "bogeyman." And even the image of his friend in Russia has changed utterly and stands out now against a murky, churning backdrop. The friend appears "lost in the vastness of Russia"; he stands in the doorway of a plundered shop, "among the wreckage of shelving and ruined wares." The father isn't finished yet with his cruel rant—now he comes to sex. Surely the fiancée was chosen merely "because she lifted her skirts," the father says, imitating "that disgusting goose" by raising his nightshirt high enough that the "war scar" on his thigh could be seen.

The disproportion has been exacerbated. The son looks on from a corner, trying to control himself. But he lets a word escape: "Comedian!" The father rails on. He accuses the son of having supplanted him, of "going through life triumphantly closing deals" that his own hard work made possible.

The calm, lazy Sunday morning in a bourgeois interior has become the stage for a ferocious duel. The son can feel this wish taking shape: "If only he'd fall over and shatter!" But the father doesn't fall. He says: "I'm still much stronger than you." Now his words bend toward their final arc. He says he's been expecting this scene with the letter for years. It's as if everything that happened between father and son were distilled in that letter. The St. Petersburg friend knew everything too. The son has one last thrust: "So you've been lying in wait for me!" But nothing can slow the father as he approaches the moment of sentencing: "And so know this: I sentence you now to death by drowning!" Standing on his bed in his night-shirt, with his stringy white hair and his toothless mouth, the father has passed judgment. The son feels driven from the room. He is concerned now only with letting as little

time as possible pass between the sentence and its execution, and so he flings himself into the river with the agility
of the "excellent gymnast he had been as a boy, much to
his parents' pride." Never had a death seemed so irrational in the telling, nor so well prepared for, proved like a
theorem. Disproportion is a compass opened so far that it
flattens on the page. That's the page on which, in a progressive palimpsest, all of Kafka's work would be written.

The nineteenth-century novel had brought about a
gradual exposure of domestic and marital horrors, culmi-
nating in the white heat of Strindberg ("the enormous
Strindberg," whom Kafka read "not to read him but
rather to lie upon his breast"). The scenes become ever
more embarrassing and ever more comical. But a father
who, standing in his bed in his nightshirt, pronounces a
death sentence on his son (specifying: "by drowning");
and a son who rushes nimbly off to carry out the sentence,
proclaiming, just before disappearing into the river, his
love for his parents, like a subversive proclaiming his
faith in the revolution to the firing squad that's about to
shoot him, except that here the revolution *is* the firing
squad—psychology, however poisoned, had never been
pushed this far. And having reached this point, the story
might be expected to sail on, into a realm where the relationship between images and actual events is seriously
destabilized and will never go back to being what it was
before.

.   .   .

The morning after he wrote "The Judgment," Kafka went "trembling" into his sisters' room and read them the story. One of his sisters said: "The apartment (in the story) is a lot like ours. I said: What do you mean? Then dad would have to be living in the bathroom." That same day, reflecting on the night of "The Judgment," Kafka thought among other things "naturally of Freud."

In the critical edition of the *Diaries*, we find a series of fragments from 1910 that were largely eliminated from previous German editions. Why? Surely because of their embarrassing repetitiveness, like a broken record. Yet it is precisely this repetitiveness that is their most important trait. There are six of these fragments, ranging in length from fourteen lines to four pages, written in succession. Let's look at the opening of each:

> If I think about it, I must say my upbringing in certain respects has done me great harm.

> If I think about it, I must say my upbringing in certain respects has done me great harm.

> Often I ponder it and then every time I must say my upbringing, in certain ways, has done me great harm.

> Often I ponder it, letting my thoughts follow their own course without interfering, and every time, however I view it, I come to the conclusion that my upbringing, in certain ways, has done me terrible harm.

Often I ponder it, letting my thoughts follow their
own course without interfering, but every time I
come to the conclusion that my upbringing has
damaged me more than I can understand.

I often ponder it, letting my thoughts follow their
own course without interfering, but every time I
come to the same conclusion, that I have been
more damaged by my upbringing than anyone
I know and more than I am able to compre-
hend.

Kafka must have been quite convinced of that incipit
to have varied it six times. But who is the "I" who speaks
here? One thinks at once of Kafka himself, since this
notebook is full of references to particular episodes of
his life. Were that the case, these incipits would almost
merit consideration as the inaugural text of that literature of psychological recrimination that would later
spread through the century. The troops of all those who
were to declare themselves damaged—by mom or dad,
by their family, by school, by their environment, by
society—could have paraded behind the heraldic insignia of that text. A vast company, mostly tedious and
querulous. But even if the expression of the psychology, as it often is in Kafka, is here oddly clear and inci-
sive, indeed almost brutal, the psychology itself is
certainly not the point of the narrative. Indeed, the psychology here will be pushed to an extreme, but as if to
ridicule it.

How can that be shown? Simply by looking at the

variations in the roster of guilty parties as it appears from one version to the next. In order:

> This reproach is aimed at a multitude of people, namely my parents, several relatives, certain house guests, various writers, a certain particular cook who accompanied me to school for a year, a heap of teachers (whom I must bundle together in my memory, otherwise I'll lose one here and there, but having bundled them together so tightly, the whole mass begins, in certain spots, to crumble away), a school inspector, slow-walking pedestrians, in brief this reproach twists like a dagger through society.

> This reproach is directed against a multitude of people, all of whom however are gathered here and as in old group photographs they don't know what to do with each other, it doesn't even occur to them to lower their eyes and they don't dare smile, because they're waiting. My parents are there, several relatives, several teachers, a certain particular cook, several girls from the dance lessons, several guests at our previous house, several writers, a swimming instructor, a ticket seller, a school inspector, then some people I met only once on the street and others I can't remember at the moment and those I'll never again remember and finally those whose instruction I, being somehow distracted, failed to pay attention to at the time; in brief, they are so numerous that one must be careful not to name any of them twice.

Implicit in this recognition is a reproach directed against a multitude of people. Among them are my parents, my relatives, a certain particular cook, my teachers, several writers, families friendly with ours, a swimming instructor, the residents of holiday resorts, several ladies in the city park who don't show certain things, a hairdresser, a beggar woman, a tax man, the family doctor, and many others besides and there would be still more if I wanted and were able to call them all by name, in brief they are so numerous that one must be careful not to name anyone in the bunch twice.

[The reproaches] are directed against a multitude of people, this can be frightening and not only I but anyone else would rather look at the river through the open window. Among them are my parents and relatives, and the fact that they harmed me out of love renders their guilt even greater, because how they could have helped me with their love, then friendly families with a spiteful gaze, who aware of their guilt resist rising up into memory, then the legion of nannies, teachers and writers and among them a certain particular cook, and then, blurring into one another as their punishment, a family doctor, a hairdresser, a tax collector, a beggar woman, a paper seller, a park warden, a swimming instructor and then certain foreign ladies in the city park who don't show certain things, several residents of holiday resorts, which make a mockery of innocent nature, and many others; there would be still more if I wanted and were able to call them all by name; in brief,

> they are so numerous that one must be careful not
> to name any of them twice.

These wild, exhilarating gallops revolve around Kafka's favorite theme: guilt. They are attempts by the writer to list all those who have, to whatever degree, harmed him. Just as Josef K., shortly before being sentenced to death, will envision a crowd of his accusers as a solid, unanimous chorus, so the young Kafka looks around and sees all those who are guilty in relation to him—guilty to the point of becoming his executioners. Certain presences are essential: his parents and relatives. But just as essential is "a certain particular cook" who had accompanied Kafka to school for a year. We finally meet her again in a letter to Milena from June 21, 1920: "Our cook, small dry and thin with a pointy nose and hollow cheeks, yellowish, but firm, energetic and superior, took me to school each morning." These words suffice to admit us to the secret memory rooms of an individual named Franz Kafka. But, even as the dim psychologist is congratulating himself for uncovering the true material concealed behind every piece of literature, Kafka the writer snatches it away and renders it meaningless. For his lucidity goes much further. Among the guilty, father and mother certainly come first. But the others step forward in an inexorable procession. We meet not only the yellowish cook, but also some people who made the mistake, on a certain day, of walking slowly, some girls from the dance school, a hairdresser, a beggar, a paper seller. And in the end they will all be arranged together, as for a group photo. They're a little embarrassed, since many don't know one another, have never even seen one another before. But all are united by guilt. Even, lost and forgotten in that crowd, his parents.

In his mad rush, Kafka sets no limits; we even find, among the procession of the guilty, some people he met once on the street and others he is *unable to remember.* Guilt, then, extends not only to everything that has been perceived, even if only faintly and only once, but also to everything that happened, unnoticed, around us. At this point, every psychology collapses from within, opening a breach that leads toward literature. First of all Kafka's.

Kafka was an expert on the feeling of being foreign or extraneous, and he began, in his last period, to consider it and represent it in his work in commonplace situations that became suddenly illuminating. For example, the family's card-game ritual. For years, in the evening, Kafka's parents played cards. For years they asked him to take part. For years the son said no. But that doesn't mean he went elsewhere. "I stayed to watch, apart, a complete outsider." One day he paused to reflect: "What does that refusal, repeated so often since childhood, mean?" The invitation to play a game represents a call to take part in the community. And the game per se, Kafka observed, "would not even have been all that boring." And yet his reply was invariably negative. From such mulishness Kafka inferred something quite profound: his behavior with his family made clear to him why "the current of life" had never swept him along, why he had always remained on the threshold of things that then eluded him. There is something slightly comic, at first, in seeing which grave consequences can be deduced from a little domestic scene. But Kafka, imperturbable, goes one step further. On an evening soon after the day he recorded these observations, he decided to take part in the game, in a manner of speaking, by "keeping score for mom." In doing so, he realized that his new situation corresponded mockingly to his typical rapport with the outside world: participating "didn't give rise to greater closeness, and whatever hint of it there might have been was drowned in weariness, boredom, and sadness over the lost time. And it would have always been that way. Only in the rarest of cases have I forsaken this borderland between solitude and community, indeed it's there that I have settled, even more than in solitude itself. How lovely and lively by comparison was Crusoe's island." Here Kafka has situated himself, defining himself almost as a geometric locus, in relation to communal life.

It was Kafka's suspicion, and this too arose from his observations of the family card game, that any practical initiatives on his part to camouflage himself in normalcy (and these could be as diverse as an office job or halfhearted attempts to devote himself to gardening or carpentry) were simply palliatives or clumsy ways of masking behavior that remained as unmistakable, in its hopeless inconsistency, "as the behavior of a man who chases the wretched beggar from his door and then when he's alone plays the benefactor by passing alms from his right hand to his left." This behavior corresponds to the sensation of going through life pressing his head "against the wall of a windowless, doorless cell." The rest—"my family, the office, my friends, the street"—were "all fantasies, some closer, some further off." Of them, "the closest" was "the woman." And thus the endless misunderstandings, with whatever woman. And thus the endless attraction, since that closest of fantasies could condense within it all the others and act as their emissary.

"Metaphors are one of the many things that make me despair of writing," noted Kafka in December 1921, commenting on the last sentence of one of his letters to Klopstock, which says only: "I warm myself by it this sad winter." A high-power lens comes upon an apparently innocuous sentence, recognizes in it the upsurge of metaphor, and despairs. Why? Kafka, a dogged naturalist of the metaphor, succeeded in bringing nearly everything, and most of all writing, back to that mysterious moment when the image breaks free from the letter—the very moment when what used to be considered real becomes precarious. But not in order to affirm the sovereignty of writing, which is already in itself a metaphor. Indeed, what gets revealed instead is its insuperable dependence on *something else.* Kafka continued: "Writing's lack of autonomy, its dependence on the maid who lights the stove, on the cat warming itself there, even on the poor old man who warms himself. Those are all autonomous activities ruled by their own laws, writing alone is helpless, doesn't dwell in itself, is diversion and despair." Let's

isolate a few words: only writing "doesn't dwell in itself"—writing, then, is first among all strangers. To recount the adventures of this stranger is therefore to give
an account of writing itself, "diversion and despair."

The outsider, the stranger, the foreigner—he wasn't
merely the constant protagonist of Kafka's writing. He
must have also been a secret companion, who appeared
and reappeared, who accompanied him without being
asked to. A few days after commenting on the last sentence of his letter to Klopstock, Kafka wrote: "I woke with
a start from a deep sleep. In the middle of the candle-lit
room, a stranger was sitting at a tiny table. He was sitting
in shadow, broad and heavy, his unbuttoned winter jacket
making him seem even broader."

Foreignness is the background noise in Kafka. Everything presupposes it, everything leads to it. Kafka knew
that feeling in its various aspects: from its most obvious,
and even banal, psychological manifestations (the sense
of being excluded by a group, by a certain type of people,
by a community) to its extreme metaphysical figurations
(the Gnostic as Stranger in the world and to the world).
At the origin of such feelings lay Kafka's hyper-acute
sense of the singularity—even the untranslatability—of
his own psychic experience. He didn't take pleasure in
this singularity but rather fought it, going so far as to seek
out the humiliation of sojourns in naturist colonies such
as Jungborn or Hellerau, where the prime attraction was

offered by the illusion of blending in with a group. (He soon realized that he stuck out even more among nudists, even if only as "the man in the bathing suit.")

All of Kafka's work is an exercise (in the way that Chopin's *Études* are exercises) on the many keys of foreignness. Karl Rossmann is the foreigner in the most radical and literal sense: the adolescent expelled from his country and thrown onto a new continent. K. is the foreigner in the traditional sense: the stranger who comes from the city to a closed and inhospitable town in the country. Josef K., as an ignorant outsider, is foreign with respect to the great organization that's sucking him in. The hunter Gracchus is foreign with respect to all the world, traveling without reprieve in the middle zone between the earth and the realm of the dead. The traveler in "In the Penal Colony" is the foreigner who visits exotic lands and records their strange customs. Gregor Samsa is the most irredeemable of foreigners, since he has, in his own room, become the unrecognizable itself: not simply foreign but biologically extraneous. At the same time, Gregor Samsa finds himself in the most common of situations. It would be easy to recognize him in certain descriptions that Kafka left of his family life. But no story discourages commentary as much as "The Metamorphosis," perhaps because of the extreme "indubitability of the story," a feeling Kafka felt for the first time when writing "The Judgment."

Before analyzing the text he had given his students at Cornell, Nabokov felt compelled to say a few simple and definitive words: "Beauty plus pity—that is the closest we can get to a definition of art. Where there is beauty there is pity for the simple reason that beauty must die: beauty always dies, the manner dies with the matter, the world dies with the individual. If Kafka's 'The Metamorphosis' strikes anyone as something more than an entomological fantasy, then I congratulate him on having joined the ranks of good and great readers."

Up until Franz's death, Hermann Kafka—as far as we can tell from the surviving photographs—didn't resemble his son. At sixty-two years of age, thus already twenty years older than Kafka would ever get, his father appears to be a hulking, strong-willed man, with short, grizzled hair and thick features. It's easy to imagine him behind a counter, but no longer that of his father's butcher shop in Wossek. He had his own wholesale fancy-goods store that now occupied the right corner of Palais Kinsky. Between his legs Hermann Kafka is holding his grandson Felix, whose birth he announced—Kafka wrote—by marching around the house in his nightshirt "as if the baby hadn't merely been born, but had also already led an honorable life and had his funeral celebrated."

Now let's shift our gaze to a photo of Hermann Kafka in 1930, six years after the death of his son and one before his own death. He's standing next to his wife, who in her long, dark overcoat seems to have grown into the ground. Hermann is thin, the neck of his shirt is too big, his over-coat is open and hangs from him, with a certain elegance, as if on a hanger. The face is that of Franz Kafka, had he grown old. Everything's the same: the hairline, the protruding ears, the slight tilt of the head, the triangular facial structure, the quiet desolation of the gaze. Only the gaze doesn't seem to correspond absolutely to his son's. But it presupposes it.

VIII. The Blanket of Moss

"The Burrow" is the closest one gets in Kafka to a testamentary piece of writing; it was composed during his last winter, 1923–1924. The story's tone is that of a scrupulous account, as if to say: if you really want to know what my life was like, you'll find the logbook here, but stripped of every inessential thing, reduced to a geometry of movements, above and below the blanket of moss that marked the entrance to my burrow. The entire story is a deductive chain descending from a single utterance, four words from the *Diaries*, written at the beginning of 1920: *"Meine Gefängniszelle—meine Festung."* "My prison cell—my fortress."

What is "The Burrow" about? A subject Kafka touched on many times, in his *Diaries* and in numerous letters. Always allusively, never systematically. It had to do with a "way of life," one that was—he came to think— irreducibly his, but that in the beginning had been almost a game, a challenge, a dare. By the end, though, it was clearly a necessity. That way of life—or rather that survival regimen—revealed itself ever more clearly and rigorously thanks to the action of what Kafka called *the writing*. But the writing in turn had simply brought to the surface that which already existed anyway: a lag, a caesura in the "current of life," in which, he knew, he had "never been swept up." He hadn't succeeded in so being, wouldn't have wanted to be, couldn't have been.

Every so often Kafka got the urge to investigate how it all began, how that "way of life," which would later become the only way of life for him, had first come into being. Once in the *Diaries*, in an entry from January 1922, he described those beginnings in language so calm and cool it sounds definitive:

> The evolution was simple. When I was still happy, I wanted to be unhappy and drove myself, using all the means that my times and my tradition made available to me, into unhappiness, yet even so I always wanted to be able to go back. In short I was always unhappy, even with my happiness. The strange thing is that the whole act, if one performs it in a sufficiently systematic way, can become real. My spiritual decadence began with a childish game, however conscious I was of its childishness. For example, I would deliberately contract the muscles of my face, or I would walk down the Graben with my arms crossed behind my head. Annoyingly puerile games, but effective. (Something similar happened with the evolution of my writing, except that later the evolution of

my writing came regrettably to a halt.) If unhappiness can be forcibly induced in this fashion, then one should be able to induce anything. However much subsequent developments seem to contradict me, and however much it conflicts in general with my nature to think this, I can't by any means accept that the origins of my unhappiness were inwardly necessary, perhaps they had some necessity of their own, but not an inward one, they swarmed in like flies and like flies could have easily been driven away.

The German language has two words that can mean "burrow": *Höhle* and *Bau*. Opposing words: *Höhle* refers to an empty space, a cavity, a cavern; *Bau* refers to the burrow as construction, edifice, articulation of space. For the animal who speaks in "The Burrow," the two words correspond to two different ways of understanding the same space. The *Höhle* is the burrow as refuge, "safety hole," pure terror reflex, attempt to escape the outside world. While *Bau*, the burrow as construction, has a self-sufficient, sovereign quality, indeed is concerned above all with continually verifying its own self-sufficiency and sovereignty. Confusion over the two meanings is practically offensive—and the unidentified animal rejects it indignantly: "But the burrow (*Bau*)," he says, "is certainly not merely a safety hole!" In fact he never once uses the word *Höhle* to describe his burrow. And for no one does he show as much disdain as for that hypothetical animal—surely "a pathetic wretch"—who would expect "to dwell where he hasn't built."

.   .   .

"The Burrow" is a single outpouring of words—the last pages are not even paragraphed—that breaks off at the beginning of a sentence. But according to the text's animating principle, the narrator could continue narrating indefinitely. Only one creature can stop him: his shadowy counterpart, should he by some chance emerge from his purely acoustic existence, ceasing to dig in the burrow as if it were his own and instead showing himself snout to snout. That would be a mortal clash. Or else that undefined, harassing creature might simply vanish, to be replaced by another supposition and other anxieties. In any case the interruption of the text would be haphazard and abrupt. Because, like the constant, relentless whistling that comes through the tunnel walls, the buzz of words from the narrating animal is unceasing. Nothing can calm it, not even certainty. "I've reached the point where I no longer even wish to feel certainty," admits the burrow's builder—and that is enough to show us the inexhaustible and compulsive nature of his enterprise.

In "The Burrow," Kafka strips away every contingency and reveals the compulsion of writing in its irreducible state, as a pure chain of gestures. Everything becomes vastly abstract, but at the same time the word, on this bare, hidden stage, takes on a pathos it has never before achieved in narrating itself. And certain sentences or sentence fragments stand out with a painful intensity, reverberating endlessly through the hollow tunnels:

the murmur of silence in the stronghold

it's as if the spring from which the burrow's silence flows had been unsealed

Precisely by virtue of being the owner of this great and vulnerable work, I am naturally defenseless in the face of any slightly more serious attack, my happiness in possessing it has spoiled me, the vulnerability of the burrow has rendered me vulnerable, its wounds pain me as if they were my own.

the great burrow stands defenseless, and I am no longer a young apprentice, but rather an old master builder, and what strength I still possess fails me when the decisive moment comes.

Gregor Samsa is a creature akin to the undefined animal who narrates "The Burrow," but he lacks that animal's constructive genius and speculative mind. He lacks, in short, a burrow. His room has undergone only the slightest of transformations, indicated by his three locked doors. Gregor simply hasn't had time to think about such things, what with having to rush through the outside world, from one train to another, spurred on by his alarm clock, in order to earn enough to maintain his family and to pay off his father's debts. But Gregor too could use a blanket of moss to conceal the entrance to his room. Lacking one, he's the most exposed of creatures. The outside world can't help but wound him, like the cruel apples his father throws at him. And though Gregor is as big as a dog when he stands, his nature as an insect—or rather as an indeterminate *Ungeziefer*, a word that already suggests noxiousness—predisposes him to his only possible end: elimination. No one needs a burrow more than he, and even the humblest kind would do, the kind that's merely a "hole for saving one's life" and as such is scorned by the wise animal who narrates "The Burrow" and harbors quite different ambitions. But Gregor won't get one. He gets nothing but bare walls over which to run madly and a couch under which to squat. He always feels like one who finds himself nude among people who are clothed, covered, protected, armed—while he, with his delicate legs, is defenseless.

"The Metamorphosis" is a story of doors that open and close. And above all doors that are locked or forced. Gregor Samsa's room has three doors. When Gregor, one rainy morning, wakes to find himself transformed into something resembling a beetle, roughly a meter in length, he immediately thinks anxiously of the late hour and the inherent torment of working as a traveling salesman who must rise early, while other salesmen can afford to "live like harem women." A little while later he hears insistent knocking on all three of his doors: first he hears his mother's voice, behind the door that leads to the living room; then his father's, behind the door that leads to the hallway; then his sister's, behind the door that leads to her room. Gregor is besieged by voices—and all three doors are locked. Because Gregor has taken "the precaution bred by his travels of locking every door at night even at home." So reasonable and quotidian is Gregor's train of thought up to that point that no one—not even Gregor—is given pause by the strangeness of this fact. To lock three doors every night within his own house, a house inhabited by a father, a mother, and a sister to whom he is very attached, is not by any means normal behavior. And not only did Gregor impose this ritual on himself, he "congratulated himself" on it. By locking those doors, he prepared a sealed space, ready for a metamorphosis. But seen through the persecuting eyes of the outside world, his door-locking gesture is a declaration of hostility. As the chief officer of his firm will say, in an accusatory tone, having come to see what happened to Gregor Samsa: "You are barricading yourself in your room." But that very room, admittedly "rather on the small side," furnished with the most commonplace of household objects, the only personal touch being the photograph of an unknown woman in a hat, boa, and fur muff, hung on a wall in a frame that Gregor himself cut with his fretsaw in a spare hour, has become a sealed and impenetrable enclosure—the precondition for achieving any metamorphosis, including the one that manifests itself in Gregor's own body. Of course, Gregor didn't know that. He must have wanted only to separate himself a little more clearly from that small community to which all his energies, especially since it was decided that he should pay off his father's debts, have been devoted. Or perhaps he didn't want such a separation. But one occurred. And every separation (even a slight one) is a total separation. This physical and metaphysical law was never the object of Gregor's reflections.

But laws hold sway regardless, even among those who are ignorant of them.

From the moment when Gregor, on his way to bed, absentmindedly locks the three doors to his room, his entire life becomes a series of doors that open and doors that close. In the beginning it is Gregor himself who won't open up, since he doesn't yet know how to control his big beetle body. In the end it's his sister, his executioner, who chases him back to his room, by now crowded with "skeins of dust and filth." Gregor will hear her scream: "Finally!" as she turns the key in the lock. Between these two extremes, a harrowing series of intermediate stations: the door that opens because the sister is bringing food for the insect; the door that again is opened so the sister and mother can remove the furniture from the room; the door that opens because Gregor, standing on his hind legs like a dog, succeeds in laboriously turning the key with his mandibles; the door that is left open in the evenings so that Gregor, "remaining in the darkness of his room, invisible from the dining room, could watch the whole family at the lamp-lit table and listen to their conversations, more or less with their consent"; and the half-open door through which Gregor is able to spy on the three bearded boarders as they chew the food his mother serves them.

In the three months of Gregor's life as an insect, his door is for him the emblem of the "borderland between solitude and community." If Kafka abandoned that region "only in the rarest of cases," Gregor manages to do so only once. Draped like Glaucus emerging from the sea, except with "bits of thread, hair, and leftover food on his back and sides" instead of algae, mosses, and shells, weakened by fasting and insomnia, still aching from the wound his father inflicted by hurling an apple at him, Gregor Samsa has "no qualms about inching across the immaculate dining room floor." His gesture is heroic—and prefigures his mystical suicide. As a man, he was indifferent to music; only in his animal metamorphosis have sounds revealed to him "the path to longed-for and unknown nourishment." For that nourishment, Gregor is prepared not only to die but to go on the attack. After having shown for weeks the most delicate modesty in hiding himself behind a sheet and under the sofa, Gregor dares to consider "taking advantage for the first time of his terrifying appearance" (much as Kafka did in writing "The Metamorphosis") in order to reach the music's source. Doing so will get him only as far as his sister and her violin, at which point he confides to her his plan to send her to the conservatory. Rising on his two hindmost legs, which are by now accustomed to such exertions, he pulls himself up to the level of her shoulders and "kiss[es] her neck," exposed in its nakedness, "without ribbons or collars." The cumbersome beetle kissing his sister's neck is the most excruciating of all *moments musicaux*. And an unbearable erotic vision as well. It would have been able to revive the great wind that "blew in from the past," from millions of years ago, to which the chimpanzee Rotpeter will one day refer in one of his academic talks. But that won't be acceptable. That great wind, observes Rotpeter with supreme irony, can now be nothing more than a "breath tickling the heels of whoever walks this earth:

the small chimpanzee and the great Achilles alike." For this reason, Gregor's reckless appearance on the dining room floor is followed, a few minutes later, by the sister's judgment: "We must try to get rid of it." The next morning the cry of the bony charwoman resounds: "Come look at this, it's croaked!"

IX. Ladies' Handkerchiefs

The apparatus—a "singular apparatus," as the officer in charge of operating it observes with warm satisfaction—is embedded in the sandy ground, in a sunny little valley of the penal colony, where one breathes a "damned, malignant tropical air." Four men stand around the apparatus: the officer; a condemned man in chains, who shows signs of animal-like devotion while waiting to be laid down into the machine; a soldier, whose task it is to supervise the condemned man; and a traveler (not a mere tourist, but an honored guest reputed to be a "great scholar"). Amid this stark masculine scene—military, correctional, colonial—a single feminine element: "two delicate ladies' handkerchiefs" that the officer has tucked between his uniform collar and his sweaty, sunburned neck. It's a heavy uniform for the tropical climate, the traveler remarks at the outset, thus eliciting from the officer a declaration of principle: of course the uniforms are heavy, "but they signify the homeland, and we don't want to lose the homeland." The delicate ladies' handkerchiefs, then, serve to mitigate the hardships the officer must face in a climate that otherwise might cause him to "lose the homeland."

Near the apparatus sits a "heap of bamboo chairs," as from an abandoned *café chantant.* The traveler is offered one so that he may witness the execution in comfort. Meanwhile the officer continues implacably to explain, in French, the workings of the machine. The traveler has trouble hiding a certain indifference and at a certain point interjects a dim little remark meant to affirm the liveliness of his interest: "So, the man is lying there." As the traveler says these words, he crosses his legs and leans back in his bamboo chair. He's ready to watch now.

Through the officer's words, the powerful figure of the "old commander" emerges. The machine's conception was entirely his, as was its creation. The traveler wants to make sure: "So he was everything himself? He was soldier, judge, builder, chemist, draftsman?" "Of course," replies the officer, proud. The old commander comes increasingly to resemble one of those titans who flourished in the nineteenth century, breaking down every barrier. They were professional geniuses, and they wanted to manipulate humanity as if it were a compliant keyboard. With his machine the old commander succeeded in realizing the most profound epistemological aspiration of his time, which Friedrich Hebbel once described in his *Diaries:* "On days like this, one feels as if the pen had been dipped, instead of into ink, directly into blood and brain." The world was marching toward the same goal but without the "as if," the final obstacle. All knowledge that was mediated—by the sound of language, by the ungraspable mind—was diminished, sapped. In order to reach a level of unquestionable truth, knowledge must be inscribed—in the sense of *incised*—on the body. Only in this way could one make sure that the word passed instantly into the blood. And the old commander had shown the way: the harrow took the pen's place and wrote "directly" (Hebbel would have said) onto the body of the condemned. The result is the only absolute knowledge, which renders superfluous every other. For this reason, the condemned man wasn't informed of his sentence. There was no need, as the officer explained: "he experiences it on his body." Kafka wrote in his *Diaries* (in 1922, eight years after the draft and three years after the publication of "In the Penal Colony") an observation that might corroborate the beliefs of the old commander (and his popularizer, the officer): "From a primitive point of view, the real, irrefutable truth, undisturbed by any outside element (martyrdom, sacrifice for a person), is only physical pain. Strange that the god of pain wasn't the principal god of the earliest religions (became so only in the later ones, perhaps). Every sick man has his household god, the man with lung disease has the god of suffocation. How can one bear his approach if one hasn't partaken of him even before the terrible union." The old commander was a devotee of that original god who never existed, that god who chooses to become manifest in the one mode that brooks no misunderstandings: physical pain. It's no longer a question, then, of symbols or metaphors or ceremonies—all belated, attenuated devices. At the same time, the old commander was a designer, an expert on gears and cogs.

And hence quite advanced. In him the archaic in its pure state (so pure that perhaps it never existed) and the modern in its pure state were conjoined. Is there any wonder that so few were able to sustain such a level of tension?

The old commander therefore succeeded in surpassing the ancients (those still dominated by the god of physical pain) while still managing to preserve some of their key doctrines. For example, that of ornament. Why is the writing on the condemned body surrounded by those fine, dense, mazy whorls, reminiscent of certain kinds of tattoos or remote decorations? How could that *horror vacui* be explained? As a sign of a still-infantile mind, or evidence of a higher wisdom? One soon sees that the latter is the case. Only ornament allows us to resolve a crucial issue: the writing "mustn't kill right away"; the condemned must be able to "spend a long time studying it." Otherwise the god will fail to give his followers sufficient time to recognize and adore him. We must consider, further, that the condemned man cannot read with his eyes the writing incised into his body. He must read it "with his wounds." So he needs a chance to adjust, to practice. That's the last reason for the ornamentation: to ensure that the condemned man has the leisure to learn to read without his eyes. Or better, to read himself, since the text by now is part of his body. Only then can the harrow run him through and dump him into the pit. Its work is done.

Meanwhile, the officer's words are also illuminating the figure of the new commander, who is first of all a reformer. Cautious but decisive, he seeks to move in a "new, gentler direction." Questions of guilt and punishment matter to him not in themselves but rather because of his fear that the colony's institutions might scandalize foreigners. For the rest, he concerns himself primarily with construction. "Harbor construction, always harbor construction!": that's what they talk about in meetings. His attitude toward foreigners is clearly that of a subordinate. He flatters the traveler, hailing him pompously as a "great scholar of the West," and though he knows that the traveler "traveled only with the intent of observing and not of course changing foreign legal institutions," he hopes the traveler will appeal to him to change the colony's current methods. As if he, with his "thunderous voice," lacks the power to act alone. Which he does not. And then there are those ladies who surround him like a swarm of Praetorians—or overage schoolgirls. Ubiquitous, capable even of latching onto the traveler's hands and "playing with his fingers." The officer's words are uttered with mournful contempt. To speak of the new commander is like speaking about modern times and their shortcomings. But the officer knows he is the only one who talks like this. The last followers of the old commander keep silent in the shadows, like some secretive sect.

This speech is the officer's pathetically resolute, last-ditch attempt to inspire in the traveler a proper, convinced admiration for the machine, but it is a hopeless task. The world has already chosen a less pure, less rigorous path, that of the new commander and his swarm of women. The truth is frightening, the officer thinks. Everyone hypocritically claims to yearn for certainty, but no one can bear to live in the world of certainty, where "guilt is always unquestionable" and the corresponding punishment is incised upon their bodies. Perfect equilibrium, unblemished transparency. It isn't by chance that one of their "technical difficulties" was devising a way to build the harrow out of glass. That is the only way to guarantee transparency. And they "spared no effort" to achieve that end. The god of physical pain can therefore finally wrap himself, as in a sash, in the perfect limpidity of the word.

And what about those ladies' handkerchiefs—the ones that protect the neck of the sweat-soaked officer? Should one conclude that even he needs to attenuate something, at least the hard rule of the uniform? And where have they come from, those handkerchiefs? That will become clear by the end. The officer has made up his mind. "The moment has come then," he says. Since the traveler hasn't yet been convinced by the machine, the officer feels obliged to take the condemned man's place in order to have these words incised on his own back: "Be just." Then his body will be pierced by numerous needles, and the machine will fall apart, gear by gear. A world will end. Before he lays himself down into the machine, the officer tosses the two handkerchiefs to the condemned man, whose liberty he has just restored. He says: "Here are your handkerchiefs." And then, turning to the traveler: "Gifts from the women." The new commander and his damned women again. So they are the ones who gave the condemned man those gauzy handkerchiefs. To mitigate his suffering, of course. Just as they stuffed him with sweets, which of course he immediately vomited up as soon as the machine began its work. And the officer in turn took the handkerchiefs away from him. Why did he do so? Out of profound meanness? Or perhaps simply because those handkerchiefs compromised the purity of the proceedings? In the end, he used them himself. Was that a failing? And now, as soon as the condemned man regains possession of his handkerchiefs, the soldier snatches them away again. The handkerchiefs just won't disappear. The blood runs, the sun beats down, the gears groan. And the handkerchiefs continue to circulate. Between the god of pain and the collapse of his machine, the whole course of history has passed. The only remaining witnesses are those two rank handkerchiefs. And a mass of rubble.

It happens in Kafka that an archaic element, with respect to which every known archaism is merely a late derivation, commingles with a contemporary element that hadn't yet had any way of manifesting itself. The result is a potent chemical compound no one knows how to handle. It surfaced once, like a coral reef, in "In the Penal Colony"—then hastily submerged itself again. It didn't let itself be looked at for long, but its presence remained noticeable beneath the water's surface.

One November evening, "with complete indifference," Kafka read his "dirty story" ("In the Penal Colony") in a Munich gallery, in front of fifty or so people and some paintings by Van Dongen and Vlaminck that hung on the wall. He felt as cold as "the empty mouth of a stove." As he read, the graphologist Max Pulver had the impression that "a faint odor of blood was spreading" through the room. At a certain point a dull thud was heard. A woman had fainted and was immediately carried outside. Others left before the end. Others complained that the reading had gone on too long.

X. Scuffles and Escapes

Karl Rossmann is the little fairy-tale hero who gets thrown into the world. Serious, tenacious, ready for anything, curious, sturdy. He encounters ogres and ogresses, other boys and girls, policemen and vagabonds, to all and each he speaks as an adult, with gravity and propriety. The sentence that precedes him, which has driven him from his homeland and his family, doesn't in his eyes compromise or cloud the world, which in America appears above all enlarged and multiplied. "How tall it is," thinks Karl of the Statue of Liberty, as his ship passes slowly by. He's not surprised when he sees the statue brandishing a sword instead of a torch. Karl observes, takes note. And this will be his approach throughout: to measure the world, its increasing quantities, its doors, its drawers, its compartments, its steps, its floors, its ever-growing number of vehicles. Nothing could be more natural for a boy who has always "been terribly interested in technology." No doubt he would have become an engineer if they hadn't sent him off to America. Karl immediately perceives whatever comes along as an element in a series.

And this seriality of the perceived alters first and foremost the eye of the perceiver. He'll come to see himself as substitutable, like one of the many dotlike figures that, seen from above, move through the streets and quickly vanish. Or else the same figures are simply reappearing again and again. The effect would be the same. Repetition of the identical looks the same as endless substitution.

An inexplicable, irrepressible cheerfulness runs through the pages of *The Missing Person*. The reason for it remains unclear. After his initial stroke of luck in meeting Edward Jakob, the proverbial "American uncle," Karl Rossmann's path becomes ever more harrowing. Every step entails some ordeal and seems to lead toward progressive degradation. But Karl has the gift of the great mystics he knows nothing about: he accepts everything that happens to him in the same spirit. He can tell when someone is hostile to him and can stand up for himself when threatened. But he never grows bitter. Karl focuses on one thing: whatever it is he must do, he wants to *do it well.* Even in the most discouraging situations he manages to tell himself: "It's just a matter of understanding the mechanism." He uses the dozens of compartments in the prodigious writing desk that his uncle procured for him with the same care and precision that he will employ in composing, from an array of half-eaten scraps, a presentable breakfast tray for the obese Brunelda.

Kafka in *The Missing Person* experimented with something that wasn't congenial to his epoch: epic naïveté. And even for him it was an isolated attempt. His trick in approaching that naïveté was to take a character who wholly embodies it and put him in a place still capable of harboring it: America, as seen through the astonished eyes of a European adolescent at the beginning of the century. On the basis of having read only "The Stoker," not knowing that it formed the first chapter of a novel, Musil got the point: "It is an intentional naïveté, but it lacks any of naïveté's unpleasantness. Because it is genuine naïveté, which in literature (exactly like the false kind; that's not where the difference lies!) is something indirect, complicated, and earned; a longing, an ideal." Soon thereafter we find the loveliest words ever written about *The Missing Person:* the novel, Musil says, is sustained by "that feeling of children's fervent prayers, and it has something of the restless care of well-done homework."

The air that circulates through *The Missing Person* is pure adventure-novel air. It's not that Karl Rossmann's experiences are so astonishing but rather that the cast of his mind is such that the world appears to him with a strange sharpness of outline. People and objects both. It's as if Karl were bringing as his gift to America that hyper-real vision that only the objective lens allows us. Stashed in his emigrant's suitcase: the hallucination of cinema.

The passengers of a European ship are disembarking in New York. A young German realizes he has forgotten his umbrella and goes back to look for it, entrusting his suitcase to a casual acquaintance. Utterly banal, one of those scenes that a novelist—even Dickens, who is Kafka's model here—devises in order to hasten toward some narrative juncture. But not this time. As soon as Karl turns around and goes back to look for his umbrella, the reader begins to experience an unusual phenomenon: that of sinking into detail. Every little thing suddenly takes on great importance. It stands out in relief, too much relief. Four lines later, when Karl Rossmann finds himself "forced to make his way through countless little spaces, continually curving passageways, short flights of stairs that followed one after the other, and an empty room with an abandoned desk," we're already obscurely aware that we're no longer merely aboard a ship, but in a new land too, where everything is subject to heightened scrutiny and the observing eye feels obliged to fix on every gesture, every step, every feature of the characters. Everything expands; each fragment takes up the entire visual field. An unreasonable tension builds. For a while we wonder why, as if that tension is preparing us for some extraordinary event. But then we forget all that, satisfied by what is already happening. If a hulking German stoker, whose name we don't even know, complains about injustices suffered at the hands of his boss, Schubal, who seems to prefer foreigners to Germans, and if Karl Rossmann, who has just met him, wants to help him make his case, this captures our interest, as if we were witnessing some divine judgment. And we're not done sinking into detail yet. As the stoker and Karl Rossmann are presenting themselves to the captain, majestic ships, their flags blowing in the wind, cross paths beyond the room's three windows—and jutting up behind them: New York. Is this perhaps the first time Karl sees the city? No, it is rather the first time Karl is seen: New York "stared at Karl with the hundred thousand windows of its skyscrapers." Thousands and thousands of eyes converge upon a single figure; they will accompany Karl through his ups and downs, never looking away. This gaze is one reason that every event he's involved in is so tense and phantasmal, without Karl's realizing it. A vast, anonymous audience is watching him. It's the birth of the cinema. But the positions are reversed: this time the audience is up high, toward the sky, and fully lit.

Kafka wanted to portray an "ultra-modern New York." Great was his disappointment when the first copy of "The Stoker" arrived. On Werfel's advice, Kurt Wolff had, for the cover image, used an etching of New York Harbor in 1840. A steamer with a tall smokestack, a few sails in the distance, the vague outline of a city in the background. A charming genre scene—but how remote from what the author had intended. No trace, in that strip of low, distant houses, of the watching eyes. Kafka hid his disappointment among expressions of gratitude. He concluded, in mandarin style, by telling Wolff that it was just as well that he hadn't been shown the cover in advance, since he would have refused it—and in so doing would have "lost that lovely image."

From the first pages of *The Missing Person*, the words fall into their rows, always with the same weight, as evenly spaced as lines in a school notebook. This evenness remains characteristic of *The Trial* and *The Castle*, even as they advance into murkier, more abstract territories. Everything is related in the manner of Karl Rossmann's journey through the ship in search of his umbrella. The surface is unfailingly compact, the density constant. Each word demands attention. The precise description of a gesture, a remark about the weather, and a digression on the law are placed on the same level and lead smoothly one into the other. Nothing is glaringly important, nothing is insignificant. Perhaps no other novelist has given readers this calm certainty, such as runners have when they feel the clay track, always uniformly firm and yielding, beneath their feet.

When Kafka was writing *The Missing Person*, the pervasive, sooty air of the big city, already encountered in Balzac, Dickens, and Dostoevsky, hadn't yet penetrated the German novel. Now, as soon as Kafka begins to describe New York, the scene stands out with the clarity of the *first time*—and of the panels of Little Nemo, still wet with Winsor McCay's colors, which Kafka had never seen.

The Missing Person is extraordinarily visual. In *The Trial* and *The Castle*, everything unfolds first of all within an individual's psyche, and images interpose themselves from time to time, beating their bat wings against the flow of thought. But here they cover, from one corner to the other, a vast external surface, over which Karl Rossmann must travel with his gaze. And so he does, like a good schoolboy. So when certain figures—his uncle, the head cook, Klara Pollunder, or Brunelda—suddenly acquire names and stories of their own, it's as if they have come to life and taken temporary leave from their stations on that surface. But their mute, cutout shapes remain. And someday they'll return to lie back down in them, as if into the still-warm depression of a bed.

New York light? It's "powerful," "tangible," always scattering and regathering—to such an extent that it seems as if "a sheet of glass that covers everything were being continually and violently smashed."

A New York peril: going out onto your own balcony, on first arriving in your room, and staring at the traffic for hours on end, like a "lost sheep."

The American spell: in his Uncle Jakob's house, a spacious freight elevator carries Karl's piano to the sixth floor. And Karl ascends beside it in the elevator for people, remaining always at the same level as the piano. All the while, he gazes through a wall of glass at "the beautiful instrument he now possessed."

The "first American poem" that Karl learns by heart is a "description of a fire." He recites the lines to his uncle, who beats the time, as they stand by a window in Karl's room and watch the darkened sky.

In the middle of New York, on the sixth floor of an iron-frame building, with the windows open wide to the roar of traffic that rises up, together with eddies of odor and dust, from the street, Karl sits at his piano and plays "an old soldier song from his homeland, which the soldiers, from the windows of their barracks in the evenings, sing to each other, from window to window, as they look out into the darkness of the square." This is Mahler in words. And Karl didn't rule out, as he lay dreaming in his bed before going to sleep, the possibility that his style of play might exert "a direct influence on the American scene."

The Pollunders welcome Karl and shower him with kindnesses. But his evening at their country house has a darkly violent undercurrent—mainly because of Green, the sinister messenger whose gestures are precise and sometimes repellent, who gives Karl the impression that their relationship "will eventually be determined by the triumph or annihilation of one or the other of them." Karl has no idea, at this point, that the moment of annihilation is nigh; it comes when Green, two hours later, reads Karl the letter with which his uncle dismisses him.

His Uncle Jakob, Pollunder, Mack, Klara, Green: these are meticulously detailed and studied figures, created by a master of his craft who specializes in rubber puppets.

Pollunder and Green sit facing each other after dinner. Each has smoked a big cigar, and now, drinks in hand, they're talking business. But what business? "Someone who didn't know Mr. Pollunder might very well have thought they were discussing criminal matters rather than business." But who really knows Mr. Pollunder?

. . .

Lyricism in *The Missing Person:* it's all the more intense because the prose doesn't make a show of it. At the Pollunders' country house, Karl enters the bedroom that has been assigned to him. He sits on the windowsill and observes the night: "A skittish bird seemed to be moving through the leafy branches of the old tree. The whistle of a New York suburban train sounded somewhere out in the countryside. The rest was silence." Nor does this lyricism need nature in order to resonate. When Karl is working as an elevator boy at the Hotel Occidental, it emerges once again in the dead of night: "He leaned heavily against the railing beside his elevator, slowly eating his apple, which from the first bite had given off a strong perfume, and he looked down, into a light well that was surrounded by the large windows of the storerooms, behind which hung masses of bananas, gleaming dimly in the dark."

Twice Karl gets cast out into the darkness. First by his parents, then by his American uncle. And each time he's pushed farther west: from Germany to New York, then from New York to California. In both cases, the preamble to his expulsion is a scuffle with a woman. A bed, a sofa. The robust Karl is smothered, flattened. The first time by a poor cook, amid eiderdowns, quilts, and pillows. The second by an "American girl," an heiress with red lips and a tight skirt, skilled in jujitsu.

Again and again Karl Rossmann is restrained, his arms or legs immobilized by the use of force and cunning. The original scuffle is the one that blurs into coitus with the maid Johanna, thereby determining Karl's fate, since Johanna gets pregnant. But other scuffles follow. First Klara, the heiress, then the head porter at the Hotel Occidental, then Robinson, then Delamarche, and finally Brunelda: they all want to block Karl's escape from some claustrophobic place. A considerable number of the novel's episodes revolve around these scenes of struggle. Meticulous, prolonged, exasperating descriptions. Observed from a certain distance, Karl's defining gesture becomes that of wriggling free—the constantly renewed effort to escape a hold or an onslaught, to regain his status as an outcast, a "missing person," a wandering foreigner. Then one day Karl finds, in the Theater of Oklahoma, the ecumenical place where everyone and everything is welcome, is registered and listed on a scoreboard. In his case, under a fictitious name: Negro—a name that evokes a race more than an individual. And it was Karl himself who wanted it that way. Perhaps he can avoid the abuse he suffers as a lone individual only by camouflaging himself in a *set*, even an abused one.

There's always something a little diabolical about the scuffles involving Karl Rossmann. They are evil's stratagems. Evil knows that "the challenge to fight" is one of its "most effective means of seduction." It knows that every fight is "like the struggle with women, which ends in bed." That's just how Karl's fate has been decided. Now he is wandering through America, waiting for a brutal hand to grab him by his jacket collar and fling him in some new direction, far away: "And he was looking nervously at the policeman's hand, which might at any moment rise to seize him."

Together with the vagabonds Robinson and Delamarche, Karl treks against a current of five unbroken lanes of traffic that are rushing toward New York. Everything that teems produces in the end a sense of stasis and quiet. Just as New York, seen from a height, will later strike him as "empty and useless," surrounded by "a smooth, lifeless ribbon of water," so now "it was the general calm that surprised Karl the most. Had it not been for the cries of animals obliviously bound for the slaughterhouse, perhaps nothing would have been heard but the clatter of hooves and the hissing of tires." These are the acoustics of the new world, as if isolated in a lab. But that's not what Karl Rossmann, still clinging to his suitcase, is thinking.

Karl Rossmann and Jakob von Gunten are kindred characters. To be a pupil in the Benjamenta Institute or an elevator boy at the Hotel Occidental is to aspire to be a zero. "Of course elevator boys mean nothing," says Karl; for his part, Jakob sees his best friend, Kraus, as "an authentic divine creation, a nothing, a servant" and himself as "a charming, utterly round zero in later life." Like Jakob, Karl knows that he might from one moment to the next be swept away, by the anger of a head waiter or a head porter, without anyone caring except perhaps Therese and the head cook, and even the cook will approve his sentence in the end. And like Jakob, Karl too could say: "Some day I'll suffer a stroke, a truly devastating stroke, and then everything, all these confusions, this longing, this ignorance, all of it . . . this thinking one knows and this never knowing, will end. And yet I want to live, I don't care how."

During the course of Karl's adventures, pride and raw humiliation are at times conjoined, as if this amalgam were the hallmark of his experience. Never is that mark so sharply felt as when Karl tries on his elevator-boy uniform at the Hotel Occidental. "On the outside," it looks "splendid, with gold buttons and braids." But when he puts it on, he shudders, "because especially under the arms the jacket was cold, stiff, and at the same time irredeemably damp with the sweat of elevator boys who had worn it before him."

It's dawn. All is still quiet in the Hotel Occidental—except in the head waiter's room, where a trial is under way. The defendant is Karl, the elevator boy. Backed by the head porter, the head waiter accuses Karl of having abandoned his post for several minutes. This scene, squeezed into the smallest of spaces, invisible to the outside world, and as near to insignificance as possible, is the originary cell of every trial, every interrogation, every sentence. Every beginning has something inconsistent and disproportionate about it, from which escape seems easy. But then it leads the defendant (or individual) toward impotence and helplessness: "It's impossible to defend oneself in the absence of good will," thinks Karl, with a lucidity that Josef K. will never manage to achieve. The point is that the world does not extend goodwill toward those who pass through it—who are always potential defendants. Something happens in the room of the head waiter of the Hotel Occidental that will spread through all the attics on the outskirts of the big city and will continue to make itself felt as far as the cathedral, or the junk room in a bank. Then too it will happen that someone will shake his head at the accused, as now the head cook does at Karl, and say: "Just causes have a just air about them, and your story, I must confess, does not." Because no story has "a just air." These words sentence him. They are spoken by the woman who up until that moment has been Karl's high protector.

While he's writing up the report of what has just happened in the barroom, the secretary Momus crumbles a pretzel with caraway seeds. The head waiter of the Hotel Occidental is studying a list and shaking the sugar from a piece of cake. K. and Karl observe them, attentive, tense. It's as if writing and reading—always mysterious acts—must be accompanied by the scattering of fine particles, by the dissolution of something friable.

When the end is in sight, someone always asks whether we aren't glad that "everything turned out so well." And occasionally there's even someone who, like Karl Rossmann, says: "But of course"—even as he's wondering "why he ought to be glad to be chased away like a thief."

The simultaneity of his affirmative answer and the silent formulation of the question in his head is decisive.

It's a mystery how *The Missing Person* manages to radiate such a sense of happiness and, at the same time, of acute despair. So disconcerting a union would be hard to find anywhere else. Karl passes from servitude to servitude, from humiliation to humiliation, from getting more and more lost to going missing in the world, all the while retaining, as if in his emigrant's suitcase along with the Verona salami, an unscathed capacity for perceiving what happens to him with a decal-like clarity that in itself prefigures happiness.

Like K.'s assistants, the two vagabonds Delamarche and Robinson are characters from whom there can be no hope of escape. "Rossmann, what would become of you without Delamarche!" says Robinson at one point—and his words sound mocking. But that's not to say he doesn't have a point. For Karl, the two vagabonds signify nothing less than a hopeless and increasingly suffocating ensnarement in life.

Dressed in red and holding a red parasol, the obese Brunelda looks out from a balcony on the eighth floor of a "huge tenement block" in a working-class neighborhood on the outskirts of the city.

Brunelda is "a fantastic singer," according to the vagabond Robinson, who is Rossmann's "living guilt." She spends her days in semidarkness, lying on a sofa that she fills entirely. She stirs herself from immobility only to swat at the occasional fly. The room is overflowing, mainly with various fabrics. Curtains, clothes, and carpets are piled high. The air is stagnant and dusty. Sitting on the sofa, legs apart, Brunelda needs help taking off her thick white stockings. In her fat little hands, she holds open a tiny fan. Brunelda snorts in her sleep, and even "at times" when she speaks. The singer is quite sensitive. She can't stand a racket. She suffers frequently from headaches and gout. She moans in her sleep, tormented by "oppressive dreams." For certain men, including Robinson and Delamarche, Brunelda's body is irresistible. "She was utterly lickable. She was utterly drinkable": that's how Robinson felt the first time he saw her, in a white dress with that red parasol.

Brunelda has become a fugitive for love. She abandoned a rich cocoa manufacturer to follow the vagabond Delamarche. Robinson recounts her deeds as if she were a romantic heroine: "Because of Delamarche, Brunelda sold everything she had and moved here with all her riches, to this apartment on the edge of town, so she could devote herself entirely to him and no one would disturb them, which was what Delamarche wanted too." Like certain great lovers of the past, Brunelda and Delamarche need solitude and servants who will attend to them in silence. Robinson and Karl are made to serve that purpose in their overstuffed, airless room. The *composition of place*, in the sense of Saint Ignatius's exercises, is so perfect that it requires no commentary, merely contemplation.

.   .   .

A particularly violent scuffle between Karl and Dela-marche. In the end, Karl's head gets slammed against a cupboard, and he loses consciousness. When he comes to, an old piece of Brunelda's lace, still wet, is wrapped like a turban around his head. Pushing aside the cur-tain, Karl creeps back into the room of his masters and jailers. "The combined breathing of the three sleepers greeted him." Brunelda, Delamarche, and Robinson form a single body, simultaneously soft and knobby, which Karl bumps against repeatedly in the semidarkness. At one point he feels Robinson's boot, at another Brunelda's overflowing flesh. The appendages of a many-headed creature, from which there can be no escape. Even the unyielding student Josef Mendel, that little Talmudist hunched in the night, studying on his balcony, advises Karl "absolutely" to remain in that room. And that word seems a decree intoned by some other voice, "deeper than that of the student," who might be one of fate's ventriloquists.

Brunelda, a fat Melusine, enjoys recalling the days when she swam in the Colorado, "the most agile of all her friends." Now, as Delamarche subjects her to endless ablutions behind chests of drawers and screens, her insid-ious call sounds again. She invites her servant Robinson to look at her nude body, but as soon as he pops his head in, she and Delamarche seize him and dunk him in the tub. It's a punishment that Brunelda would like to inflict on Karl too. She's already lying in wait—and she calls him "our little fellow."

. . .

And then the panicked search for Brunelda's perfume, among "matted, stuck-together stuff" and through drawers that overflow with powder boxes, hairbrushes, sheet music, letters, English novels. Drawers that, once opened, can't be closed again. But Karl doesn't lose heart, because he never loses heart, and he says: "What work can be done now?" Whether it's learning English, playing the piano, accompanying guests on the elevator, or preparing Brunelda's breakfast tray, Karl is always ready to apply himself—his good disposition is unassailable. And just as, in the beginning, he came forward to address the ship's captain on the stoker's behalf, so now he offers to stand up for the maltreated Robinson, heedless of where he is and of who might be listening with a smirk.

The deeper Karl goes into the vast spaces of America, the more stuck he gets. Not only because someone is always violently detaining him, but also because he is surrounded by boggy terrain. The central source: Brunelda's room. Robinson explains that the singer "isn't transportable"—not because she's sick but because she's too heavy. To be with her is to sink. A little later we see Karl in a hallway trying, with care and skill, to compose an acceptable breakfast from the remains of the breakfasts of many strangers. He cleans knives and spoons, trims partially eaten rolls, collects leftover milk, scrapes away dribbles of butter, all in order to "remove the evidence of use." This is the most desperate moment of his adventures. But it is Karl's gift to be unaware of that. He is focused on his task, even though Robinson assures him that it's pointless, since "breakfast had often looked much worse." And, with Brunelda already wolfing it down, reaching out with her "soft, fat hand that could flatten anything," Karl reflects, like a technician judging his own work, and tells himself: "The first time I didn't know how it should all be done; I'll do better next time."

At first light, the streets empty, Karl pushes a cart that wobbles beneath a shapeless burden, covered by a gray cloth. Sacks of potatoes, one man thinks. Sacks of apples, Karl tells another. But it is Brunelda. Robinson and Delamarche will not be heard from again. Karl, having taken yet another step on the road to the irreparable, is now alone with his burden, which will be hard to shed. Finally they come to the "dark narrow alleyway where Enterprise No. 25 was located." There, Karl and the singer meet a man who is waiting impatiently. But what is Enterprise No. 25? An office? A factory? A brothel? A freak show? A circus? We'll never know, though the brief description we're left with, before the manuscript breaks off for good, suggests a brothel. The paint on the walls is reasonably fresh, and the artificial palm trees are "only slightly dusty," but Karl is struck most by a particular quality of the place: a dirtiness that "wasn't tangible." This is a metaphysical obstacle; it goes beyond the physical facts. Here "everything was greasy and repulsive, as though everything had been put to some ill use and by now no amount of cleaning could have remedied it." Here even Karl, the most upbeat, open-minded, and willing of all the heroes, finds himself for the first time at a loss as he confronts the irredeemable: "Karl, when he first came to a place, loved to think about what might be improved there and what a pleasure it would be to get to work at once, heedless of the potentially endless work involved. But this time he didn't know what could be done." On the road to abjection—a thoroughly unintentional abjection, shaped by circumstance—Karl has reached the dead end. For the first time, Kafka writes, he didn't know what could be done.

The Theater of Oklahoma is certainly the "biggest theater in the world"—some say it's "nearly limitless." But the few who pause outside the racetrack are a bit suspicious, as if its banners conceal some catch. Karl may have guessed why: "It's possible that the enticements used in the recruitment campaign are failing precisely because of their grandiosity." There is an inescapable disproportion between this spectacle that is almost coextensive with the world and the inhabitants of the world itself. The spectacle is too vast, too boundless. It exists apart, in a sort of cosmic autism. At best, one might be able to get a walk-on role, as Fanny does with her trumpet—as Karl himself does when, on that same trumpet, he plays a few bars of a song he heard once in some pub.

Exegetes of various stripes agree that the Theater of Oklahoma inspires both dismay and euphoria. For some it's the only apparition of happiness in Kafka's work. For

Adorno, it is also the only plausible image of that utopia that pervaded his thought. It's as if the call of the poster inviting people to the Clayton racetrack were addressed to each person individually. But the world is full of posters—and "no one believed in posters anymore." This one, however, sounds like an eschatological announcement (the model, after all, for posters): "The great Theater of Oklahama is calling you! It's calling only today, only once!" The appeal is directed at the individual reading it. And the individual learns that he is everyone: "All are welcome!" But this total openness is paired with the cruel temporal arbitrariness: "Everything closes at midnight, never to reopen!" To which is appended the merciless codicil of every eschatology: "Cursed be those who don't believe us!"

If there was one place in the twentieth century that came to represent mathematical, irresponsible happiness, it was the set of the Hollywood musical. But when Kafka was writing *The Missing Person*, the musical didn't exist yet. Neither did the sound track, which burst into metahistory, accompanying and anticipating history, with the messy chorus of trumpets that greets Karl in front of the Clayton racetrack. The vision that unfurls there before his eyes is the original scene of the musical: a variation that finally upsets the symmetry of the angel formations in Dante's paradise. The direction is at once simple and grandiose. Every detail stands out, but especially this one: *hundreds of women* standing together.

In front of the entrance to the racetrack a long, low platform had been built, on which hundreds of women dressed as angels, with white robes and great wings on their backs, played long gleaming golden trumpets. They weren't standing directly on the platform, rather each stood on a pedestal, which however was hidden from sight by the long flowing robes of the angel costume. But since the pedestals were quite tall, some indeed as tall as two meters, the figures of the women appeared gigantic; it was only their little heads that to some degree disturbed the impression of great size, and their loose hair too seemed strangely short and faintly ridiculous in the way it fell between and around their great wings. In order to avoid any uniformity, they had used pedestals of varying heights, and there were very low women who appeared only slightly taller than their actual size beside others who soared to such heights that the slightest breeze seemed to threaten them. And now these women were playing in unison.

These words suffice to convey an almost unbearable sense of happiness—and this time an unmotivated happiness, free from any worry of election or exclusion. It's a pure visual and auditory fact. Nothing more is required. The perfect life would need no other introduction.

In 1914, between August and October, Kafka found himself writing a new novel, *The Trial*, and at the same time trying to finish an interrupted novel, *The Missing Person*. A year later he made this observation: "Rossmann and K., the innocent and the guilty, in the end both alike killed in punishment, the innocent with a lighter hand, more pushed aside than taken down." Such words could resolve many of the exegetes' doubts. Finally we learn, from an authoritative source, that Josef K. is guilty, without further ado, and that Karl Rossmann is innocent, without further ado. But none of that matters to a higher power that wants only to kill them. By execution, in K.'s case. As for Karl Rossmann, he simply needs to be pushed off the edge of the road, like an animal hit by a car.

XI. The Riskiest Moment

Everything remains in its senseless, inscrutable place.
—from "A Fratricide"

"The strange thing is that when one wakes up in the morning, one generally finds things in the same places they were the previous evening. And yet in sleep and in dreams one finds oneself, at least apparently, in a state fundamentally different from wakefulness, and upon opening one's eyes an infinite presence of mind is required, or rather quickness of wit, in order to catch everything, so to speak, in the same place one left it the evening before." These lines, which are the fundamental chord of *The Trial*, were crossed out by Kafka (and again one suspects that he crossed out whatever gave too much evidence of the thought behind the text). We encounter them in the opening scene, when Josef K. begins talking with the guards. He recalls then what an unspecified "someone" once told him about the fact that waking is "the riskiest moment." And that unknown person had added: "If you can manage to get through it without being dragged out of place, you can relax for the rest of the day." *The Trial* is the story of a forced awakening. Josef

K. is the one for whom nothing will ever return to its
proper place.

In the beginning, Josef K. is certainly not the foreigner
to whom absolutely anything might happen. He's an exec-
utive in a large bank. His immediate goal is to undermine
the current vice director and install himself in his place (a
word that is already tormenting him). At his office, he's
known to have a particular talent for organization. He has
a good memory. He can speak decent Italian. He knows a
little about art history. He is a member, representing the
bank, of the society for the preservation of the city's monuments. He rents a room in the apartment of a respectable
woman who takes in boarders. His lover is a dancer who
performs at night in a tavern and receives him during the
day once a week.

Josef K.'s existence is rooted deeply in order. At the
bank, he can keep his clients waiting, even if they are important entrepreneurs. Time vibrates, "the hours hurtle
by"—and Josef K. wants to enjoy them "like a young
man." A thought troubles him: will his superiors at the
bank view him with sufficient benevolence to offer him
the post of vice director?

Josef K. doesn't know that all these facts predispose
him to being put on trial. Like a fragrant, friable substance, he will during handling reveal new qualities,
among them the pathetic beauty of the defendant—if it's
true that "defendants are the loveliest of all."

. . .

Josef K.'s situation, as his trial begins, greatly resembles Franz Kafka's in the spring of 1908. Both are brilliant employees. Kafka, younger by five years, is about to be hired, following flattering recommendations, by the Workers' Accident Insurance Institute, after having resigned from another insurance company (Assicurazioni Generali). Both permit themselves to "enjoy the brief evenings and nights." Kafka frequents the Trocadero and the Eldorado, eloquent emblems of the Prague demimonde. He once concocted a plan to show up in those places after five in the morning, like a tired, dissipated millionaire. Josef K. keeps in his wallet a photo of his lover, Elsa, who "by day received visitors only in bed." Kafka recounts one of his late-afternoon visits to the enchanting Hansi Szokoll. He sat on the sofa by Hansi's bed; her "boy's body" was covered by a red blanket.

Hansi introduced herself on her calling cards as *"Artistin"* or *"Modistin,"* two terms sufficiently vague as to rule nothing out. According to Brod, Kafka once said of her that "entire cavalry regiments had ridden over her body." Again according to Brod, Hansi made Kafka suffer during their "liaison." We know this much for sure: they posed together for Kafka's loveliest surviving photograph. Elegant in his buttoned-up frock coat and derby, Kafka is resting his right hand on a German shepherd that looks like an ectoplasmic emanation. But someone else is petting the dog: Hansi, whose figure has countless times been cropped out of the photo as if it were a Soviet document. She is smiling beneath a panoply of presumably auburn curls, topped by a little round hat. Kafka and Hansi are seated, posing, symmetrical. The out-of-focus, demonic dog sits between them—and their hands are almost touching.

According to Brod, Kafka in that photo has the look of one "who would like to run away the next moment." But that's a spiteful interpretation. His expression seems closer to absorbed melancholy. On the other hand we must be suspicious when Kafka smiles in a photograph, as in that silly pose at the Prater with three friends, facing a painted airplane. There Kafka is, in fact, the only one smiling, yet we know that in those very hours he was suffering from acute despair.

K. and Karl Rossmann are two figurations of the foreigner, he who sets foot in a world about which he knows nothing and through which he must make his way, step by step. But their gaze always retains, deep in their eyes, the reflection of another life. Josef K. is quite different: not only does he not start out as the foreigner, but he gets asked by his superiors to serve as guide for a foreigner who is passing through their city. The foreigner is he who is forced to understand, who must take it as his calling to understand, if he wants to survive. Josef K., on the other hand, is the native, and he's completely at home in the bank where he works, to such a degree that he can be chosen to represent the company. It's not required of him that he understand so much as that he submit to the order of which he is a part.

K. and Karl Rossmann live in a state of protracted wakefulness and chronic alarm. Josef K. is subjected to a forced awakening, thanks to two guards, who may even be impostors. The moment they choose is early morning, the moment that corresponds to physiological awakening. When the two kinds of awakening merge, one can be sure that a strange, ungovernable event is about to take place: everything is becoming literal. And so more dangerous. From the moment of his forced awakening, Josef K. is compelled not to understand but to recognize the existence of an ulterior world that has always been concealed within his city, mostly in anonymous, dreary places: the offices of the court that has issued the order for his arrest. With respect to that world, Josef K. will finally find himself in the position of the foreigner, a position he doesn't like and hasn't sought.

Josef K. thus has an *acquired* foreignness. He is the one forced to become foreign, whereas Karl Rossmann and K. are foreign from the start—Karl by order of his parents, K. by his own choice. Karl is the only one with a long line of precursors behind him: all those who, under adverse circumstances, have had to leave home and seek their fortune in the world. The antecedents of Josef K. and K., on the other hand, are not as clear, their relatives not as numerous. The simple K that marks them announces the disappearance of that jewel box of details that defines the Balzacian variety of novelistic character. That letter becomes an algebraic symbol, which designates a range of possibility. But this shift doesn't imply a greater abstraction. Indeed, by now characters with thick identification files have become an atavism. Much more common is the cohabitation under the same name—or under the same insignia—of many people, even incompatible ones, who often cross one another's paths without recognition, perhaps a few seconds apart, like daily riders of the subway.

Josef K. first grasps the gravity of his situation when he sees the two guards who have come to arrest him "sitting by the open window." What are they doing? "They're devouring his breakfast." The verb Kafka uses, *verzehren*, is stronger than the usual *essen*, "to eat." The voracity of the two guards presumes their total autonomy and the insignificance of whomever the breakfast was meant for. In an instant, life strips Josef K. of all authority. As with his breakfast, so with his undergarments, which the guards have already confiscated, going so far as to say: "You're better off giving these things to us rather than the depository."

No less intimate than undergarments, breakfast marks the end of the delicate phase of awakening and the entrance into the normal course of the day. But it is precisely this from which the guards want to exclude Josef K. From now on, he will have to remain perpetually exposed, vulnerable, defenseless, like a man just shaken from sleep who hasn't yet got his bearings. Now he will have to get used to his new state, until it comes to seem normal. There will be no more breakfasts. At most, he'll be allowed to bite the apple he left on his bedside table. The guards imply all this when they dip the bread and butter into the honey. For Josef K., this scene is like the gaze of the guard Franz: "likely full of meaning, but incomprehensible."

.   .   .

When Josef K. realizes that two unknown persons have come to arrest him, he thinks at first that it's all a joke, indeed a "crude joke," being played on him by "his colleagues at the bank, for unknown reasons, perhaps because it was his thirtieth birthday." He is comforted in any case by the thought that he lives "in a state governed by law," where "peace reigned everywhere and all the laws were in force."

And yet, when he withdraws briefly into his room, he finds it surprising—or "he found it surprising at least according to the guards' way of thinking"—that "they had driven him into his room and left him alone there, where it would be ten times easier to kill himself." Resuming then for a moment "his way of thinking," Josef K. wonders "what motive he could possibly have for doing so." He answers himself at once: "Perhaps because those two were sitting in the next room and had taken his breakfast?" This is the most delicate of passages. From the very beginning, Josef K. has tried to "insinuate himself somehow into the guards' thoughts," in order to sway them in his favor (a vice or virtue he will frequently indulge during the various phases of his trial). In so doing, he has discovered that his arrest is tantamount to a death sentence, and hence the risk of suicide, which would seek to preempt the sentence. But immediately following this insight, when he wonders about the possible motive for suicide, he reenters *his own* "way of thinking"—and it is there that he formulates the laughable hypothesis according to which his suicide might be provoked by the fact that the guards have taken his breakfast. Josef K. judges this thought "absurd," and yet it's the most lucid thought he has had so far: the sight of the guards devouring his breakfast implies that he has been notified of his death sentence. It implies too that notification and execution tend to coincide. The breakfast that the guards are devouring is already the breakfast of a dead man. By now the psychic commingling has begun; it will become increasingly difficult for Josef K. to distinguish between his own "way of thinking" and that of his persecutors. Blunders will become increasingly likely.

In a very brief time, the same event—the arrest—has seemed both a foolish waste of energy and a death sentence, with the attendant danger that the condemned man might try to escape the sentence through suicide. As for the suicide, it could also be prompted by the fact that the guards were eating Josef K.'s breakfast. Josef K. rejects these absurdities, as anyone would. He doesn't notice, however, that they were all formulated in his own head in the course of a few instants: the joke (a poor one), the death sentence, the suicide as preemption of the sentence, and the suicide as protest against the commandeering of his breakfast. Josef K. *is* all this. If in the end, in place of the guards, there appear two executioners who stick a knife in his chest and twist it, this too happens as a result of a thought he had in those early moments. He told himself then that the suicide idea had a flaw: "It would be so absurd to kill himself that, even had he wanted to, the absurdity would have prevented him." Accordingly, when one day he is taken away by the executioners, among his last thoughts is that it is "his duty to seize the knife, which sailed over him from one hand to the other, and stab himself." Of course, by now the gesture seems much less absurd. But Josef K. will still be unable to perform it.

Josef K. looks at the guards who have come to arrest him with distaste. They seem too lowly. He thinks: "Their confidence is made possible only by their stupidity." And yet one of the guards has just told him something that could cast light on what will happen to him: "Our authorities, as far as I understand them, and I understand them only on the most basic level, don't seek out guilt among the populace, but are, as the law says, attracted to guilt and have to send us guards out. That's the law." The law recognizes explicitly the attraction exerted by guilt, the one magnet of all action. The law is like an animal sniffing its prey: it follows only the call that emanates from guilt. From life in general.

Josef K. makes one mistake after another. At the beginning, he actually shows "contempt" for his trial, as if it were a painful and indecorous inconvenience. He doesn't understand that its wretched aspects allude, by antiphrasis, to the majesty of the trial itself. Then, after having observed his lawyer, Huld, pretending "for months already" to be hard at work on his case, he decides to intervene directly. The trial seems to him then like one of the many negotiations that he has had to expedite at the bank. If the court is, as it seems, a "great organization," then any dealing with it must constitute a "major transaction," which, like any transaction, could result in a profit or a loss. Such a transaction, then, certainly wouldn't involve "thoughts of any kind of guilt." Indeed, and here Josef K. allows himself to be extreme in his reflections: "There wasn't any guilt." *Guilt* and *transaction* are words that belong to completely different spheres. With the enterprise of a star employee, Josef K. decides to treat his life like *a bank transaction.* His is a delirium with all the appearance of rationality—he now identifies with a bank. But in the subsequent passage he falls back into the most embarrassing intimacy: as soon as he decides to write his memorial to the court on his own, he realizes that such a document would necessarily resemble a general confession, which he can't think about without "a feeling of shame"—the same "shame" that would "survive" him after his death sentence is carried out. All these stories of the trial and of writing in connection with the trial are steeped in *shame* as their essential element. It's the air surrounding them. There are only two kinds of air we can breathe: the air of paradise and the air of shame. Those are the only two kinds that Adam breathed.

Josef K.'s defense strategy. In order to demonstrate his innocence, he will examine his own life, aspiring to that high level of organization and that capacity for scrutiny that are normally attributed to the court itself: "It all had to be organized and scrutinized, at last the court would come across a defendant who knew how to stand up for his rights." The accused individual lays claim to the same instruments used by the vague, powerful court. He wants to beat it at its own game. But at the same time he feels overwhelmed by the "difficulty" of the enterprise he's preparing to undertake, a difficulty tied not only to the contents of the memorial to the court but also to the very fact of *writing*. The only way—he thinks at once—would be to write it "at home, at night."

From this point on, what's said about the memorial applies also to writing in general as Kafka conceived it:

> Anything but stopping half way, that was the most foolish thing of all, not only in business, but anywhere, any time. Of course, the memorial would entail almost infinite labor. One needn't be especially faint of heart to jump to the conclusion that it would be impossible ever to finish the memorial. Not because of laziness or deceit, which would alone be enough to prevent the lawyer from finishing it, but rather because, since he was in the dark about the existing charges and all their possible ramifications, his whole life down to the smallest action and event would need to be called back up, exposed, and examined from all angles. And what a sad job that would be besides.

Understood radically, the "memorial" presumes a gap-free knowledge of one's own life. This is literature's delusion of omnipotence, a delusion inextricably bound to its origin, which presupposes guilt—or at least accusation. And this delusion itself is the origin of every doubt, of every suspicion of impotence and inadequacy. The endless oscillation between the suspicion of total futility and the desire for total dominion is such that the feelings associated with this practice take on a tonality of sadness. *Sad is what it is*, this writing, this elaboration of a complete consciousness that Josef K. feels obliged to make. It's a task at once boundless and infantile, like literature. And also, to be brutal about it, senile: a job "well suited perhaps for keeping the mind occupied once it has become childish, after retirement, and for helping it get through those long days."

Josef K.'s double in his life outside his trial is the vice director. On one hand, Josef K. would like nothing better than to usurp him. On the other, "the vice director was good at appropriating everything K. was now forced to abandon." Each of them wants to appropriate the role of the other. Their essence is substitutability. The vice director comes into Josef K.'s office and pokes around "in the bookcase as if it were his own." Josef K. feels the same anxiety, perceives the same intrusiveness as when the vice director, in order to illustrate a funny story about the stock market, begins to draw on the notepad intended for Josef K.'s memorial to the court. In the same way, the vice director soon thereafter appropriates clients who had waited at length and in vain to speak with Josef K. And it will be the vice director—not Josef K., as originally planned—who closes the deal with the manufacturer. "A charming man, your vice director, but certainly not harmless," the manufacturer will later tell Josef K., as if in warning. As soon as Josef K. turns his back to step out into the unmentionable world of the trial, he knows that someone else will take his place and complete the tasks that ought to fall to him. Even before he's out the door, the vice director is foraging among the papers in his office. He's looking for a contract, it seems, and he quickly leaves saying he has found it. But under his arm he has "a thick stack of papers" that certainly contains much more than the contract. Every responsibility that Josef K. sheds in the course of the trial gets instantly assimilated by the vice director, strengthening him: on his face, even the "deep clean lines seemed less a sign of age than of vigor."

Behind all this lies Josef K.'s memory of the guards who devoured his breakfast. This expropriating power is always at work, manifesting itself obliquely, as if by chance, but with absolute assurance.

Josef K. has spent two hours, in his office, lost in thoughts of the memorial he wants to write. He has kept various clients waiting. When at last he receives the first, a manufacturer, the vice director enters the room; he is "not quite clear, as if behind a gauzy veil." This image alerts us to what by now we already know: the vice director isn't a typical character, with distinguishing traits that are clearly defined and often in evidence. The vice director is a larval form of Josef K. Wherever he appears, something delicate is happening to Josef K., within Josef K. This time the vice director begins talking cordially with the client—and soon the two figures *overshadow* Josef K. If a lens were now to focus on this scene, isolating it from everything else, this is what we would see: Josef K. is sitting at his desk, and, lifting his gaze, he has the im-

pression that "above his head two men, whose size he
mentally exaggerated, were in negotiations over him.
Slowly, turning his eyes cautiously upward, he tried to as-
certain what was happening above him, and without
looking he took a sheet of paper from his desk, placed it
on the palm of his hand, and lifted it little by little toward
the two gentlemen, as he himself stood up." Two giants
discuss, in coded language, the life of an inferior creature
who is nearly flattened by their bodies and who, to get
their attention, slowly lifts toward them a page on the
palm of his hand. But who, in a normal office, ever offers
a page to someone by lifting it slowly on the palm of one
hand? Josef K. knows this perfectly well: "He wasn't
thinking of anything in particular, he acted only out of a
feeling that he would have to behave in this way once he
had composed the great memorial that would completely
unburden him." For Josef K., events are arranged on two
very distinct planes: on one hand, in the normal worka-
day world, there unfolds a commonplace office scene
among three people—two bank officers and one client—
who are discussing business; on the other, in the secret
world of the trial, there looms something that may happen in the future, after Josef K. has successfully completed the act that will decide his fate, the only act that
could "completely unburden him": writing his "great memorial." To reach that moment, one must offer a written
document *from low to high*, taking the risk that the offer
will not be noticed, or else—and this, the worst-case scenario, is promptly played out—that it will be deemed de-
void of interest. "Thanks, I already know all that," says

the vice director, after barely glancing at the page. But why is the vice director so dismissive? "Because whatever was important to the chief officer wasn't important to him." On one hand, then, the "great memorial" that Josef K. has resolved to write must contain every least detail of his life, reaching levels of extreme, unutterable intimacy; on the other, it runs the risk of not even being taken into consideration because it's *too personal*. Why, indeed, should what matters to Josef K. matter to the vice director? A nasty, paralyzing question. Josef K. doesn't know how to escape it. Meanwhile, the vice director is one of two giants who are discussing his fate, who in fact may have already decided it.

In an obscure, mocking way, the vice director seems to know what's going on in Josef K.'s mind. He knows because he *is* in his mind. If Josef K. imagines the moment when the memorial will "completely unburden [*entlasten*] him," a few moments later the vice director says that Josef K. looks "overburdened [*überlastet*]"—and thus incapable of discussing anything. And he adds: "The people in the antechamber have been waiting for him for hours now." The vice director's observation gives rise to a most unpleasant suspicion: that Josef K., who already feels persecuted by an elusive authority, behaves the same way it does, capriciously making the bank's clients wait just as the judges make him wait. The superimposition seems perfect. When it's made clear that Josef K. isn't even thinking of admitting another client, the text says: "admitting any other party [*irgendeine andere Partei*]," using the same word, *Partei*, that designates the other parties we encounter—not just those summoned for trials, but also those who will appear one day, radiant with mystery, in the speculations that Bürgel addresses to K., toward the end of *The Castle*.

A "great memorial," such as Josef K. conceives, must first of all be unmistakable. It must be the very voice of some peculiarity. But how does the world treat peculiarity? "Every individual is peculiar and called on to act out of the strength of his peculiarity, but he must take pleasure in his peculiarity," Kafka once wrote. Then this drastic sentence: "As for my own experience, both in school and at home, the desired goal was to erase this peculiarity." If the individual in general, then, is characterized by *being peculiar*, it's also true that the earliest collective powers with whom he comes in contact (family, school) immediately take it upon themselves to *erase* that which defines him. Everyone conspires to ensure that no individual will "take pleasure in his peculiarity."

The third sentence is even more ruthless: "Doing so made the work of education easier, but it also made life easier for the child, who however first had to savor the pain caused by restriction." The erosion of the individual's primary attribute (his peculiarity) is therefore both a part of the "work" of education and an aid to help the new being through life. For life to be livable, one's peculiarity must be extinguished. But this idea seems somehow monstrous and unthinkable, as would, from a child's point of view, the request to stop reading an "exciting story" and go to bed. The monstrosity is implicit in the disproportion of the elements: for the reading child, "everything was infinite or else faded into the distance," so that he found it inconsistent when "arguments limited only to him" were used to persuade him to interrupt his reading, so inconsistent in fact that they "failed to reach even the threshold of what merited serious consideration." The child's peculiarity lay precisely in that determination "to keep reading." For the adult, it will become the determination to keep writing. In both cases, at night. Then, "even the night was infinite."

In the child's view, the sense of the "wrong that had been done him" was linked *only* to himself, as if that injustice had been specially devised for that occasion. As a result, notes the child at a distance of years, "there developed the beginnings of the hatred that determined my family life and from then on, in certain ways, my entire life."

Two words are particularly striking: *work* and *hatred*—words that emerge from the process of the *erasure of peculiarity*. We are thrown, from the scene of the child immersed in reading and forced to go to bed, into a menacing, oppressive landscape. Thus we arrive at the decisive passage: "My peculiarity went unrecognized; but, since I felt it, I had to recognize in this behavior toward me a disapproval, all the more since I was very sensitive in that regard and always on the alert." That disapproval is the prelude to a sentence. Peculiarity and guilt converge. Or rather, the first thing we're guilty of is peculiarity. The sentence comes down from the outside world, but soon it is carried out internally by the child himself, who "kept [certain peculiarities] hidden because he himself recognized in them a small wrong." Now we are on a slippery slope, at the bottom of which can only be self-condemnation: "If however I kept a peculiarity hidden, the consequence was that I hated myself or my destiny—considered myself bad or cursed." The climate has imperceptibly changed: the circle of light around the reading child is now the spotlight isolating the defendant. By now it is no longer a question of *peculiarities* that must be defended but rather of *confessions* that must be rendered. Suddenly we find ourselves back with Josef K. as he tries to decide how to compose his "great memorial" to the court. And whether it's even possible. The answer (a negative one) is given here: "The peculiarities I revealed multiplied the closer I got to the life that was accessible to me. But this didn't bring with it liberation, the mass of what was kept secret didn't diminish as a result, but rather a sharpening power of observation made it clear that it had never been possible to confess everything, that even the apparently complete confessions of earlier times had, as it turned out, left their hidden root within me." Here the texture of *The Trial* emerges: he speaks of "apparently complete confessions," of "the mass of what was kept secret," of the ineradicable "root" of something that must be considered a source of guilt. Such words can be grasped only within the territory of *The Trial*. Indeed they are located at its outermost edges. The problem here is the impossibility of confessing the secret—and therefore of exhausting it. And since the secret has to do with peculiarity, and peculiarities are guilt itself, we're left with the inextinguishability of the guilt we carry with us. And having reached the peak of lucidity, the analysis now falls back into the vortex: "This wasn't a delusion, only a particular form of the knowledge that, at least among the living, no one can rid himself of himself." At this point, suspended in the void, we barely notice that parenthetical: "at least among the living."

It isn't sufficient to write, by oneself, a memorial in one's own defense, thinks Josef K.: one must then submit it "immediately and pressure them, every day if possible, to examine it." And here an extraneous splinter wedges its way in: "To that end, it wouldn't of course be enough for K. to sit in the hall with the others, placing his hat beneath the bench. He himself or the women or other messengers would have to besiege the officials day after day, forcing them to sit down at their desks and examine K.'s statement instead of staring into the hall through the grille." *The women*, says Josef K. But which women? Who are these women he mentions, who will have to "besiege" the officials to make them read some pages he has written? Miss Bürstner, Mrs. Grubach, the washerwoman, the nurse Leni, the dancer Elsa: those are the only ones we know about. They don't have much in common, but then we remember another insight that came to Josef K. as Leni was sitting on his lap: "I'm seeking help from women, he thought, almost amazed—first Miss Bürstner, then the court usher's wife, and now this little nurse, who seems to feel some inexplicable need for me." This insight raises an issue that isn't easily explained and that is enough to derail his train of thought: this "inexplicable need" for him that a woman he has just met seems to feel, very like what other women—Frieda, Pepi, Olga—will seem to feel toward K. in the village beneath the Castle. But how can that inexplicable feminine need be put to use as part of the rigorous plan of self-defense that Josef K. is preparing? And what about those "messengers" who might, if necessary, replace the women? They are even more perplexing. This momentary and almost imperceptible vacillation of his argument risks vitiating it entirely, the way a paranoiac's hasty parenthetical remark can open and then immediately close again the peephole into his vast delirium, canceling out an otherwise impeccable line of reasoning. Josef K.'s idea that "the women," in general, might help him compel the court officials to read his memorial seems already somehow incongruous, comical, or overly specific, even if it's a specificity that eludes the reader. It won't elude the prison chaplain, who will one day tell him: "You seek too much help from others and especially from women."

And the "messengers"? Josef K. hasn't mentioned them before—and it's hard to imagine what their function might be. Which messengers? Used to communicate what? And invested with what powers? No answers can be abstracted from any of Josef K.'s prior thoughts. We're completely in the dark. But if we gaze ahead into the distance, we glimpse the silhouette of Barnabas in his silver livery, in the as yet unconceived *Castle*. It's as if the crosshatched contours of another world are emerging, where the world of *The Trial* is destined to be continued.

The court offices are located in the places of things one wants to forget: in the attics of the big city. But the court itself is incapable of forgetting. It's the universal preserve, the *horreum* of memory spoken of by Giordano Bruno, the "granary" of what happens. Its limits can't be known, because any attic might continue on into the next, into even more extensive offices. What the court demands, if an individual dares—as Josef K. does—to write up his own memorial, is complete knowledge of his own life, reconstructed down to the last detail. Clearly no one is capable of responding satisfactorily. And this inability establishes once and for all the disparity between the court and the individual. Consequently the court may oppress the individual without the slightest effort, simply because its task is to keep alive the traces of everything that has ever happened. Sometimes dangerously alive.

The life of the court is found, like Odradek, in junk rooms—places where even the poor store what they no longer use, where the power feared by everyone, beginning with those who serve it, is exercised. And so, in a room at Josef K.'s workplace, among "old unusable printed matter and ceramic ink pots, empty and overturned," we find a representative of the court at work: the flogger with his naked arms, his "savage, ruddy face," and his sailor's tan, wrapped in a dark leather girdle as if he had just left an S/M club. He has been entrusted with a special kind of punishment: sordid, secret, suited to lowly characters such as the guards who arrested Josef K. and took possession of his undergarments. He must flog them, perhaps to death, because Josef K. denounced them in his deposition. And we know that the court wants "to make a good impression."

Josef K. tries to intervene, then runs away terrified by the thought of being discovered there by some bank clerk. With formidable agility, he quickly develops a series of justifications for his behavior, throwing in for good measure a vague threat against "the truly guilty, the high-level officials, none of whom had yet dared show themselves to him," as if they were the ones who were obliged to respond to him—and not he to them. This baldly inconsistent reversal signals that Josef K. is by now in a state of extreme weakness. The terror is in him. But not only because of the unmitigated ferocity of the scene he has just witnessed. At work, the next day, he "still couldn't get the guards off his mind." He wonders: where are they now? He opens the junk-room door and finds again the exact scene from the previous evening, down to the last detail. There's nothing left to do but shut the door again and pound his fists against it, "as if that might close it better."

The flogger episode reveals to Josef K. something for which no remedy exists: the court hasn't merely insinuated itself, via attics and junk rooms, into the recesses of space; it has also sequestered time. The flow of time is pierced in every instant by a succession of *tableaux vivants.* The flogger perpetually raises his naked arm against the two groaning guards. The closed door always opens on the same scene. And no new instant is capable of clearing the room.

Returning from a visit to his brother-in-law's abhorred (and no doubt deadly) asbestos factory, of which he had been forced to become a silent partner, Kafka observed that one feels less foreign in a foreign city than one does on the outskirts of one's own city. In a foreign city, one can easily bypass such feelings, even "forgo comparisons," as if it were a hallucination or a landscape unreeling beyond the window of a train. A few tram stops, however, or a half-hour walk, can carry one across the imperceptible border that delimits the "wretched, dark fringe, scored with furrows like a great gorge," that is the periphery of one's own city. "Therefore," he continued, "I always enter the periphery with mixed feelings of anxiety, distress, pity, curiosity, haughtiness, wanderlust, and virility, and I return with a sense of well-being, of gravity, of calm." The court before which Josef K. had to appear was based, shrewdly, in the periphery. By the time the defendant arrives there, he is already weakened, vulnerable, exposed to the unknown, and yet what he sees there is utterly commonplace, scenes that repeat themselves everywhere: children playing, strangers looking out a window or crossing a courtyard. The most serious changes are of such a nature: modest in terms of the distance covered, barely noticeable while in progress, overwhelming by the time one is welcomed into the "dark fringe" of meaning.

.   .   .

The charges Josef K. levels against the court, in his bold, vehement deposition—his first and only—are those that, by age-old tradition, are customarily leveled against every center of power: that it's based on arbitrariness and injustice (as an example, Josef K. cites the story of his arrest), on brutality and dishonesty (even among the audience in the hearing room are "persons who are being directed from up here"); that, on the other hand, despite its rough-hewn outward appearance, one can glimpse a "great organization" behind it. Corruption is obviously essential to the functioning of the machine, corruption that no doubt extends from the simple guards all the way to the "highest judge." And in addition to "the innumerable, indispensable retinue" of those who collaborate with the machine, along with the "ushers, copyists, gendarmes and other assistants," Josef K. doesn't shrink from including "perhaps even executioners." Only a small part of all this would be more than enough to charge him with contempt of court. But the examining magistrate is unruffled. He wants only to make it clear that, with his deposition, Josef K. has deprived himself "of the advantages that an interrogation invariably offers the arrested man."

The court doesn't seem to fear the appalling accusations Josef K. has made public: such accusations are found in every history book. If the court were merely a corrupt, arbitrary center of power, prone to any sort of malfeasance, it would lose its peculiarity and its profile would blur together with so many others. And yet, in Josef K.'s impassioned speech, given not in his own name but in the name of the many who suffer similar abuses and who, he supposes, are present in the audience ("I'm fighting for them, not for myself," he says, in the tone of a tribune), there lurks a passage whose implications might truly worry the court: "What is the point of this great organization, gentlemen? It consists in arresting innocent people and starting proceedings against them that are senseless and that, in most cases, including my own, go nowhere." Corruption may even be necessary in order to sustain the "senselessness of the whole thing." A new perspective has come to light here: the goal of the "great organization" isn't to obtain power or money or to impose some idea—the three forms of which history offers examples in such abundance. The goal is to arrest the innocent and then to punish them. The goal is punishment for its own sake, a self-sufficient activity, like art. And recognizable by the splendor of its "senselessness."

But Josef K. isn't able to pursue this course any further—and perhaps he doesn't even realize the power of what he's just said. The room is already abuzz, the audience choosing now the role of voyeur, as the student subdues and gropes the washerwoman "in a corner by the door." And when Josef K. turns around to look, all the observers—no longer just some among them—appear to him to be infiltrators from the court: "You're all officials, I see, you're the corrupt band I was speaking against." In a matter of moments, the oppressed populace in whose defense he had risen has become a compact representation of the oppressors. All Josef K. can do now is grab his hat and leave the scene. As he runs down the stairs, he is followed by "the noise of the assembly, which had come to life again, probably to discuss what had happened as students might."

One Sunday morning, Josef K. visits the court offices "out of curiosity." He sees other defendants sitting on benches and waiting, as if out of habit. Their clothes look "neglected," but various signs make it clear that most of them "belonged to the upper classes." Social rank is quite relevant to the court. It isn't attracted to the guilt of the common people. It is among the bourgeoisie—that metamorphic class that is willing and able to take the shape of everything else, to imitate the aristocracy and seep into the working class—that guilt flourishes. There is little to differentiate these defendants from those men at the bank who wait in the antechamber outside Josef K.'s office, except their careless dress. And a terrible hypersensitivity: "Defendants in general are so sensitive," observes the court usher when a distinguished gentleman, Josef K.'s "colleague" insofar as he's a defendant, suddenly yells as if Josef K. "had touched him not with two fingers but with red-hot tongs."

The court that tries Josef K. "isn't very well known among the common people"; it seems to have an esoteric purview. It wants to make a good first impression, however, and thus it has appointed an information officer, charged with giving out "any information the waiting parties may need." This man has two characteristics: "he knows an answer for every question," and he is elegant, sporting "a gray waistcoat that ended in two long sharp points." His clothes were acquired thanks to a collection taken up from among the court employees and the defendants, since the administration proved "rather strange" about it. In the attics that host the court offices, as well as in the distressing corridor where the defendants sit waiting, hats beneath their benches, this man moves with the ease of a master of ceremonies in the halls of a Grand Hôtel. But sometimes he can't help laughing in the defendants' faces—as he does with Josef K. A female employee next to Josef K. explains: "Everything's set to make a good impression, but then he ruins it all with his laugh, which scares people." The information officer is an embodiment of the court: long steeped in the stagnant attic air, he can't stand fresh air, as if he were afraid of dissolving outside those offices where he is both genius loci and tour guide. He is ceremonious and cruel. "He really knows how to talk to the parties," the woman whispers to Josef K., who nods.

Josef K. tries to speak with a defendant, who wants only to be left alone to wait ("I thought I could wait here, it's Sunday, I have some time and won't bother anyone here," he pleads). The stale air makes it hard to breathe. A sort of "seasickness" overtakes Josef K. From the end of the hall he hears "a roar of pelting waves, as if the hallway were pitching back and forth and the defendants on either side were rising and falling with it." He finally knows where he is now. The information officer's laugh and the sly sarcasm of his words reverberate: "Just as I said. It's only here that the gentleman feels unwell, not in general." *Only here:* But Josef K. has now ascertained the vastness of that *here:* it's a sea that lifts and sweeps away everything in its path. These offices are linked by an obscure equation to the work of punishment, and Josef K. is on the verge of recognizing this link when he is overcome by vertigo. But there's no need to worry: "Almost everyone has an attack like this the first time they come," the woman tells him gently.

In the same attic rooms, depending on the day, either laundry is hung out to dry or the court hearings take place. But what's the difference between laundry drying on a line and the work of the court? To a large extent they coincide, or at least each infuses the other. The court is a hallucination superimposed on everything else. It overruns everything from below, from the margins, from above. It thrives on the periphery, in poor neighborhoods, in attics. It generates suffocating heat and clouds of steam. However, if one prefers, there's always a sensible explanation: "You can't completely prohibit the tenants" from hanging their laundry in the attics, remarks the employee who helps Josef K. and whose face bears the "severe expression that certain women have even in the bloom of youth." And she adds: "That's why these rooms aren't very well suited for offices, even if in other ways they offer great advantages." She doesn't specify what these "great advantages" might be.

Mrs. Grubach takes Josef K.'s "happiness" to heart, for he is "her best and dearest boarder," but she doesn't give much weight to his arrest. For her, it isn't as "serious" as being arrested for stealing. No, his is an arrest that seems "like something scholarly." Thus she can say: "I don't understand it, but then one doesn't need to understand it." Josef K. replies as though he has immediately grasped her meaning, but suggests that the arrest, rather than "something scholarly," ought to be considered a "nothing." He adds: "I was caught by surprise, that's all." And he goes on to explain: "If immediately upon awakening, without letting myself be thrown off by the fact that Anna hadn't appeared, I'd risen immediately and, ignoring anyone in my path, had come to you and eaten breakfast in the kitchen for a change, if I'd had you bring my clothes from my room, in short if I had behaved reasonably, nothing else would have happened. Everything that wanted to come into being would have been stifled."

This conversation between Josef K. and his landlady, as she patiently darns a pile of stockings into which he "from time to time buried his hand," is one of the most vertiginous exchanges in all of *The Trial*. But neither of the two interlocutors grasps its import, and neither of course does the reader, for the story has just begun. The words exist and act on their own, occasionally passing through people but never belonging to them—indeed they are immediately forgotten. Only a writer's hand will one day be able to gather them and set them in their place, at the nerve center of events.

To counter Mrs. Grubach's theory, according to which some doctrine, perhaps a complex, ancient one, lies behind his arrest, Josef K. wants to reduce it to a pure physiological fact. The arrest is something "that wanted to come into being" but that could have been "stifled" had he shown sufficient quickness in the moment of awakening ("immediately," *gleich*, appears twice in three lines). What follows is comic in its labored detail—he should have moved immediately into the kitchen, had breakfast in the kitchen, had clothes brought from his room—but immensely serious in its aim: "to stifle" something that is about to come into being. The implicit thesis is this: if one acted "reasonably," one could ensure that "everything that wanted to come into being" would be "stifled." Bold metaphysical thesis. The ancient terror of becoming is caught in the instant of awakening, therefore at the source of that which is becoming. And that includes all things, since the world itself is something "that wanted to come into being." But awakening requires this virtue: a quick reaction time, which only the prepared can count on. And here Josef K. is forced to admit, as if ruminating: "We are so poorly prepared." That fact alone explains how one can get mixed up in a trial. But what is required in order to be prepared (and therefore to act "reasonably")? At the very least, an office. Josef K. adds: "At the bank, for example, I'm prepared, nothing like this could ever happen to me there." Certain consequences can be inferred from his ominous aside, including, above all, this one: that in order to act "reasonably" one needs to contain within oneself the equivalent of an office, since one can't expect the awakening to take place in an actual office. Further, the "reasonable" action has, among its functions, that of stifling certain things that want to happen. If events take another course, if two strangers devour our breakfast, if the same strangers confiscate our clothes, then there has been a disturbance in our awakening, which is "the riskiest moment." Josef K.'s entire story shows us what the risk is: that revelation may transform into persecution.

Awakening, the *bodhi* that is continually spoken of in Indian thought from the Vedas to the Buddha, is something that happens during wakefulness, an invisible shift, a sudden change in distances and in the mental pace, thanks to which consciousness is able to observe itself— and is therefore able to observe itself in its typical role as observer. The most effective metaphor for this event is the awakening from sleep, the passage from dream to wakefulness. That auroral moment of fullness and astonishment—but also sometimes of bewilderment and anxiety—suggests another fullness that can characterize every instant of waking life. Few people experience awakening as a perpetually renewed act, within wakefulness— such an act is definitive only in the Buddha. And yet such people are the only ones, according to some, who can be said to think. Everyone, however, experiences the act of waking, of rousing oneself from sleep. But this phenomenon that everyone experiences daily is merely an example, a hint, a rough figuration of that other phenomenon, of which most remain unaware.

One rainy morning, Josef K. is preparing to leave his office in order to take an Italian client of his bank on a tour of the monuments of his city. He gets a phone call. It's Leni, who asks him how he is. He replies that he has an appointment at the cathedral, explains why. Leni "suddenly" tells him: "They're hunting you down." Josef K. replaces the receiver, disturbed by the warning. And he tells himself: "Yes, they're hunting me down."

This is perhaps the moment of purest terror in Josef K.'s story. Behind the voice of the invisible Leni, we sense an unknown, sinister immensity yawning open. And again, only a woman is capable of auguring its existence. Until that moment, Josef K. thought that having to show the client around the city was merely an inconvenient duty, since "every hour away from the office troubled him." A minor annoyance, part of the course of daily life. But as soon as he replies to Leni, he senses something fatal—and preordained—about this appointment at the cathedral, something to which he is alerted by an inner voice that harmonizes perfectly with hers. Their two voices blur: "Yes, they're hunting me down." Normal office life has now become a fragile, transparent shell, beneath which can be recognized, by its slow, lethal breath, an abysmal creature: the indomitable life of the trial.

Diary entry from November 2, 1911: "This morning for the first time in a long time the joy again at the thought of a knife being turned in my heart." Antepenultimate sentence of *The Trial:* ". . . while the other stuck the knife into his heart and turned it there twice." One notices first the repetition: already in 1911, the knife in the heart is like an old acquaintance who has reappeared.

Then the attention to the gesture, as if the decisive element of the whole scene were the verb *drehen*, "to turn." And finally the "joy" the thought inspires. That's a rare word in Kafka. Up until the very end, Josef K. rebels against—and collaborates with—the power that wants to kill him. When the two executioners come to take him away, he is ready. His outfit even matches theirs. They wear frock coats "with seemingly immovable top hats." Josef K. is "dressed in black" with "new gloves that were snug on his fingers." He's sitting near the door "with the look of one who expects guests." As the trio walks down the street, the two executioners hold him tightly between them, forming "a unit of the sort usually formed only by lifeless matter." His last rebellious line of reasoning, then, is utterly disinterested, having no chance by this point to help his case, and it's subtle enough to offer itself as a brainteaser: "Were there objections that had been forgotten? Of course there were. Logic is, no doubt, unshakable, but it's no match for a man who wants to live." As for him, he had stopped being "a man who wants to live" a year ago.

The two executioners want Josef K.'s head to rest nicely on a "loose block of stone" in a "suitable spot" in the quarry that has been preselected for the killing. They struggle to get him into the right position, a task made easier by "K.'s cooperation with them." And yet his "position remained quite forced and implausible." This is the true end point of *The Trial*. Even when the executioners and the condemned man join forces, the victim's position remains "implausible." The execution is real; the actions have something incongruous and distorted about them. That imbalance is the hallmark of the whole affair. Maybe that's what Josef K. is thinking, moments later, as he watches the two executioners pass the butcher knife back and forth but declines to take it in hand and drive it home himself. In the end, he can't "relieve the authorities of all the work." Thus he commits one "final error," of course: but who bears "the responsibility" for the error, if not "the one who had denied him the remnant of strength required"? And who might that be? Whose task is it to strip Josef K. of that last bit of strength he needs not only to help the executioners position his head properly on the stone block but also to open up his body with the butcher knife? This is the extreme question that *The Trial* leaves hanging. And the most frightening. But it's easily over-looked: the unfolding series of actions is too vivid for one to pay much attention to Josef K.'s final cogitation.

A moment later, a light goes on in a window on "the top floor of a building next to the quarry," and a figure appears there in silhouette. This figure—it could be a man or a woman—is the last of many who have appeared in windows. It recalls the figures who, from the facing windows, observed Josef K.'s arrest.

If the fact that Josef K. can't find the strength to stick the butcher knife in his own chest is a "final error," then the trial, in its pure, ideal form, must have been plotting his suicide from the very start. But in all the key moments, Josef K. turns out to lack sufficient strength, either to remain awake long enough to listen to the revelatory words, or to perform, with his own hand, the resolving gesture. Thus his two executioners have the air of tenors or vaudeville extras. They are "fleeting improvised men," Judge Schreber would have said, and serve only for that momentary task of plunging the knife into Josef K.'s body. If the order of the world were more perfect, they would be unnecessary. Josef K. would act alone. But would there be, in that case, a trial? Or wouldn't the trial coincide with the act of creation, with that long suicide?

XII. The Stuff of Legends

For generation upon generation, the painters charged with painting the portraits of the court judges have passed down "rules that are numerous, varied, and above all secret." The latest artist called on to apply them is Titorelli, a painter of mythological scenes with a penchant for heathscapes. As Reynolds painted the great ladies of his day in the attitudes of Diana or Minerva, so Titorelli paints a judge in the semblance of a goddess: the Goddess of Justice, of course. Though she could also be the Goddess of Victory, the artist notes. Or maybe even, after some final retouches, which Titorelli performs in Josef K.'s presence, the Goddess of the Hunt. She is depicted mid-chase, with wings on her ankles. Surely every jolt must unbalance those scales of justice. A blindfolded woman running: that's what Titorelli is painting. More than a goddess, she's a riddle, one whose solution isn't clear. Is she solemn? Derisive? This is all we know for sure: the Goddess of Justice is visible at once, and the Goddess of the Hunt is the last to reveal herself. Does this, perhaps, foretell the court's ultimate, esoteric meaning?

. . .

Josef K. and K. experience their decisive revelations while sitting on the edge of a bed: K. on Bürgel's bed, Josef K. on Titorelli's. Less important, but still significant, is proximity to a bed: Gardena beside K.'s bed in the maids' room, K. beside the superintendent's bed. Even the position one assumes on the bed is meaningful, as we can see from Titorelli's behavior. It isn't enough for him that Josef K. sit on the edge of the bed. Instead the painter "pushed him back into the eiderdown and the cushions." Only when Josef K. is sinking toward the middle of the bed does Titorelli ask his "first actual question": "Are you innocent?" And Josef K. answers: "Yes."

The edge of the bed is the threshold of another world, and one must sink into that other world before the most essential, most direct question can be asked. Only in Titorelli's studio, in that oppressive burrow, two strides wide in each direction, only in that stale air, can such words be uttered. And what Titorelli says now hasn't been heard before. First: "The court can never be swayed." If it has seen guilt, no one can persuade it that the guilt isn't there. This is a valuable, if indirect, rejoinder to the declaration of innocence that Josef K. has just made. Second: the corrupt girls who play on the stairs and who guided Josef K. to Titorelli "belong to the court." Indeed, the painter adds, "everything belongs to the court." With his ceremonious, indifferent manner, and above all with these last words, added "half in jest, half in explanation," Titorelli has offered Josef K. revelations that could carry

great weight, if only he didn't find them, thanks to his unshakable mistrust, "unbelievable."

Josef K. already has an "opinion" about the court, even
if he prolongs his captious interrogation in an effort to
"uncover contradictions" in the painter's words, and he
too now has something to say about it, which, in its terseness, seems like a final judgment: "A single executioner
could take the place of the entire court." That executioner
is death itself, which acts without consulting instructions or verdicts, just as the Goddess of the Hunt, whom
Josef K. thought he recognized in the painting propped on
Titorelli's easel, strikes in the mazy forest without the
authorization of any preliminary judgment. Josef K. has
lucidly perceived that the court is the place where the
Goddess of Justice and the Goddess of the Hunt blur into
a single figure. Titorelli suggests that the Goddess of Victory can be seen in the same figure. But that's a superfluous addendum. Victory, for the court, is a given for every
moment of the world's existence.

In the eyes of the manufacturer who first speaks to
Josef K. about him, Titorelli is a postulant, "almost a beggar," as every artist is, in principle. In Josef K.'s eyes he is
first of all a "poor man," precisely what he himself will
seem in Titorelli's eyes. And yet that "poor man," thanks
to his profession, is the only one who has direct access to
the remote past, to the "legends."

The subject of legends comes up when Titorelli is
explaining to Josef K. that there are three types of absolu-

tion: "real acquittal, apparent acquittal, and protraction." Titorelli knows of no case of real acquittal. But he knows that some real acquittals "are said to have occurred," at least among the legal cases handed down in legend.

When they speak of legends in *The Trial*, they may as well be speaking of myth, a word Kafka doesn't use here, perhaps because it brings in something superfluous or academic. The legends tell of judgments that are otherwise inaccessible: the court's ancient verdicts, which "are not published." This alone should render them valuable. An abyss, however, divides us from those legends. Certainly they are "very beautiful," and one can even attribute to them "a kind of truth"—and here, rustling behind Titorelli's words, we hear the age-old dispute over myth: Plato is watching us—"but they are not provable." And what is a court if not the place where proof must be offered? Is it possible, then, Josef K. asks, "to appeal to such legends in court?" Of course not, the painter replies. He even laughs. A terrible laugh. The court is steeped in legends, right down to the portraits of its judges—and these legends are the only means of accessing a part of its history. If nothing else, they offer beauty and "a kind of truth." But they can't be utilized, and so, Josef K. concludes, "it's useless to talk about them."

This ferocious amputation has many consequences: above all, it becomes pointless to consider "real acquittal," because real acquittal is treated only in the legends—and it's useless to talk about legends. It's as if the world agreed, with a simple gesture, to abolish a part of itself. And the only part, furthermore, where the adjective "real" is applicable. All the rest of the world, which soon will be considered the whole world, is divided up between "apparent acquittal" and "protraction." Within that world things can be proved, but they may not be real. As for any acquittal that one might obtain there, it will certainly not be "real." This brief exchange in Titorelli's cramped, stifling studio, between two people who have just met, has a grave consequence: in the name of reality, reality is left aside. With the haste of a man who is after tangible results, Josef K. says at once: "Then let's leave real acquittal aside." What remains? Apparent acquittal and protraction. Only they have applications; only of them is it useful to speak. In the meantime, Titorelli asks Josef K.: "But don't you want to take your jacket off before we discuss them? You must be very hot." Josef K. agrees—and says: "It's nearly unbearable." He finds it nearly unbearable mainly because he has come too close to grasping the nature of his situation. Thus, just as he is getting ready to talk about what can be most useful to him, he has "the feeling of being totally cut off from air." Here begins a brief, dense back-and-forth between him and Titorelli on air, fog, windows, heat, doors. In *The Trial*, any mention of windows or air or breathing is a signal—like a conversation about clothes in *The Castle*—that we have entered an intense, highly sensitive zone.

What Josef K. wants to find out can never be breathed. Titorelli knows that—and nods "as though he understood

K.'s malaise very well." The close, oppressive air of Titorelli's garret is now ready to flow out over the vast wasteland of apparent acquittal and protraction.

Does the fact that legends can't be used as evidence reflect one of their intrinsic weaknesses—or one of their privileges? Since the legends deal with "ancient legal cases" for which "the court's final verdicts are not published," one might assume that their inadmissibility as evidence stems from the impossibility of verifying their contents. Titorelli's account, however, doesn't say that *in the past* the court's final verdicts were not published. The painter asserts, rather, that such verdicts are *never* published. If that's the case, not only the legends but also all other evidence, of any kind, would be inadequate. It would always be unverifiable. As for the legends, they would then be the only texts that at least "contain real acquittals," the only ones, therefore, that incorporate some of the final verdicts. Of course, the legends may all be frauds. But they may also be the last surviving vestige of the court's final verdicts. The last vestige of something "real" in a world as cut off from reality as Josef K. is from air.

For a long time, during the greater part of human history, myth was the prime source of wisdom. Then it became a sequence of insidious, pointless stories, meaningful only to the degree that they helped us understand how people lived in the past. The sources of wisdom shifted. Matters myth had once told stories about were now proved and applied. But there were those who noticed that some of myth's wisdom had been sealed off within the new wisdom. No big deal, most felt. We'll know a little less about our past, but what does the past matter when before us lies the immensity of the present? Others, however, persisted. They noticed that the inaccessible part of myth dealt with the "court's final verdicts." And no other text did, since those verdicts "are not published." Thus the hope was born, in a few, that one might, through the myths, come to know things that one could never otherwise discover. Most considered such hope a serious delusion, but they couldn't prove it, since the court's recent verdicts, which might have countered the ancient ones, were also inaccessible. For even now the verdicts were not published. Meanwhile the world continued to be embroiled in trials and verdicts, which, however, were never final. The trials were all visible, the verdicts all provisional. Reality had been taken away, everything became a snarl of appearance and protraction.

Why aren't the real acquittals published? In order to guard some secret? So that "the highest court" can protect its exclusive right to grant "final acquittals," thereby ensuring the inaccessibility of the secret? Nothing indeed is as inaccessible as what isn't there. And many claim it isn't, convinced that the barricade erected around the secret serves above all to allow the greatest freedom of action at the highest levels. But this explanation, however plausible and seductive, addresses only the secret's easiest, most external aspect. Its foundation appears when Titorelli describes what happens in the event of a real acquittal: "The court acts must all be set aside, they disappear totally from the proceedings; not only is the charge destroyed, but also the trial and even the acquittal, everything is destroyed." If everything is destroyed, one can see why real acquittal is never made public: because it is destroyed in the very moment it comes into being. The extinction of the *acts*—and here again, as we move beyond the surface sense of "judicial acts," the literal meaning shows through: that of *acts* as *karma*—is the only way out of the trial, following the exertion, on the part of the highest judges, of their "great power to free a person from the charge." All the rest is made of ropes that slacken or tighten according to the will of ordinary judges, who enjoy only "the power to unbind a person from the charge."

As for apparent acquittals: it's clear that these cover a vast share of the possibilities—and Titorelli lets it be understood that the most congenial solution for Josef K. lies in this area. Apparent acquittal is characterized by its tendency to grant the relief of temporary victory, but only in the context of ongoing anxiety. One who obtains an apparent acquittal and returns contentedly home can never be sure he won't find someone waiting for him there, ready to arrest him again on the same charge. The charge, by its nature, tends to remain "alive" and "continues to hover over" the defendant like a dark bird. It's no surprise that, "as soon as the high order comes," the charge can "immediately take effect" again. And here

Titorelli touches on a crucial point: a trial may lead to a verdict, but "the proceeding remains active." The trial is only a temporary dramatization of something that never ceases but rather "continues pendulum-like, with larger or smaller oscillations, with longer or shorter interruptions"—and that's the "proceeding." Titorelli's meticulous description only confirms Josef K.'s recent insight: "A single executioner could take the place of the entire court." Behind all its imposing apparatus, the court "serves no purpose." It certainly doesn't serve to determine guilt, given that in every case "the court is firmly convinced of the defendant's guilt" from the start. Why, then, does the court continue to exist? Couldn't a single executioner eliminate the interminable series of acts, all of which have a predetermined outcome? And isn't this like saying that every life could be immediately ended by death, without having to develop through all manner of branching and leafing? Maybe Titorelli would have hinted at an answer had Josef K. not been in such a hurry to get out of that stifling garret. But where would he go to breathe easier? Into the hallways of the court, with which that room communicates via the door behind the painter's bed.

In his work at the bank, Josef K. deals with laws and courts of every kind. And that multiplicity comforts him, because it seems to limit each individual power. Speaking with Titorelli, however, he realizes that his convictions are mistaken. Everything converges toward a single court— and that court extends everywhere. More disconcerting even than its omnipresence is its talent for mimicry. The court is pervasive, yet it can pass unnoticed or be confused with other courts. The court's activities are widely known, but at the same time one isn't bound to be aware of them. Many people are familiar with Josef K.'s trial, but only because they have something to do with the court. Otherwise his trial would be a secret. This is the real terror: that some normal life may exist, that it may be proceeding smoothly along, but that it may contain within it another life, one with radically different aims, working quietly, as if protected by the sheath of the normal life. If that's true, it will no longer be possible to appeal to normality, and even less to nature, for both will be suspected of serving as mere covers for another process, which proceeds along a completely different course. And whose proceedings have a completely different meaning.

"No acts get lost, the court doesn't forget anything": this is still Titorelli speaking. Everything piles up and coalesces. But, in the course of this vast procession of proceedings, does anything final, transparent, or unquestionable manage to survive? It would seem not. The real acquittals are destroyed the moment they are pronounced. And the convictions? There are none. Beyond the void left by the destruction of the real acquittals, there remain only cases of apparent acquittal—which are by their nature never final, since "the proceeding remains active," like an ember beneath ash—and cases of protraction, where the trial is cunningly kept "at the lowest stage," so that it never gets as far as a verdict and a possible conviction. The procession of proceedings seems in the end unable to produce not only acquittals but convictions as well. Yet Josef K. will be convicted and killed in the most atrocious manner: "like a dog." One day the secretary Bürgel, who is the prison chaplain's secular counterpart, will explain to Josef K. that "there are things that founder for no other reason than themselves."

Even if "everything belongs to the court," only in two cases are particular people said to belong to the court: Titorelli says this about the corrupt girls who surround him, and the priest says it about himself in the cathedral. The girls mock Josef K., and the priest is more "friendly" toward him than anyone else has been. In both cases, we're dealing with manifestations of the court, which must be compatible with each other, or else the entire construction would collapse. At most, they may play different roles within the same "great organism," where we know that "everything is interconnected" and effortlessly "remains unchanged" even in the presence of disturbances. Perhaps now we can begin to grasp the words the chaplain will eventually say to Josef K.: "You don't have to regard everything as true, you only have to regard it as necessary." Nothing is stranger, or more misleading, or more deceptive, than necessity. In this sense, Josef K. has grounds for declaring: "The lie becomes the order of the world." But as soon as it becomes such, it spreads out over every manifestation, and hence even over the judgment that condemns it. Without knowing it, Josef K. himself belongs in that moment to the court and to its lie.

．　．　．

There are always at least two worlds, and between them no direct contact is permitted. It's rumored, however, that such contact does occasionally take place, in violation of every rule. And it is always looming, like a threat or an omen, discernible even in a door set into a wall. Josef K. noticed that door in Titorelli's garret and immediately wondered what it was for. Later someone told him that the court offices were in communication with the painter's room. That door was the thinnest interspace between the two worlds. Speaking with Titorelli, Josef K. had come as close as possible to the court. But he didn't trust what he heard, just as K., late one night, hesitated to believe what Bürgel was saying. A door like the one in Titorelli's studio might look something like this:

> In my apartment there's a door I've never paid attention to. It's in my bedroom, in the wall shared with the house next door. I've never thought anything of it, indeed I never even realized it was there. And yet it's quite visible; the lower part is blocked by the beds, but it rises high above them, it's not like a regular door, it's more like a main entryway. Yesterday it was opened. I was in the dining room, which is separated by another room from the bedroom. I had come home very late for lunch, no one else was home, only the maid working in the kitchen. Then the racket began in the bedroom. I rush over there at once and see that the door, the door I've been unaware of until this

moment, is being slowly opened and at the same time, with gigantic strength, the beds are being pushed out of the way. I yell: "Who is it? What do you want? Easy! Careful!" and I expect to see a swarm of violent men come bursting in, but instead it's just a skinny young man who, as soon as the gap is wide enough for him to pass, slips through and greets me cheerfully.

When he was writing, Kafka never knew what would come out of that gap in the wall: "a swarm of violent men," or a "skinny young man" who might resemble himself so closely as to be indistinguishable.

XIII. Lawyer Visits

Josef K. goes to see his lawyer, Huld, to remove him from the case. He explains that in the early stages "unless he was somehow violently reminded of it," he was able to forget completely about his trial. But now, he says, "the trial is steadily closing in on me." The original—*immer näher an den Leib rückt*—means literally: the trial "is moving ever closer to my body." And he adds: *förmlich im Geheimen*, "in complete secrecy." The trial is a machine that comes ever closer to the body of the accused. When contact is finally made, the sentence is incised, as with the machine in the penal colony. But for now no one except the accused himself can see the machine. This terrifying vision, an early intimation of the story's conclusion, is unleashed by the fact that a dead metaphor (the expression *an den Leib rücken*) has come back to life—and no longer as a metaphor but as a literal description of events.

With her large, sad, black eyes that bulge slightly, with her round doll's face and her long white apron, Leni presides over everything that happens in Huld's office—and in his bedroom too, which is, as always, the place of revelation. She is at once both nurse and jailer. She doles out both pleasure and punishment to the accused. The guardian of their metamorphoses, she plunges them ever deeper into guilt, thereby exalting their beauty. Like Gardena and Frieda with respect to the Castle, Leni has an insider's knowledge of the court's mysteries. Her every word is valuable and suggestive. But it would be illusory to think her on one's side. If Leni loves all the accused and is lavishly promiscuous with them, that doesn't mean she wants to help them. She's the Eros of the law, amorously circling those to whom it is applied, before piercing them.

Leni gives herself to all the defendants, on principle, for she finds them all beautiful. "She clings to all of them, loves them all, and seems to be loved by them in return," as is Ushas (Dawn) by those who, awakened, welcome her and offer her their first sacrifice. Then Leni returns to Huld and tells him about her affairs "to entertain him." Of course, explains the lawyer, to recognize the defendants' beauty one must have "an eye for it." And Leni certainly does. From the moment Josef K. first sees her "large black eyes" through the peephole in the door, they give him the impression, perhaps deceptive, of being "sad." But Leni, as we will learn, is behind every door, like a suction cup on the visible world. The touch of Leni's body is the defendants' guarantee that their beauty is flowering, that the proceeding is exerting its effect on them. In this, the court is impartial. Through Leni, it acknowledges its foundation: sexual attraction to guilt.

. . .

"There was total silence. The lawyer drank, Josef K. squeezed Leni's hand, and Leni sometimes dared to caress Josef K.'s hair." On another occasion too, Leni runs her fingers "very delicately and cautiously," through Josef K.'s hair, much as the gentlemen in the barroom run their fingers through Pepi's curls—though not delicately of course, but "avidly." It's the hallmark of intimacy and of the trial, of some obscure event unfolding.

Josef K. is he who waits, who observes—all the while looking for another way, as he squeezes Leni's hand: the way of women. Leni doesn't discourage him. Indeed, she risks an amorous gesture. In the silence, Huld drinks his tea "with a sort of rapacity." Leaning over his cup, he seems unaware of what's taking place around him. But we sense that nothing escapes him.

In the scenes where Josef K. is granted much more detailed "insight into the judicial system" than parties normally receive—as happens during his conversations with Titorelli and with Huld—feminine ears are always listening, hidden. The corrupt girls are huddled beyond the cracks in Titorelli's walls. Leni, who appears in Huld's bedroom "almost simultaneously with the sound of the bell," has clearly had an ear to the door. The feminine presence behind these scenes signals their initiatory nature. Titorelli's corrupt girls even have the impudence to intervene, like haughty priestesses, urging the painter not to paint the portrait of "such an ugly man" as Josef K. Could his ugliness be due to the fact that he is still "a newcomer, a youth" in terms of his trial, which itself is still so "young" that it hasn't yet had time to take full hold of him and bring his beauty to light? Is he perhaps still too raw, as yet insufficiently ripened and refined by his "proceeding"?

All the legal proceedings, dauntingly complex, rigorous, and gradual, are merely preparatory to a judgment that is immediate and aesthetic—if that's how we want to describe the physiognomic judgment that determines innocence or guilt "on the basis of the defendant's face, and especially the line of his lips." That's the basis, according to superstition. And though Block calls it "ridiculous," he's quick to add that, according to several defendants, Josef K. faces "certain conviction, and soon," a conviction they infer "from his lips." But is superstition really such a silly thing? Or is it "the repository of all truths," as Baudelaire wrote? If the latter, guilt would no longer reside in a person's will, whether conscious or unconscious, but in his very shape. In that case, the task of the lawyers and the court alike would be to help make plain a conviction that has always existed.

The defendant in *The Trial* becomes the party in *The Castle*. A slight shift: it's clear, after all, that every *party* is in the first place *guilty*. The dominant Eros is that which comes down from above toward the external, excluded world: from the court toward defendants, from the Castle officials toward parties. It's the Eros of predators, detecting the scent of the unknown. It's parallel to the Eros that

belongs to the external world, to shapeless appearance—
and so to parties and defendants—and that wants to enter
the place of authority and law. The disparity between
these two trajectories is beyond repair. One always,
though perhaps by a slow, tortuous route, reaches its goal.
The other, almost never.

Does guilt heighten beauty? Such an audacious question might never have been asked before. But as he listens
to Huld speaking from bed, Josef K. is forced to put it to
himself. "Defendants are the loveliest of all": this is the
undeniable reality Huld describes. But how can it be explained? Does the seriousness of the guilt determine the
intensity of the beauty? That can't be, Huld asserts, as if
alarmed: "It can't be guilt that renders them beautiful."
But he quickly adds: "At least as a lawyer I have to talk
that way." This aside strips the preceding assertion of all
meaning. Indeed a lawyer, as part of his job, must above
all maintain the innocence of his clients. Consequently, he
must at all costs deny that their undeniable beauty is a
product of their guilt, which he would otherwise be admitting. But where else might their beauty come from? At
this point Huld advances a hypothesis that may be more
alarming than the first: "It must result from the proceedings being brought against them, which somehow adhere
to them." It's true, then, what Block the merchant—"that
wretched worm" (Huld's words) who nevertheless partakes of the beauty of defendants—observed moments
earlier when he told Josef K.: "You must keep in mind
that in this proceeding things the intellect can't handle are

continually being made explicit." Leaving aside the question of guilt, and in the absence of any valid argument against its indissoluble connection with beauty, one arrives at the supposition that the "proceeding" itself, with its various elements that exceed the capacity of the intellect, has the power to adhere physically to the defendants, like the alchemic *opus* to the *prima materia*. The process of the trial is thus like any other process that entails the transformation of a substance. That substance is the defendant. And guilt seems to be the original state of every substance. The more the proceeding cuts into the defendant's life, the more beautiful he becomes, and the worse his guilt can be assumed to be. And ripeness, the perfection of beauty, is that telos that also signifies the end, death: a capital sentence. Presumably, the defendant's beauty in that moment is almost blinding.

Josef K. quickly realizes, with dismay, that everyone knows about his trial. But that fact, as Huld explains to his client, doesn't mean that the proceeding is public. It certainly may become so, "if the court deems it necessary, but the law doesn't require it."

At this point, Josef K. may glimpse the brand-new archaism of his situation. There have been periods, of course, when no distinction was made between public and private, and others when such concepts didn't even exist. But over time, ever more precise rules and definitions arose to circumscribe the scope and meaning of those two words. Now, however, it seems they must again be applied to an indistinct situation, while at the same time the various distinctions elaborated over the centuries continue to be relied on. Everyone knows that Josef K. has been accused, but "the record of the accusation is not available to the defendant or his lawyers," meaning that the defense's initial memorial to the court would be able to address "matters relevant to the case only by chance." Observed from a certain distance, and once its unnerving elusiveness is grasped, the situation undeniably reveals a striking coherence: in every trial the first priority is to guard the sovereignty of the unknown. *Ignotum per ignotius* seems to be the court's motto. Any move on the defendant's part to gain some control, however limited, over the case (*Sache*), which in German is also the *thing*, is at every step discouraged, rebuffed, derided. Huld continues talking, eventually revealing to his client the all-governing principle: "In general the proceeding is kept secret not only from the public but from the defendant as well." The first thing excluded is knowledge itself. The proceeding is, by nature, an underground river. If it occasionally becomes visible to the defendant, his lawyer, or the public, it does so only by accident. The whole thing could begin and end without ever becoming manifest. The defendant could live and die without ever knowing that he's on trial or that he has been sentenced. And perhaps even without realizing that the sentence is being carried out. As for the general state of things, little would change.

Huld must be in the revealing vein this day, since he even grants his client a few glimpses into the lives of the officials. To begin with, it isn't true that their power makes their lives easy. One should remember, as a fact noteworthy in itself, how "extraordinarily seriously the gentlemen take their occupations," how they can even fall into "great despair" when faced with "obstacles that, by their very nature, can't be overcome." But what of the nature of the officials, the gentlemen? Hard to say, since one has such a limited view of it from outside the court. But one thing is clear: "the officials lack contact with the common people." That's precisely why these gentlemen, paradoxically, sometimes show up in the offices of the lawyers, a group generally mistreated and despised. Evidently the gentlemen want to learn something about the world. They fear they lack "a proper sense of human relations," perhaps because they are "constantly constricted, day and night, within their law." It's as if the officials, longing to have some relationship with the outside world, have ventured, with understandable caution, into a clearly ambiguous and treacherous middle ground: lawyers' offices. But if their approach to the outside world reflects uncertainty and bewilderment, their experience within the court proves equally vexing. And here once again, with magnanimous indulgence, Huld explains a general principle, which helps us get our bearings: "The court's hierarchies and ever-increasing ranks are infinite and, even for initiates, ungraspable." To belong to the court is simply to find oneself on one of its steps, without knowing how many come before and especially how many come after. The same state of obligatory ignorance that is peculiar to the defendant is replicated to some (also uncertain) degree within the court. Thus the proceeding that is usually hidden from the defendant, as Huld has already

revealed, may also be hidden from "the lower officials."
For them too (again: as for the defendant) "the legal case
appears within their field of vision often without their
knowing where it came from, and it continues on without
their knowing where it's headed."

The more Huld refers to the narrowness of the visual
field of individuals—be they defendants, lawyers, or low-
ranking officials—the greater our sense, by contrast, of
the immensity of the whole. The court is truly a "great organism," a vast cosmic animal whose imposing nature we
may grasp, but not its overall shape. Whatever happens,
"this great judicial organism remains somehow eternally
suspended" (but where? one wonders; in which regions of
the sky?), and if anything ever damages or wounds one
part of it, "it easily compensates for the slight disturbance
in some other part—after all, everything is interconnected—and it remains unchanged; indeed it becomes, if
anything, and this is quite likely, even more closed, even
more watchful, even more severe, even more cruel." These
lines might refer, point by point, to the self-regulating ca-
pacities of a brain, to the emanations of a divine pleroma,
to the operating procedures of an information network, or
to a secret cipher. But even before we pause to wonder
about the identity of the object that Huld is describing, we
are struck by the hints of its psychological characteristics.
The "great organism" he speaks of is, above all, a closed
system that rebuffs every "suggestion for improvement,"
which indeed only the most ingenuous creatures—unfailingly defendants, especially the fresh ones still in the first
phases of their trials—would dare offer. Huld here has the

delicacy not to mention, as an example of one who has engaged in this ill-advised behavior, his own client, Josef K. But the description fits him to a T.

Further, the "great organism" is attentive. Constant wakefulness is its supreme quality, the one on which all others depend. The great organism is conscious, acutely conscious, perennially conscious. Each attack on it can only enhance its powers of mental acuity. Thus—and this is Huld's most useful piece of advice—one must "above all not attract attention." Those who know the great organism best are distinguished, as the Greeks were with regard to their deities, by their ability to go unnoticed by it. If the officials are already "irascible," we might suppose that the great organism of which they are only tiny cells is even more so. In speaking of its attention, one speaks of the keystone of the organism's existence: its uninterrupted mental life. But this implies certain behavioral traits. First of all, the "great organism" will be "severe." And why? Because there's a pact between wakefulness and the law. Indeed one might even suppose that the law is the partner of wakefulness, as if wakefulness were inconceivable except in connection with some law. Pure contemplation, content with itself, without any governing purpose, is obviously out of the question, which brings us to the final characteristic of the great organism: a certain wickedness. Wakefulness is linked, by some obscure mechanism that Huld doesn't even begin to address, to a punitive aspect, a sharp-eyed will to strike. Can there be a wakefulness that doesn't punish? That doesn't need to be accompanied by the rigor of law? Huld doesn't say—he adds only the advice that concerns him, the foundations of which he has now laid: "Let's let your lawyer work, then, instead of disturbing him."

Block, the grain dealer, is also represented by Josef K.'s lawyer, in his "business cases" as well as in a trial of the kind Josef K. is undergoing. This fact is of immediate interest to Josef K., who asks: "So the lawyer takes on ordinary cases too?" At Block's affirmative reply, Josef K. appears relieved: "That connection between the court and jurisprudence seemed extremely reassuring to K." Until this moment, a corrosive suspicion has been building in him: that the court has *nothing* to do with the law and the legal codes. Perhaps the court is simply a powerful, impenetrable apparatus superimposed upon juridical praxis and terminology, but in the end completely separate, resting on other premises. Block's answer is at first blush "reassuring," because it makes the court's very existence seem less foreign and opaque. Ultimately it might be one of many courts, one that simply by chance hasn't come to Josef K.'s attention sooner. But in the very next moment, these thoughts open the door to an even more disturbing suspicion: the court might indeed be part of that "jurisprudence," and the process of passing into its ambit from that of the ordinary cases might even be easy, one habit among many for certain men of the law, just as it is possible to sit calmly down in a café without realizing that one is surrounded only by costumed extras. And another suspicion arises: what if all the courts that deal with "ordinary cases" are only a cumbersome, misleading front for the one true court, that which judges Josef K. and prefers to camouflage itself among the normal courts?

Block is the assimilated Jew whose arrival is "always ill-timed," even when he has been "summoned." Whatever he does is the wrong thing, and yet it corresponds precisely to what is asked of him. Only he would think to boast of having "studied closely what decency, duty, and judicial custom demand." Who else but Block would decide to "study" what "decency" demands? That itself is an indecent admission.

Though as defendants they share a common condition, Josef K. subjects the merchant to those violent oscillations between attraction and aversion that assimilated Jews endured in the period between the first emancipations and Hitler. Josef K. listens to Block's stories with the greatest attention, leaning toward him. He has the impression that Block has "very important things" to say and knows how to say them. And yet, moments later, "K. suddenly couldn't bear the sight of the merchant." There's something shameless in the way Block reveals his suffering. Josef K. watches him and thinks that the merchant is certainly experienced, "but those experiences had cost him dearly." Block is a magnet for humiliation. It's as if his body is the repository for that supplement of uncertainty, fatigue, and anxiety from which the Jew in the big city cannot escape.

Only once, in a letter to Milena, did Kafka speak of Jews directly and at length. He was writing in response to a question of Milena's that had taken him aback and that must have seemed improbable ("You ask me if I'm Jewish, perhaps this is only a joke"). It was the perfect opportunity. He wrote:

> The insecure position of Jews, insecure within themselves, insecure among people, should explain better than anything else why they might think they own only what they hold in their hands or between their teeth, that furthermore only tangible possessions give them a right to live and that once they have lost something they will never again regain it, rather it will drift blissfully away from them forever. Jews are threatened with dangers from the most unlikely quarters or, to be more precise, forget dangers and let's say "they are threatened by threats."

With Block one has the impression that he holds his trial documents "between his teeth." In any case, they are never out of his sight. In the unlit room where Block sleeps, there is "a niche in the wall, by the head of his bed, in which he had carefully arranged a candle, an inkpot and pen, and also a bundle of papers, probably trial documents."

Block's voluntary humiliation at the bedside of his lawyer, Huld, and in the presence of Leni and Josef K., is an impious parody of monotheistic devotion, with respect to which every anti-Semitic caricature seems timid. That's why the scene "nearly degraded the onlooker"—and the reader.

Even when first entering the bedroom, Block is unable to look at the lawyer, "as if the sight of his interlocutor were too dazzling to bear." From this point on, each gesture takes on an additional resonance: biblical, devotional, ritual. Block begins to tremble, as the lawyer, his back turned, addresses him. His face would be an unbearable sight. Block stoops as if to kneel on the fur rug beside the bed. The lawyer and the merchant exchange these words: "'Who is your lawyer?' 'You are,' said Block. 'And other than me?' asked the lawyer. 'None but you,' said Block. 'Then do not follow any other,' said the lawyer." It's a profession of faith. Its model is Moses before Yahweh. A little later Block kneels on the bedside rug: "'I'm on my knees, my lawyer,' he said." Then, encouraged by Leni, he kisses the lawyer's hand, twice. Leni stretches her supple body and leans over to whisper something in Huld's ear. Perhaps she is interceding on Block's behalf, so that the lawyer will speak to him. Now the lawyer begins to speak and Block listens "with his head lowered, as if listening transgressed some rule (*Gebot*)." But *Gebot* is also "commandment." At this point, Josef K. has a strong, decisive sensation: the scene isn't taking shape before his eyes but is the repetition of something "that had repeated itself many times before and would repeat itself many times again, and only for Block could it retain its newness." This is a definition of ritual. Indeed, it's a definition of ritual that makes plain its affinity with obsessional neurosis, as defined by Freud.

The lawyer and Leni, those two harmonious accomplices, are ready to lead Block to his final abjection, which is the performance of ritual gestures for some alien purpose. This is the most subtle of profanations, and Block is compliant. They treat him like a caged and rather repulsive animal. The lawyer has already dubbed him "that wretched worm." Now he asks Leni: "How has he behaved today?" In the manner of a John Willie governess with a leather bodice and a riding crop, Leni replies, "He's been quiet and diligent." Huld aims to transform his client into a "lawyer's dog," and Block is presented to Josef K. as model and prefiguration of what he himself could become. "If [the lawyer] had ordered him to crawl under the bed as into a kennel and to start barking, he would have done so gladly." In order that his abjection be crystal clear, his devotional gestures must be fused with the repertoire of animal gestures.

Leni proceeds in her description of Block's day, as she observed it through the peephole in his cell. "He was kneeling on his bed the whole time, he had the documents you loaned him open on the windowsill and was reading them there." Thin, small, with a bushy beard, kneeling before a text, Block now appears to us as a Hasid immersed in the Torah. According to Leni, his devotion is a sign of obedience to the lawyer: "That made a good impression; the window in fact opens only onto an air shaft and gives barely any light. That Block was nevertheless reading showed me how obedient he is." At this point Huld breaks in like the perfect straight man who knows how to take things further, even when they seem extreme already: "But does he at least understand what he reads?" And Leni, without missing a beat, retorts: "At any rate I could tell he was reading closely." If there's one image that has over the centuries characterized Jews, it's *reading closely*. A Jew reading, as in Rembrandt, seems to reach the highest summits of intensity and concentration. That this is the image implied by Leni is confirmed at once: "He read the same page all day, and as he was reading he followed the lines with his finger." Leni has in mind the little silver hand used to keep one's place in the Torah. Block doesn't possess one, he doesn't possess anything anymore, but he revives the gesture. His life, Leni assures us, consists now only of study, "almost without interruption." If he does pause, it's only to ask for a glass of water—and he did that "just once." So, she adds, "I gave him a glass through the peephole." We know that Leni can also be "affectionate" with Block. She doesn't deny him a glass of water. After all, the beauty of defendants shines even on him.

While Leni and the lawyer trade lines in their mise-en-scène, Block, still kneeling on the fur rug by the bed, "moved more freely and shifted from side to side on his knees." These are signs of satisfaction, as a dog might show, because Block has the impression that they are saying "something flattering" about him. It's a good moment to resume the torture—and the lawyer seizes it, saying to Leni, in a reproachful tone: "You praise him. But that's just what makes it difficult to speak. The judge's pronouncements were not indeed favorable, regarding neither Block nor his trial." This is what Huld has been leading up to. But like an actor carried away with his part, he keeps going, recounting his conversation with the judge, using it as a pretext to humiliate Block further while pretending to defend him. He reports that, among other things, he told the judge: "Of course, [Block] as a person is unpleasant, has bad manners and is dirty, but from a procedural standpoint he's irreproachable." Even this cruelty, which might seem superfluous, has its function: it refines the torture. No doubt Block "has gained a great deal of experience" with trial procedures. His life by now consists of that experience and nothing else. At this point the lawyer launches his final attack: "What would he say if he were to learn that his trial hasn't even begun?" It's a hard blow, and in keeping with his doglike nature, Block becomes agitated, even wants to stand back up. Then he yields and sinks down to his knees again. The lawyer is quick to reassure him: "Don't be afraid of every word. . . . One can't begin a sentence without you staring as if your final judgment were coming"—a biblical expression again. And the lawyer continues: "What senseless fear! You must have read somewhere that in certain cases the final judgment comes unexpectedly, from a random mouth at a random moment." Indeed, Block must have read something of that nature. One could even guess where. And the lawyer confirms that, "despite numerous reservations, that's no doubt true." Nothing is as exasperating, nothing as mocking, as the lawyer's reservations—which now assume a sorrowful tone, for he can see in Block's attitude "a lack of the necessary trust." With this reproof, the lawyer seems to have concluded his peroration. But one lethal detail still remains. At bottom, Block's only remaining pretense is that he's able to understand—

able to understand perhaps only a minute part but at least something of the trial that is by now his entire life and that perhaps, as he has just been told, hasn't even begun. And it's precisely that frantic eagerness to understand that "disgusts" Huld. For the death blow, the lawyer decides then to reveal the undisclosed, indeed strictly esoteric, premise of his activity. At this point, extraordinarily, he turns directly to Block: "You know that various opinions accumulate around the proceeding until they render it impenetrable." Wanting to understand is above all useless. And this is the true ending. "Embarrassed," Block plunges his fingers into the fur of the bedside mat. He turns the judge's words over and over. Leni senses that the moment has come to end the scene. She lifts Block by the collar. And she commands: "Now leave that fur alone and listen to the lawyer."

The humiliations and torments suffered by Block are used by Huld to show Josef K., as in an anatomy lesson, what awaits him. Not only does Block's case resemble Josef K.'s and prefigure what it might look like at a riper stage but—and this is the most wounding point—Block himself resembles Josef K. as well. Block is the *only* other defendant Josef K. has spoken with at length up to now, and he can't help recognizing himself in Block as in a repellent mirror. And when Josef K. nonetheless behaves toward Block like a lordly gentleman who must maintain the greatest possible distance, Block strikes back at once, with the quickness of a wounded animal and with concentrated venom: "You're no better a person than I am, for you too are a defendant and you too are on trial. If, despite this, you're still a gentleman, then I'm just as much a gentleman, if not a greater one." Without ever saying the word *Jew*, which is unutterable in *The Trial*, Block wants to remind Josef K.: You are an assimilated Jew just as I am. It's futile for you to make a show of despising me. Your existence too is "always ill-timed."

Each time that Josef K. is doubled, it's by a figure who embarrasses—and ultimately horrifies—him: in his normal life, which is his office life, it's the vice director; in his life as a defendant, it's Block. When Josef K. is summoned by telephone to his first interrogation, the person waiting to use the phone next is the vice director, who immediately asks, "Bad news?" for no reason other than "to get K. away from the phone." Then he immediately invites him on a sailing trip, for the very Sunday when his interrogation is scheduled. As for Block, who is defended by the same lawyer, as soon as Josef K. decides to dismiss the lawyer, he discovers that Block has sought out five others, or rather six. And if Josef K. anticipates having to devote the better part of his energies to his trial, Block reveals that he has for some time devoted *all* his energies to his trial; he has gradually withdrawn from his business, having "spent everything [he] had on the trial." He has even withdrawn from his offices and is reduced now to occupying only a "little back room, where [he] work[s] with an apprentice." Of course Josef K. at first finds Block "ridiculous" but then is "extremely interested" in what he says. Might Block, Josef K. now wonders, be his most reliable source of information about the trial? When Block's trial is "about the same age" as Josef K.'s, he isn't "particularly happy" with Huld either. One might almost say that Josef K. is following, step by step, Block's path. For this reason Josef K. "still had many questions and didn't want Leni to discover him in that private conversation with the merchant." He even goes so far as to think, while Block is speaking: "I'm learning everything here," a feeling he never had with Titorelli or with Huld. This is the point where the figure of Block and that of Josef K. nearly merge. But one difference still remains: Block has entrusted the lawyer with the task of writing his memorials to the court. Josef K., on the other hand, wants to claim the task for himself. He wants to write by himself that which concerns him. Block professes to have determined that memorials are "completely worthless," but Josef K. remains convinced that a single memorial, written by himself, can be decisive: it will be his "great memorial." But despite this difference, Josef K. is ready now to recognize Block as a "man of some value, who at least had experience in these matters and knew how to convey it." And Block, indefatigable, continues speaking. "He's as dear as he is gossipy," observes Leni when she returns to the scene. It doesn't escape Josef K. that Leni "spoke to the merchant affectionately, but also with condescension."

If Josef K. had not been awakened one morning by a guard dressed in a "traveler's outfit," what would have become of him? Perhaps he would have continued his bank career until the day he died, without ever becoming any the wiser. Or perhaps one day he would have been visited by a dream that finally would have both illuminated and resolved his situation, a dream that Kafka dreamed seven years after the draft of *The Trial:*

> My brother has committed a crime, a murder I think, and I and others are accessories to his crime; punishment, resolution, liberation come from afar, they approach fearsomely, many signs point to their unstoppable advance, my sister, I think, announces each of these signs, and I greet them all with rapturous exclamations, my rapture increasing the closer they come. My exclamations were brief phrases, I thought that because of their obviousness I would never be able to forget them, and now I can't remember any exactly. I could manage only exclamations because it took a huge effort for me to speak, I had to puff out my cheeks and twist my mouth at the same time, as with a toothache, before I could get a word out. Happiness consisted in this: that punishment was coming and I welcomed it so freely and with such conviction and joy, a sight that must have moved the gods, and I could feel the gods' emotions almost to the point of tears.

In order for both the gods and the man contemplating them to be moved, punishment, announced by imperious signs, must arrive. Only then can one be sure that the gods and the man feel the same thing. And, since punishment is the consequence of a murder committed by a man, punishment—insofar as it is welcomed by both men and gods, indeed can move them both in exactly the same way—might be that which in other epochs was called *sacrifice*.

XIV. Nighttime Interrogations

In a narrow room of the Gentlemen's Inn, a room filled mainly by his bed, the secretary Bürgel peeks out from under the covers. Except for the bed, there's only a night table and a lamp. K. enters the room by mistake and sits on the edge of the bed. Bürgel's words—more revealing than anything else we've heard about the Castle—get lost in the fog of exhaustion that envelops K. At a certain point, as K. tries to shift positions, heavy with sleep, he grabs one of Bürgel's feet, "which was sticking out from under the covers." This is the only contact he'll have with a representative of the Castle, and hence with the Castle itself. And Bürgel doesn't remove K.'s hand, "no matter how irksome it must have been." Then K. falls asleep, and Bürgel lights a cigarette. "He sprawled back on the pillows and looked at the ceiling, letting his smoke rise toward it"—Kafka added in a deleted passage. For K., this is the point of maximum proximity to his goal. He sleeps, squeezing an official's foot, and neither the official nor the Castle denies him that contact. The Castle lets itself be touched, but only by one who has fallen into a deep sleep brought on by an obsessive quest for contact with the Castle.

Nothing has meaning except in relation to the Castle. One must therefore make contact with the Castle. But constant contact with it would make life unlivable. Castle representatives are in an analogous, if reversed, position. By means of incessant work that is difficult to distinguish from inertia, the officials concern themselves constantly with that *party* that is the world beyond the Castle. But they couldn't stand it if the party were always right in front of them. Indeed, they flee the party in every possible way, resorting to every kind of guile. But there's one block of time they can't control, during which the unexpected or overwhelming may occur: that of the nighttime interrogations. It is essential, as a rule, that no contact take place even then.

The words with which Bürgel, from his bed, dismisses K. are also the only gentle—and hopeless—words that the Castle grants that party that is the world: "No, why should you ever need to make excuses for your sleepiness? Physical strength has its limit; can one help it if that particular limit also carries other kinds of meanings? No, one can't help that. That's how the world corrects its course and maintains its equilibrium. It's an excellent system; in the end it always seems unimaginably excellent, though in a certain way unconsoling." Here, suddenly, in the person of the chubby official Bürgel, the order of the world takes the floor. And it isn't some generic *order of things*, but rather the Vedic *rta* that appears intact before us (*The Castle* is its novel). What could ever threaten that? What if, by chance, someone—and it won't be K.—managed to "extricate himself from sleep"—what would happen then? The world, we infer from Bürgel's words, would lose its equilibrium. Or at least would no longer be able to homeostatically correct its course. But why? Why should the world fear the wakefulness of a single man? Bürgel doesn't say, though he makes it clear that the mechanism that regulates the order of the world is, in itself, an "excellent" thing. What more could one ask for: that it exceed excellence? Perennial wakefulness could only disturb that mechanism—perhaps leaving it out of order forever.

Of course, the "excellent system," seen from a different viewpoint, is "unconsoling," *trostlos*. Might he be thinking of the parties' viewpoint (which is everyone's viewpoint, since each person is equally a party)? Again, he doesn't say. The order of the world declares itself laconically—and rarely. What matters to Bürgel is demonstrating, for the first time, that authority is no stranger to leniency. But it's a special case; the Castle is gentle and understanding only toward those who are exhausted. The Castle asks for no excuses from those who have reached the limits of their physical strength—without having reached anything else.

One of the most mysterious aphorisms of Zürau: "The good is, in a certain sense, unconsoling (*trostlos*)." *In gewissem Sinne*, "in a certain sense." *Iva*, the Vedic seers would have said.

The Castle organization is "gap-free," according to Bürgel, the liaison secretary. And it's a "great, living organization." But his officials suffer from constant exhaustion. "Everyone here is tired," Bürgel observes. Why? A worry is eating away at them: the thought that someone might find a gap, that "a peculiar, perfectly shaped, clever, tiny little grain" might succeed in slipping through the Castle's "incomparable sieve." This would be enough to hamper its ability to remain undamaged by the world, enough to bring about the unlikeliest of events: the "little grain," which is to say the party, with his burden of "poor life," could find himself suddenly "controlling everything." Then he would have to do nothing more than "somehow present his request, whose fulfillment already awaits it, is indeed leaning toward it." The organization's very raison d'être, which is first of all to be diligent and vigilant in ensuring that no request gets granted, would thus fall away. An insuperable barrier must separate the mind that formulates a desire and the appearance of the object of desire. The need for such a barrier is what justifies the imposing nature of the organization, within which, as one who approaches it perceives, "many things seem predisposed to terrify." But the approacher doesn't know that his mere approach sows terror within the organization as well, among the ranks of officials. Upon those twin terrors, each parallel and indifferent to the other, the world's course runs.

In his impassioned peroration, Bürgel responds to some of the rashest questions but avoids the one that's at the root of all the others: why must the secretaries strive, using every trick in the book, to ensure that the nighttime interrogations *don't* happen—and hence that there is no chance, however slim, for a party's request to be satisfied? The party's request is a desire, a mental act. If the desire's fulfillment were guaranteed (*gebürgt* is Bürgel's verb), the world would no longer be unresponsive to the mind. It would no longer present itself as a mysterious, opaque expanse. Each mental act would have an effect. Everything would be reduced to a nexus of theurgical whirlwinds. But wouldn't the world thus lose its thrill, its supreme uncertainty that derives from the fact that it doesn't obey the mind? Perhaps Bürgel, out of politeness, doesn't want to say so explicitly, but that's what he may be thinking when, just before dismissing K., he defines the world as an "excellent" and yet "unconsoling" system. The Castle, he implies, is neither benevolent nor malevolent. Or at least, it is no more so than the world itself.

Josef K.'s conversation with the chaplain in the cathedral corresponds to K.'s nighttime conversation in Bürgel's bedroom. In both cases the key element is exhaustion, which comes on, in both cases, as soon as the acme of lucidity has been reached. K.'s exhaustion is like Arjuna's dismay in the face of the epiphany of Krishna, like Job's mute astonishment when Yahweh evokes the Leviathan. But in place of these silences before an overwhelming vision, we find an irresistible sleepiness, which is better suited to an epoch unable to bow to epiphanies and no longer accustomed to encountering them.

After the arguments are revealed comes that which reveals itself: epiphany. And that which reveals itself is vastly more powerful. And it might even be sleep. Because in this case what reveals itself is nothing less than the "world [that] corrects its course and maintains its equilibrium," utilizing the occasional or constant torpor of its inhabitants.

The people who belong to the court are shady in various ways, skillful as tormentors, and thoroughly dubious in word and appearance. The only one to depart from this profile is the prison chaplain, a "young man with a smooth, dark face" and a "powerful, trained voice," whose solemn words echo in the vast cavity of the cathedral. After listening to him, Josef K. says: "You are an exception among all those who belong to the court." The chaplain doesn't comment, but in his parting words to Josef K. he affirms: "I too belong to the court." What, then, is the secret face of the court? Is it the austere, solitary face of the chaplain, or the face of the girls on Titorelli's stairs, with their "mixture of childishness and abjection"? After all, even those girls are said to "belong to the court."

Josef K.'s story turns on this point: is the court a deception? The chaplain denies that it is as soon as he comes down from the pulpit and begins speaking with Josef K. on his level: "You're deceiving yourself about the court." On the heels of these words comes the "story"—found "in the introductory writings to the Law"—about the man from the country and the doorkeeper. The story deals with precisely "such deception" (that into which Josef K. has fallen in considering the court itself a deception), and the chaplain presents it as an illustration of how one might avoid it. Josef K., however, sees deception at work in the story as well; above all, he thinks that the man from the country who presents himself at the door to the Law is deceived, but so is the doorkeeper himself. It is the chaplain's "well-founded" argument that leads Josef K. to this last conclusion: "Now I too believe that the doorkeeper was deceived." And this seems to him a confirmation of the other deception, because "if the doorkeeper is deceived, then his deception will necessarily be passed on to the man." The chaplain, conceding nothing, observes that in "the letter of the text" of that story "nothing is said about deception." The conversation proceeds now as if coaxed, by both parties, toward some end: "'No,' the chaplain said, 'you don't have to regard everything as true, you only have to regard it as necessary.' 'A gloomy opinion,' says Josef K. 'The lie becomes the order of the world.'" In the beginning, deception characterized the court, then the story of the doorkeeper of the Law, and now at last the order of the world; instead of diminishing, deception has spread to the far edge of the whole of things. But if the whole is deception, then what's left?

The chaplain doesn't object to Josef K.'s contemptuous statement, "though it certainly didn't accord with his own opinion." Thus the conversation dies away, inconclusive. The chaplain has already rebuked him for being unable to look two steps ahead, but with this statement—even though he didn't consider it a "final judgment"—Josef K. takes another step forward, perhaps one step beyond those "two steps." Now it's no longer a matter of the court or of law, but of the "order of the world," *Weltordnung*, an expression with an ordinary usage, referring to the rules of everyday life, and a metaphysical usage, referring to the order that holds together that which is. But at this very point, when everything, however it is understood, ought to change its name, Josef K. stops short.

What holds Josef K. back after his statement about the order of the world is an irresistible exhaustion, of the same kind that overcomes K. during his nighttime conversation with Bürgel. Bürgel dismisses K. with revealing words, which touch directly on the order of the world and which also apply to Josef K.'s situation in the cathedral. As soon as thought has gone far enough to confront "the order of the world," that order shrouds it in a fog that's invaluable to it; because "that's how the world corrects its course and maintains its equilibrium." The arrangement is one of "unimaginable excellence," but it's also "unconsoling," says Bürgel, echoing Josef K., who describes as "gloomy" (*trübselig*) the chaplain's view regarding the necessity that substitutes for truth. If K.'s mind could remain awake and vigilant, the world would be disturbed by it, just as Josef K. is disturbed when a stranger appears in his room to arrest him. And then it would be the world on trial. But doesn't such a hypothesis negate itself? Or is it simply another novel? In any case, in realizing that he's "too tired to follow all the consequences of the story" (the story of the doorkeeper of the Law), because "it led him down unfamiliar paths of thought," Josef K. also recognizes that the court officials are much better prepared to venture down those paths than he. And yet, moments earlier he described them as biased ("they're all prejudiced against me") and so lascivious that "if you show an examining magistrate a woman in the distance, he'll knock over his table and the defendant just to get to her first."

Many are the glosses and commentaries on the story, which the priest tells Josef K. in the dark cathedral, about the doorkeeper of the Law. The longest, most persuasive gloss is by Kafka himself—it's *The Castle*. To understand it, one must read all of *The Castle*, after having replaced each occurrence of the word *Castle* with the word *Law*.

The spell of *The Castle* also derives from the way it leaves law behind, from its ability to render that word superfluous, because implicit. Now one speaks not of laws but of regulations, as if such regulations constitute a further level, beyond the law. Compared with the dialogue between the chaplain and Josef K., Bürgel's monologue is striking first of all because it doesn't permit itself any reference to ancient stories and never abandons its apparently arid terrain: that of administrative practices. There is no philosophy or theology to appeal to—at most there is custom. And yet Bürgel's words assume at times a pathos the priest can't muster, even if he ought to be familiar with it: the pathos of the Gospels. As Bürgel speaks, the great order seems gradually to abandon its various defensive frameworks, choosing to show itself *almost* as it appears to itself, in its solitude and in its irrepressible desire to welcome something foreign into its tautological autism.

. . .

With his head leaning on his arm and his arm stretched toward the post of Bürgel's large bed (the only object in the room apart from the night table and lamp), K. listens to the most lucid, most precise words that he's yet heard about the Castle. They are also the only words spoken about the Castle from within. Cautious words, they make explicit the doubts and the sense of impotence about resolving them that the Castle produces among its own officials, who feel they lack "the proper distance" for answering certain questions. But who, then, would have the "proper distance"? The landlady of the Gentlemen's Inn? Or Count Westwest? Or perhaps K. himself?

Nonetheless, drunk with weariness, K. finds Bürgel "amateurish" and so must strive not to "underestimate him," as he is instinctively inclined to do—much as Josef K. instinctively mistrusts Titorelli. Meanwhile, Bürgel's words tumble toward the secret. They reveal to K. things that no one has told him before, things on which everything depends. Why, for example, are the secretaries required "to conduct most village interrogations at night"?

The great danger of the "nighttime interrogations" arises because, on such occasions, the barriers between parties and officials tend to come down. Previously inadmissible considerations begin to filter in, such as the parties' "troubles and fears," and resistances weaken, until in the end there may be "an absolutely inappropriate trading of places between the persons involved"—parties becoming officials and vice versa. In the middle of the night, the parties would find themselves, as if after a dance step, in the places previously occupied by the secretaries they had been besieging daily. An unheard-of reversal would take place, wounding the great order: that which is perennially external to it would infiltrate its most delicate mechanisms. The pure chance nature of the individual party would take on the voice of necessity. There can be no greater risk.

The nighttime interrogations are not necessarily harmful—Bürgel himself speaks of their "perhaps only apparent disadvantages"—but they are certainly frightening. They are the perpetual shadow of the regulations. The officials, then, take "measures" to fortify themselves against the interrogations. And because they occupy the lowest ranks of the hierarchy—those closest to the parties—the secretaries in particular develop an "extraordinary sensibility in such matters," constantly inventing tricks to reduce their risk. They are "as resistant as they are vulnerable." In their border outposts, they understand that every order—no matter how ubiquitous and flexible—contains a vulnerable point, which is exposed in those rare moments when a party becomes able to "achieve more through a word, through a glance, through a show of trust, than through a lifetime of arduous effort." Of course, Bürgel adds, those opportunities "are never taken advantage of"—a fact that surely plays a part in the general scheme of things. But to the heightened sensibility of a secretary, it's enough that such "opportunities" exist.

They have something in common with K., "a surveyor without surveying work," who nevertheless exists and has the potential to disturb. His situation is considered "surprising" and perhaps unsettling, since—as Bürgel makes clear—"our circumstances here are certainly not such that we can let technical ability go to waste."

What is the relationship between the regulations and the nighttime interrogations? It's true that nighttime interrogations are not prescribed by any regulation, but it's also true that the very nature of things—"the overabundance of work, the manner in which the officials are employed at the Castle, their lack of accessibility, the requirement that the interrogations of the parties happen only after the usual investigations have been completed, but then immediately"—makes nighttime interrogations an "unavoidable necessity." Bürgel even dares to make a claim that some of his colleagues might consider impious: "But if they have now become a necessity—as I say—that is still, albeit indirectly, a result of the regulations."

As soon as necessity is named, we enter the realm of the regulations. Thus "finding fault with the nature of the nighttime interrogations," Bürgel adds, as if shocked at his own audacity, would be like "finding fault with the regulations." The nighttime interrogations, these abnormal, pernicious entities, are therefore themselves the offspring of the regulations. They are members of the same family. For this reason alone we can see as baseless the claim that the regulations reach into every corner, that nothing exists beyond the regulations and their "iron-clad observance and execution," as Bürgel puts it. Alongside them, the nighttime interrogations will always manage to persist. And K. has, without knowing it, sought out that dark, amorphous, elusive zone, which is the only place that could welcome him, despite his less than limpid past and his burden of "troubles and fears." Only "during the night" would it be possible "to judge things from a private point of view," thus doing justice to the peculiarity of the person and of his difficult circumstances—a peculiarity that the person could then, at last, describe in all its strangeness. In just that moment, however, overcome by exhaustion, K. finds that he can no longer even recognize the voice of the man who is revealing all this; he doesn't even see him as a person now but rather as "a something that prevented him from sleeping and whose deeper significance he couldn't fathom."

Bürgel is the psychopomp who introduces K. to the secret of nighttime interrogations. But every secret looks different depending on the point of view. Seen from the highly significant viewpoint of the landlady of the Gentlemen's Inn, hence from the viewpoint of officialdom, the nighttime interrogations have a completely different nature and purpose. According to the landlady, they have "the sole purpose of allowing those parties whom the gentlemen couldn't bear to see by day to be quickly interrogated by artificial light at night, so that the gentlemen had the chance immediately after the interrogation to forget all the ugliness in sleep."

Mysteries are always a little shady. That's why the early

Christian Fathers used Eleusis as a principal argument for defaming pagans. But the landlady's view, as always the view of the orthodoxy, isn't merely reductive. It's true that the "gentlemen's boundless delicacy" is sorely tested by the nighttime interrogations. And it's quite possible that they feel a certain disgust when faced with that shapeless mass of singularity, as party after party scurries past them, each one potentially capable of upsetting them, making it "difficult or downright impossible to maintain fully the official character of the hearings." And K., according to the landlady, is one of the worst examples of that sort of thing. Not only does he make a "mockery of all the security measures." Not only does he hang around like a ghost where he doesn't belong, but—unlike ghosts—he refuses to vanish in the morning, indeed he "remained there, hands in his pockets," as if everything else—the gentlemen and their rooms—was just some apparition and he himself the only reality. And that's not all: in the end he even witnessed the distribution of records, a ceremony that must be conducted behind "nearly closed doors," such an "important, fundamental" task that not even "the landlord and landlady had ever been allowed to watch, though it took place in their own house." K., that disrespectful, inconsiderate, sneaky foreigner, had thus managed, as if accidentally but really through perverse insistence, to witness the true mystery: the distribution of records, of fates—a scene that once upon a time was spoken of only in legends, and that no one had dared to *watch.* The last one to speak of it was Er the Pamphylian, and Plato has left us his story.

.   .   .

The most revelatory conversations for Josef K. and
K.—those with Huld, with Titorelli, with Bürgel—are repeatedly counterpointed by something that alternates,
contrasts, and mingles with the speaking voice. To begin
with, there are the female spies. Every word uttered by
Huld and Titorelli seems to require their presence. Behind
Huld's door we sense Leni's soft breath. Through the
cracks in Titorelli's door we glimpse the eyes of the "corrupt" girls who infest his stairs—one of whom keeps
moving "a piece of straw slowly up and down" through
one of those cracks. Only Bürgel's words seem undisturbed, except by K.'s sleepiness and his dreams. Here
that phenomenon we can't help associating with Kafka
occurs before our eyes: the osmosis between dream and
reality. As Bürgel speaks, K. falls into a sleep in which "he
heard Bürgel's words perhaps better than earlier when listening to them awake and exhausted." Now that his "an-
noying consciousness had disappeared," K. is listening to
each word and, at the same time, celebrating a victory—
even "raising a glass of champagne in honor of the victory." But once again the revelatory words call for and
call forth a counterpoint, even if only in sleep. At first it
isn't a woman, or a girl, but rather "a secretary, nude." Is
it Bürgel? One of his colleagues? Who knows. All we
know for sure is that the secretary looks "very like the
statue of a Greek god." And K. attacks him, as the secretary, like some Artemis surprised during a bath, tries to
hide his nakedness. Then we hear his voice, as Bürgel's
words continue crumbling into the background. And it's a
feminine voice: "This Greek god squeaked like a little girl

being tickled." This time, too, the counterpoint has a female voice.

No critic, from the dullest to the greatest, has failed to consider *dreams* when speaking of Kafka. But *dream*—like *unconscious*—is in this case a lifeless word. It interrupts the flow of thought rather than guiding it. Unless we're talking about the type of dream that Kafka described once in his *Diaries* (and that could also be an excellent description of *The Castle*): "a wildly branching dream, which simultaneously contains a thousand correlations that all become clear in a flash." Such dreams are one way the mind may represent a certain quality of wakefulness, a quality that wakefulness itself has difficulty attaining, clouded as it is by an indomitable will to control. But wakefulness is always the subject, even if—thanks to an irony encountered both in the world and in Kafka—its most precise, most effective image is attained not through continual, conscious effort but "in a flash" during a dream. This too is a trick of wakefulness.

As K. dreams, Bürgel continues his monologue, having now reached the point where he must address an extreme case, the only case in which the parties—despite all the "security measures"—might have the audacity to "take advantage" of the Castle. At issue is the "nighttime weakness of the secretaries," which presents what is certainly "a very rare opportunity, which is to say it almost never arises." But does its rarity diminish its gravity? Certainly not for the secretaries, whose lives are plagued by the thought of it. The opportunity "consists in this, that the party shows up unannounced in the middle of the night." With this phrase, which immediately evokes the evangelical "thief in the night," Bürgel seems to have exceeded the limits of what he is able to say. Immediately afterward, as if falling back on professional constraint in order to mask his excessive disclosures, he turns all his energies to a grueling bureaucratic exposition, probing the differences between competent and incompetent secretaries. As if shaken by a demon, he calms down only after a thirteen-line sentence. Now the words have gone back, for a moment, to spreading their thick protective fog.

K. nods and smiles, half asleep. "Now he believed he understood everything perfectly." But this means only that he feels close to falling fast asleep again, "this time with no dreams or disturbances." That "gap-free organization," as Bürgel himself calls the Castle, with its swarms of secretaries, competent and otherwise, was too tedious and torturous. Maybe it would be better just to let things go, not to insist. And thus, finally, to "escape from them all." This is the only time K. comes close to anything like liberation. But there's never any respite. After retreating into the most rigorous official jargon, Bürgel seems to have regained his strength. His revelations are not yet at an end.

Bürgel is speaking of an extremely unlikely possibility, indeed "the unlikeliest of all." Yet he is also describing, like a faithful chronicler, what's happening in the very moment he is speaking. We come to this exercise of transcendental acrobatics after having passed through such numerous and surprising turns of argument that our attention is blunted and we have a hard time grasping the absolute newness of what's taking place. Bürgel now tells K. that *the party* "can't, on his own, figure anything out. Exhausted, disappointed, inconsiderate, and indifferent, he has, because of his fatigue and disappointment— though he probably attributes it to some indifferent, accidental cause—entered a room other than the one he wanted, and there he sits, ignorant, and his mind, if it is filled with anything at all, is filled with thoughts of his error and his weariness": these words are the meticulous description of what's happening in those very moments to K., as he sits on the edge of Bürgel's bed—and, behind K., in the mind of the reader, who may be wondering how much longer this laborious digression will last. But Bürgel is at the same time describing that extremely rare opportunity for escape, around which gathers the imposing skein of regulations that govern the lives of the Castle officials. The greatest generality and the most irreducible singularity coincide for a moment. As do the unlikeliest thing in the world and the simple procedural recording of a fact. The event is so prodigious that Bürgel is overcome by the "loquaciousness of the happy." And he asks himself: "But can one abandon the party at that point? No, one cannot." Indeed, "one must explain everything to him." This is the pinnacle of *The Castle.* But could the Castle survive a complete explanation of itself? Probably not. Or if it did, it would remain forever wounded, because the party's request, when granted, "truly tears the official organization apart—and this is the worst thing that could happen in the course of one's duty." But it won't happen, because K. is already sleeping deeply and is "cut off from everything around him."

For a Castle official to be caught up in the "loquaciousness of the happy" is unheard of, if only because the allure of the Castle—and, by extension, of its representatives—resides first of all in silence. Each time K. lifts his eyes to look at the Castle itself, he fails to detect "the slightest sign of life." It might be simply a matter of distance. But for some reason a sign is important: "his eyes demanded it and refused to tolerate the silence." A risky demand.

What, then, is that silence like? "Someone sitting calmly, looking straight ahead, not lost in thought and thus cut off from everything else, but free and indifferent, as if he were alone and unobserved; and yet he must have known he was being observed, but that didn't in the least disturb his tranquility, and in fact—whether through cause or effect was uncertain—the observer's gaze couldn't hold and turned away." This image of the Castle appears to K. one day as an early darkness falls, and it is the clearest image that the Castle has allowed of itself. But it's still an image. Going beyond the image is like secretly drinking Klamm's cognac, transforming "something that seemed merely the vehicle for a sweet perfume into a drink fit for coachmen."

Not only is the Castle there in place of the apparent emptiness that K. perceives on his arrival in the village, but the Castle itself is like a being looking out into emptiness, or in any case staring at something that never clouds its "free and indifferent" gaze. Two different figures of emptiness confront each other. They can't collide, because one emptiness can't clash with another. But one emptiness could enter the other. Could let itself be absorbed by the other.

There's only one way to win the game with the Castle. Contravening the perpetual elusiveness of his colleagues, Bürgel describes it to K. when he speaks of the possibility of becoming "a peculiar, perfectly shaped, clever, tiny little grain," which, once it has assumed its shape, could slip through that "incomparable sieve" that is the Castle organization. These seem like instructions for escaping a maximum-security prison. Do they apply? On this point, Bürgel answers himself; in fact he gives two contradictory replies. The first: "You think this can never happen? You're right, it can never happen." But the other one follows immediately: "But one night—who can guarantee [*bürgen*] everything?—it does happen." And this is the moment of greatest tension in his monologue. What follows is a series of further lucubrations outlining the gravity of the possible damages such an event would cause, an event, he emphasizes, whose existence is unconfirmed, except by "rumor." But even this is not sufficiently reassuring. It's much more effective "to prove, as is easily done," that such an event has "no place in the world"—just as K. has always feared that there's no place for him in the Castle.

Bürgel's monologue is so effective because he always speaks from within the Castle and the thought of sabotaging it never even occurs to him. His admissions are all the more eloquent—and all the more probative. When Bürgel approaches the final threshold, even his language changes. It suddenly becomes simple, direct:

> Of course, when the party is in the room, the situation is already an ugly one. It tugs at one's heart. "How long can you resist?" one asks oneself. But there won't be any resistance, we know that. You just have to imagine the situation properly. Before us sits the party, the party on whom we've never laid eyes, for whom we've always been waiting, and with real thirst, but whom we have always, and quite reasonably, considered unreachable. His mute presence alone is an invitation to penetrate his poor life, to make oneself at home in it and to partake of the suffering born of his vain demands. Such an invitation in the dead of night is enthralling. One accepts it and in that moment one ceases to be an official.

Indeed, one is no longer an official but rather a great mystic.

What Bürgel in the end reveals is the great order's hidden helplessness. To grant the party's request "truly tears the official organization apart," which is the deepest misfortune—and shame—an official can know. The party forces the order, hence the official, to perform some task that goes beyond the order itself. And here Bürgel returns to the evangelical image of the "thief in the night": now the party is described as a "robber in the woods who in the night exacts from us sacrifices we would never otherwise have been capable of making." The official at this point feels hopeless but also happy. "How suicidal happiness can be," Bürgel says—you'd think he was quoting a line from Kafka's *Diaries*.

But could the world go forward, were such a thing to happen? On one condition only: if the party, also overcome with weariness, remains unaware of all this, lost in other thoughts, thoughts of his "error" or his "weariness," since he has "entered a room other than the one he wanted." And, thanks to his oblivion, the order remains intact. Bürgel is now describing what's happening in that very moment between himself and K. But the scene isn't over. The extreme tension has produced an excess: the "loquaciousness of the happy."

In Bürgel's case, it's a hopeless happiness. The party cannot be left to himself, to his distraction and his weariness, but must be shown "precisely what has happened and why it happened"—and above all how the party himself, on that rarest of occasions, passes briefly from that deeply rooted state of utter helplessness into a condition wherein he "can control everything," provided that he can "somehow present his request, whose fulfillment already awaits it." Indeed—Bürgel explains—the fulfillment is by now "leaning toward" the request. With this passage, "that which is most necessary has taken place," in the sense that necessity has been stretched to the breaking point, to the point of transferring to the party the power that has always been denied him—a *translatio imperii* that would shake the world to its foundations. But there's no proof that such a thing has taken place, or that it could. At this point, Bürgel concludes, there's nothing left to do but "be content and wait." How could this scene be defined? It's "the official's most trying hour." Nothing implies that the scene takes place. But "all this must be shown." The parties must at least be *told the story. The Castle* must at least be written.

XV. Veiled Splendor

Kafka spent eight months in Zürau, in the Bohemian countryside, at his sister Ottla's house, between September 1917 and April 1918. The tuberculosis had declared itself a month before, when he coughed up blood in the night. The sick man didn't hide a certain sense of relief. Writing to Felix Weltsch, he compared himself to the "happy lover" who exclaims: "All the previous times were but illusions, only now do I truly love." Illness was the final lover, which allowed him to close the old accounts. The first of those accounts was the idea of marriage, which had tortured him (and Felice) for five years. Another was his business career. Another was Prague and his family.

After arriving in Zürau, Kafka chose not to write anything the first day, because the place was "too pleasing" and he feared his every word would be "evil's cue." Whatever he wrote, before he thought of the reader he thought of demons—and of his unsettled account with them. Not even illness was enough to settle it.

. . .

Zürau was a tiny village among rolling hills, surrounded by scattered woods and meadows. The focal point of life there was the hop harvest. As for its inhabitants, animals were more in evidence than people. Kafka immediately saw the place as "a zoo organized according to new principles." Ottla's house was on the market square, beside the church. Except for the friends and relatives who threatened constantly to visit, the situation approached that reduction to the minimum number of elements toward which Kafka naturally tended in his writing—and which he would have liked to extend to his life in general.

In his only period of near happiness, he found himself surrounded by semi-free animals. Theirs, after all, was a condition quite familiar to him. There exists an invisible chain, of a generous length, that allows one to wander here and there without noticing it, as long as one doesn't go too far in any single direction. If one does, the chain will suddenly make itself felt. But Kafka was never self-indulgent enough to view this state of affairs, as many do, as a dirty trick played on him alone. This is how he expressed it in the sixty-sixth Zürau aphorism, describing a "he" who signifies "anyone":

> He is a free and secure citizen of the earth, since he is bound by a chain long enough to allow free access to every place on earth, yet short enough that nothing can drag him beyond the earth's confines. But at the same time he is also a free and

secure citizen of heaven, since he is bound also by a heavenly chain that functions similarly. Thus he is choked if he tries to move toward the earth by his heavenly collar, and if he tries to move toward heaven, by his earthly one. And despite this, every possibility is his, he can feel it, indeed he refuses to trace this all back to an error made by chaining him in the first place.

Never does Kafka seem to find his situation as agreeable as he does during those months in Zürau. Only there can he escape everything: family, office, women—the principal powers that have always hounded him. Further, he is protected by the barrier of illness, which, as if by magic, now shows no "visible signs." Indeed, Kafka will write to Oskar Baum, in a provocative parenthesis: "(on the other hand I've never felt better, as far as my health is concerned)." In Zürau the world has been nearly emptied of human beings. It's this emptiness, above all else, that gives rise in Kafka to a feeling of slight euphoria. The animals remain: "A goose was fattened to death, the sorrel has mange, the nanny goats have been taken to the billy goat (who must have been quite a handsome fellow; one of the nannies, after having already been taken to him once, had a sudden flash of memory and ran the long road from our house back to the billy), and the pig will no doubt be butchered at any moment." These words are enough to suggest the superimposed scenes of an ongoing tragicomedy. Kafka added: "This is a compressed image of life and death." The reduction to the prime elements

has been completed in a Bohemian village where the theater of life is left to the animals—and to the commonest of
them. And it's a relief. But, just as Strindberg had experienced, hell is ready to burst forth at any moment, her-
alded by noise. In Zürau, it will be the noise of mice.

We find the first account, like a war bulletin, in a letter
to Felix Weltsch (mid-November 1917):

> Dear Felix, the first great flaw of Zürau: a night of
> mice, a frightening experience. I am unscathed
> and my hair is no whiter than yesterday, but it
> was the most horrifying thing in the world. For
> some time now I've heard them here and there
> (my writing is continually interrupted, you'll soon
> see why), every now and then at night I've been
> hearing a soft nibbling, once I even got out of bed,
> trembling, to take a look, and then it stopped at
> once—but this time it was an uproar. What a
> dreadful, mute, and noisy race. At two I was
> awakened by a rustling near my bed and it didn't
> let up from then until morning. Up the coal box,
> down the coal box, crossing the room diagonally,
> running in circles, nibbling the woodwork, whis-
> tling softly when not moving, and all the while the
> sensation of silence, of the clandestine labor of
> an oppressed proletarian race to whom the night
> belongs.

But wasn't it Kafka himself to whom the night belonged?
Now he discovered that beside him, behind him, above
him, the same belief held sway among an "oppressed pro-
letarian race" that worked without respite. His anxiety

was brought on more than anything else by the sensation that those multitudes had "already perforated all the surrounding walls a hundred times, and were lying in wait there." (This was the same race that was waiting, unseen, to obsess the builder of "The Burrow," who one day said: "What an incessantly industrious race and how bothersome their zeal can be.") Their smallness rendered them elusive and unattackable, and thus all the more terrifying. As for Kafka's coveted nocturnal solitude, it now seemed more like confinement at the center of a porous surface, pierced by countless malevolent eyes.

After that first night, no matter to whom he was writing—whether Brod or Baum or Weltsch—Kafka spoke of mice. The subject lent itself to endless variations, all the more so when Kafka introduced, in self-defense, the presence of a cat, which raised further questions: "I can drive the mice away using the cat, but then how will I drive the cat away? Do you imagine you have nothing against mice? Naturally, you don't have anything against cannibals either, but if at night they crept out from under all the cupboards gnashing their teeth, you surely couldn't bear them any longer. Anyway, I'm now trying to harden myself, observing the field mice on my walks; they're not so bad, but my room isn't a field and sleeping isn't walking." The same amalgam of the outrageously comic and the appalling—a gift of Kafka's, like the mysterious irreducibility of certain Shakespearean verses—characterizes all his epistolary accounts of the Zürau mice, out of which will someday grow the speculations of "The Burrow" and

the events of "Josephine the Singer, or the Mouse Folk."
The "mouse folk" would remain for Kafka the ultimate
image of community.

Brod, who could lend a touch of kitsch to anything, described Kafka's stay in Zürau as an "escape from the
world into purity." He also viewed it—he wrote to his
friend—as a "successful and admirable" enterprise. It
would be hard to find two adjectives that irritated Kafka
more. He replied to Brod with a closely argued letter in
which he explained that the only sensible conclusion he
had ever reached in his life was "not suicide, but the
thought of suicide." If he didn't go beyond the thought, it
was due to a further reflection: "You who can't manage to
do anything, you want to do this?" And here was his closest friend speaking to him of success, of admiration, of
purity. In his reply, Kafka invoked for the first time (the
only other instance was in his *Letter to His Father*) the
final sentence of *The Trial*, applying it to himself: "It
seemed as though the shame must outlive him."

On September 15, after three days in Zürau, Kafka
wrote: "You have the chance, if ever there was one, to
begin again. Don't waste it." He had understood the manifestation of his illness as a provisional leave of absence
from the torment of normal life. He was entering what
would prove to be a unique period. Looking back on his
time in Zürau, he would one day write to Milena, referring to himself in the second person: "Consider also that
what may have been the best period of your life, which

you haven't yet spoken about adequately to anyone, were those eight months in a village, about two years ago, when you thought you had settled every account, when you confined yourself only to that which is unquestionably within you, without letters, without the five-year postal connection to Berlin, protected by your illness, and when you didn't have to change much of yourself, but had only to retrace more firmly the old narrow features of your being (your face, beneath the gray hair, has hardly changed since you were six)." Confining his own field of action to what lay "unquestionably" within himself seems to have been Kafka's lifelong aim. But if there was a time when he tried to pursue it with absolute rigor, in part because his external circumstances conspired to assist ("the voices of the world becoming quieter and less numerous"), it was during the Zürau months. It is in this context that we must understand, as a kind of daring experiment made possible only under these conditions, the appearance of a new form: the aphorism. New first of all in a physical, tactile sense: Kafka typically wrote, in pen or in pencil, in school notebooks, barely even marking divisions between one text and the next as he filled them; now, however, he puts together a sequence of 103 individual slips of onionskin paper, each measuring 14.5 centimeters by 11.5 centimeters, each containing, with rare exceptions, a single numbered fragment, generally aphoristic. The sequence has no title. Brod's suggestion—*Reflections on Sin, Suffering, Hope and the True Way*—is both appealing and, in its solemnity, misleading, but it rightly suggests the fact that these slips of paper constitute the only text in which Kafka directly confronts theological themes. If there is a theology in Kafka, this is the only place where he himself comes close to declaring it. But even in these aphorisms, abstraction is rarely permitted to break free of the image to live its own life, as if it has to serve time for having been autonomous and capricious for too long, in that remote and reckless age when philosophers and theologians still existed.

Prior to transcribing them on those slips of onionskin, Kafka had written the Zürau aphorisms in two octavo notebooks, among other fragments, some of the same nature and equally penetrating. The numbering follows, almost without exception, the order in which the aphorisms appear in the two notebooks. It is thus impossible to attribute to the sequence a reasoned organization, as we can for example in the case of Wittgenstein's *Tractatus.* It's also impossible to determine why some of the aphorisms on the onionskin sheets are crossed out: they are not of a particular type, and what's more, some of them are among the most noteworthy. Kafka himself never alluded to these aphorisms either in letters or in his other writings. No evidence exists, therefore, not even indirect evidence, that he intended to publish them. But their very mode of presentation suggests a book of roughly a hundred pages, where each page would correspond to one of the slips of onionskin. This book is like a pure diamond, buried among the vast carboniferous deposits of Kafka's interior. It would be pointless to seek, among twentieth-century collections of aphorisms, another as intense and

enigmatic. If published one after the other, these fragments would occupy twenty or so pages and would be almost suffocating—because each fragment is an aphorism
in the Kierkegaardian sense, an "isolated" entity, which
must be surrounded by an empty space in order to
breathe. This need explains the point of transcribing them
one to a page. But even the definition of *aphorism* is misleading, if we understand that word as currently used to
mean "maxim." Some of these fragments are narrative
(for example, 8/9, 10, 20, 107), others are single images
(15, 16, 42, 87), and others are parables (32, 39, 88). We
find a similarly various texture in Kafka's *Diaries*, but
here every redundancy, every arbitrariness, every insis-
tency, has been stripped away. In their terseness and in
their deceptive clarity, these sentences have an air of final-
ity. They are the rapid brushstrokes of an exceedingly old
master, who distills everything into these brief flicks of his
wrist, guided by an "eye that simplifies to the point of
utter desolation." That's how Kafka defined his gaze in a
letter of that period.

It's pointless to set the Zürau aphorisms beside some of
the pinnacles of the past. The comparison skews, as
though resting on an unstable base. If Kafka writes that
"impatience and inertia" are "man's two deadly sins,
from which all the others derive," it's futile to look elsewhere for related sentences, whether comparable or conflicting, on the same themes. The same is true when he
writes of the three forms of free will, concluding that the
three forms are really one and don't presuppose any will,

free or not. Why is this the case? Perhaps because he had "a kind of congenital indifference to received ideas." Even to the *great* received ideas. One always gets the impression that Kafka lacked common ground with other great writers, even though he venerated at least a few of them (Pascal, Hebbel, Kierkegaard). But the peculiarity of his aphorisms, their steep, irreducible singularity, reaches such heights as to allow comparison only with other fragments marked by the same peculiarity. Kafka can communicate only with Kafka—and he can't always do that. It's hard to tell just how aphorism 8/9—which speaks only of a "stinking bitch, which has littered many times and is already decomposing in places"—relates to those that come before or after it. Indeed Brod quietly deleted it. (Perhaps he thought it clashed with the noble title he had chosen.) And yet this sequence is precisely where all randomness or connection through mere juxtaposition is denied. It's the only instance of Kafka's taking pains to give one of his works a visually and spatially unambiguous shape, almost to the point of determining the typographical layout. Each of those sentences presents itself as if the greatest possible generality were intrinsic to it. And at the same time each seems to emerge from vast deposits of dark matter.

Max Brod was a tireless practitioner of a style of psychological analysis not very different from what would one day become the preferred style in women's magazines, though his is denser and fuzzier and has occasional

theological complications. Every so often he dared to pro-
voke Kafka: "Why then do you fear love in particular
more than earthly existence in general?" Kafka replied as
if from an astral distance: "You write: 'Why be more
afraid of love than of other things in life?' And just before
that: 'I experienced the intermittently divine for the first
time, and more frequently than elsewhere, in love.' If you
conjoin these two sentences, it's as if you had said: 'Why
not fear every bush in the same way that you fear the
burning bush?'"

Kafka was not a collector of theologies. The word itself
was not congenial to him. He rarely named the gods, and
he resorted to ruses in order not to attract their attention.
To believe in a personal God seemed to him to be, above
all else, one of the ways of allowing the "indestructible
something" in us to "remain hidden." That's the enigmatic formulation found in the fiftieth Zürau aphorism.

He generally spoke of the gods in an oblique fashion.
One might argue that his boldest assertion is concealed
in a line of his *Diaries* that says only: "The passage in
Hebel's letter on polytheism." The reference is to a letter
from Johann Peter Hebel to F. W. Hitzig, where one reads:
"If the Theological Society still existed, this time I would
have written a paper for them on polytheism. I confess to
you—since a confession between friends is no less sacred
than one before the altar—that it seems more and more
obvious to me, and that only the state of captivity and
childishness we're kept in by the faith in which we're

baptized and raised and subjected to homilies has prevented me until now from erecting little churches to the
blessed gods."

Taking all this into account, Kafka's embarrassment—
when subjected by Brod to the manuscript of his most
ambitious opus, which would appear in 1921 in two volumes totaling 650 pages, bearing the vaguely grotesque
title *Paganism Christianity Judaism*—could not have
been small. Brod had lavished on this book his talent for
frightening oversimplification.

Kafka read the manuscript immediately and offered
Brod his thoughts on it in a letter. At first we find rather
general praise. Then, having endured long explanations
of what constitutes paganism, Kafka takes the opportunity to say what the ancient Greeks mean to him—using
arguments that have nothing to do, not even polemically,
with Brod's book. Instead we look on with astonishment
as Kafka sketches a vision of Greece that includes himself
in one corner, like the donor in a medieval altarpiece:

> In short, I don't believe in "paganism" as you de-
> fine it. The Greeks, for example, were perfectly fa-
> miliar with a certain dualism, otherwise what
> could we make of *moira* and other such concepts?
> It's just that they were a rather humble people—as
> far as religion is concerned—a sort of Lutheran
> sect. As for the decisively divine, they could never
> imagine it far enough from themselves; the whole
> world of the gods was only a way to keep that
> which was decisive at a distance from the earthly
> body, to provide air for human breath. It was a

great method of national education, which held and linked the gaze of the people, and it was less profound than Hebrew law, but perhaps more democratic (no leaders or founders of religions here), perhaps freer (it held and linked them, but I don't know with what), perhaps humbler (because their vision of the gods' world gave rise to this awareness: so, we are not gods at all, and if we were gods, what would we be?). The closest I can come to your conception might be to say: in theory, there exists a perfect earthly possibility for happiness, that is, to believe in the decisively divine and *not* to aspire to attain it. This possibility for happiness is as blasphemous as it is unattainable, but the Greeks were perhaps closer to it than many others.

"In theory, there exists a perfect earthly possibility for happiness, that is, to believe in the decisively divine and *not* to aspire to attain it": that's from the letter to Brod (1920). "In theory, there exists a perfect possibility for happiness: to believe in the indestructible within us and not to aspire to attain it": this is from the sixty-ninth Zürau aphorism (1918). The sentence in the letter reiterates the aphorism, except for one point: where the aphorism speaks of "the indestructible," the letter speaks of "the decisively divine." This is the only time Kafka hints at what he means by "the indestructible." Now we at least know that "the decisively divine" can be superimposed on it. (But what do we make of that "decisively"?) As for the word *indestructible*, it appears exclusively in four of the 109 Zürau aphorisms. It certainly makes for memorable sentences, but why did that word appear only there? Why was it never explained? Why was it chosen?

Appearances can be fleeting, inconsistent, deceptive. But at a certain point one encounters something unyielding. Kafka called it "the indestructible." This word brings to mind the Vedic *akshara* more than it does any term used in less remote traditions. Kafka chose never to explain its meaning. He wanted only to distinguish it clearly from any faith in a "personal God." Indeed he went so far as to assert that "belief in a personal God" is nothing more than "one possible expression" of a widespread phenomenon: the tendency of "the indestructible" to "remain hidden." And yet "man cannot live without an ever-present trust in something indestructible within himself." Those who act (and everyone without exception acts) can't help feeling, during the moment in which they act, immortal. And what could lead a man to this mirage if not a vague awareness of "something indestructible within himself"? The indestructible is something we can't help noticing, like the sensation of being alive. But what the indestructible might be tends to remain hidden from us. And perhaps it's best that way.

Kafka treated paradise in six of the Zürau aphorisms (3, 64, 74, 82, 84, 86). That these are linked to the ones that treat the indestructible is made clear: "If that which must have been destroyed in paradise was destructible, then it wasn't decisive; but, if it was indestructible, then we're living in a false belief." For Kafka, the whole world was "a false belief"—and that was the subject of his writings: the enormous, inexhaustible, tortuous developments of that false belief. Where did they originate? In a fatal misunderstanding regarding the two trees that grow in the center of paradise. Humans are convinced that they were kicked out of that place for eating the fruit of the Tree of the Knowledge of Good and Evil. But this is an illusion. That wasn't their sin. Their sin lay in not having yet eaten from the Tree of Life. The expulsion from paradise was a pretext to prevent them from doing just that. We are sinful not because we were kicked out of paradise but because our expulsion has rendered us unable to perform one task: to eat from the Tree of Life.

Kafka, who was ill with knowledge, in the end devalued knowledge. In fact, he tells us with hidden sarcasm, "After original sin we have been essentially equal in our capacity to know good and evil." All the differences we pride ourselves on are of little importance, because "the true differences begin beyond that knowledge." But what can such a knowledge be, which begins beyond knowledge? Simply the "effort to act in accordance with it." Here every mental construction comes to ruin, for that capacity simply wasn't given to us. And in our vain attempt to put knowledge into action, we can only fail. For man that means: to die. Kafka adds, in parentheses: "Perhaps this is also the original meaning of natural death." Man dies, then, because he "must destroy himself" in his anxiety to act in accord with whatever knowledge he possesses. And meanwhile he overlooks the Tree of Life, whose leafy branches continue rustling, intact. This process, this trial, is in progress at every moment. For Kafka, paradise wasn't a place where people lived in the past and of which a memory has survived, but rather a perennial, hidden presence. In every moment, an immense, encompassing obstacle prevents us from seeing it. That obstacle is nothing other than the expulsion from paradise—a process Kafka called "eternal in its principal aspect."

But what might that "principal aspect" be? Only the terrible misunderstanding about knowledge. This is a truth that partakes of the "unconsoling" nature of the good, but it also, we soon realize, implies something that no one any longer would dare to hope: if the expulsion from paradise is an "eternal process"—at least in its "principal aspect"—then that "makes it possible not only that we will be able to remain permanently in paradise, but also that in fact we are permanently there, and it doesn't matter whether we know it here or not." Like the indestructible, paradise too may remain hidden. Indeed, in the normal course of life it does. Perhaps only in this way is life possible. Yet we recall that "we were created to live in paradise"—and nowhere does it say that the intended purpose of paradise has been changed. Hence everything that happens does so, "in its principal part," in paradise, even if during the very moment in which we are being expelled.

Magic was discredited primarily by those who equated it with a kind of creation, and creation was thought to have operated ex nihilo. Doubly naïve. Kafka never wrote about magic, but he had an exact notion of it, so exact that he was able to define it once with sovereign coolness: "It's entirely conceivable that life's splendor surrounds us all, and always in its complete fullness, accessible but veiled, beneath the surface, invisible, far away. But there it lies—not hostile, not reluctant, not deaf. If we call it by the right word, by the right name, then it comes. This is the essence of magic, which doesn't create but calls." The worship of idols is more than anything an attempt to evoke life's splendor with names that are, time after time, right. Such a recognition ought to be sufficient to put an end to the atavistic struggle against the gods— a struggle that fails to understand that the singular is one modality of the plural, and the plural one way to catch a flashing glimpse of the veiled splendor.

In his first days in Zürau, Kafka wrote these lines: "O beautiful hour, masterful state, garden gone wild. You turn from the house and see, rushing toward you on the garden path, the goddess of happiness." A goddess he named only that once.

Sources

The first number refers to the page, the second to the line or lines of text where the quotation appears. For Kafka's writings, I have referred to line numbers as well as page numbers in the case of volumes that appeared as part of the critical edition (*Kritische Ausgabe*, eds. Jürgen Born, Gerhard Neumann, Malcolm Pasley, and Jost Schillemeit; Frankfurt: S. Fischer, 1982–); where reference is made to the apparatuses, I have used "App" or "Komm."

I. The Saturnine Sovereign

3, 2–3: Franz Kafka, *Das Schloss* (The castle), ed. Malcolm Pasley, in *Kritische Ausgabe*, 1982, 7, 8.

6, 7: Ibid., 119, 4.

6, 12–14: Ibid., 95, 12–14.

6, 20–21: Ibid., 96, 15.

6, 22–23: Ibid., 15–16.

6, 27: Ibid., 26–27.

7, 11–13: Ibid., 100, 2–4.

7, 22: Ibid., 101, 11–12.

7, 24: Ibid., 109, 25–26.

7, 25: Ibid., 110, 1.

7, 25–26: Ibid., 5–7.

7, 28–29: Ibid., 8.

8, 2–4: Ibid., 23–25.

8, 14–15: Ibid., 116, 12–13.

8, 22: Ibid., 12.

8, 27–29: Ibid., 118, 15–18.

9, 13–14: Franz Kafka, *Der Process* (The trial), ed. Malcolm Pasley, in *Kritische Ausgabe* (1990), 85, 6–7.

9, 25–26: Ibid., 22, 3.

9, 26–28: Kafka, *Der Process*, App, 168.

10, 1–2: Kafka, *Der Process*, 34, 13–15.

10, 12–13: Kafka, *Das Schloss*, 215, 18–19.

11, 12: Kafka, *Der Process*, 77, 17.

11, 19–20: Franz Kafka, *Tagebücher* (Diaries), eds. Hans-Gerd Koch, Michael Müller, and Malcolm Pasley, in *Kritische Ausgabe* (1990), 135, 15–16.

11, 21–23: Ibid., 17–18.

12, 2–3: Kafka, *Das Schloss*, 215, 20.

12, 4: Ibid., 21.

12, 4–5: Ibid., 23.

12, 5–6: Ibid., 23–25.

12, 9: Ibid., 19.

12, 27–28: Kafka, *Der Process*, 126, 22–23.

13, 1–2: Kafka, *Tagebücher*, 135, 18.

13, 12: Kafka, *Das Schloss*, 414, 25.

14, 10: Ibid., 95, 27.

Sources

14, 17–18: Ibid., 406, 1.

14, 18: Kafka, *Der Process*, 158, 18.

14, 24: Ibid., 160, 20.

15, 13: Ibid., 162, 4.

15, 15–17: Ibid., 6–8.

15, 30: Ibid., 154, 24–25.

16, 1: Ibid., 26.

16, 1–2: Ibid., 25–26.

16, 2: Ibid., 155, 2.

16, 6: Kafka, *Das Schloss*, 336, 27.

16, 10–11: Ibid., 337, 1.

16, 17: Ibid., 11, 7.

16, 19–20: Ibid., 8, 12–13.

17, 1–3: Ibid., 113, 20–21.

17, 13–14: Ibid., 119, 21–23.

17, 23–24: Ibid., 107, 5–6.

17, 28: Ibid., 119, 18–19.

19, 7: Ibid., 4.

19, 8–9: Ibid., 95, 27.

19, 18–20: Ibid., 119, 2–5.

19, 23–24: Ibid., 5–7.

20, 1–3: Ibid., 118, 24–26.

20, 7: Ibid., 119, 8–9.

20, 16–18: Franz Kafka, *Nachgelassene Schriften und Fragmente* (Posthumous writings and fragments), vol. 2, ed. Jost Schillemeit, in *Kritische Ausgabe* (1992), 114, 11–12.

20, 21–23: Kafka, *Tagebücher*, 517, 14–17.

21, 6–9: Kafka, *Nachgelassene Schriften*, vol. 2, 373, 1–2.

21, 11–14: Ibid., 3–4.

21, 18–28: Ibid., 4–13.

22, 25–26: Kafka, *Das Schloss*, 411, 13.

22, 28–29: Ibid., 13–15.

23, 3–4: Ibid., 410, 21–22.

23, 13–14: Ibid., 488, 17–18.

23, 18: Ibid., 493, 21.

24, 17–18: Ibid., 455, 11–12.

24, 20–23: Ibid., 16–19.

24, 25: Ibid., 444, 13–14.

26, 26: Kafka, *Der Process*, 290, 7.

27, 14–21: Kafka, *Nachgelassene Schriften*, vol. 2, 331, 13–20.

27, 23–24: Elias Canetti, *Der andere Prozess* (The other trial) (Munich: Hanser, 1969), 94.

28, 9–10: Ibid., 86.

28, 15–16: Kafka, *Nachgelassene Schriften*, vol. 2, 331, 19–20.

28, 26–27: Kafka, *Das Schloss*, 17, 21–22.

28, 28: Ibid., 18, 16.

29, 1: Ibid., 20.

29, 2: Ibid., 23.

29, 11–12: Kafka, *Nachgelassene Schriften*, vol. 2, 16, 3.

29, 14–15: Ibid., 4.

29, 16–18: Ibid., 5–8.

30, 12–13: Ibid., 1–2.

30, 14: Kafka, *Tagebücher*, 135, 18.

30, 25–27: Kafka, *Nachgelassene Schriften*, vol. 2, 16, 9–11.

II. From Pepi's Dreams

31, 2–3: Franz Kafka, *Das Schloss* (The castle), ed. Malcolm Pasley, in *Kritische Ausgabe* (1982), 458, 12–14.

31, 7–8: Ibid., 23–24.

31, 11: Ibid., 6.

31, 13–14: Ibid., 14–15.

31, 16–17: Ibid., 15–16.

31, 19 — 32, 1: Lautréamont, *Les Chants de Maldoror* (The songs of Maldoror), in *Œuvres complètes*, ed. Pierre-Olivier Walzer (Paris: Gallimard, 1970), 85.

32, 9–12: Kafka, *Das Schloss*, 458, 25–27—459, 1.

32, 25: Ibid., 459, 13.

33, 5–6: Ibid., 459, 17–18.

34, 8: Ibid., 471, 7–8.

34, 10–14: Ibid., 8–12.

34, 18–19: Kafka, *Das Schloss*, App., 472.

34, 26–27: Kafka, *Das Schloss*, 485, 7–8.

34, 27–30—35, 1–2: Ibid., 14–20.

35, 3–4: Ibid., 486, 17.

35, 9–10: Ibid., 487, 12–13.

35, 12–14: Ibid., 486, 15–17.

35, 27: Ibid., 485, 23.

36, 7: Ibid., 488, 17–18.

36, 9–10: Ibid., 22–23.

36, 12–13: Ibid., 23–24.

36, 20–21: Ibid., 485, 19–20.

36, 21–22: Ibid., 487, 22–23.

36, 26–27: Ibid., 486, 13–14.

36, 29: Ibid., 487, 7.

36, 30—37, 1: Ibid., 486, 12–13.

37, 1–2: Ibid., 8–9.

37, 3: Ibid., 5.

37, 4–6: Ibid., 22–24.

37, 12–13: Ibid., 467, 26–27.

37, 15–16: Ibid., 468, 3–4.

37, 18–20: Ibid., 487, 17–20.

37, 20–22: Ibid., 487, 27—488, 1–2.

37, 30: Ibid., 455, 20.

38, 1: Ibid., 18–19.

38, 6–8: Ibid., 487, 23–26.

38, 10: Ibid., 26–27.

38, 24: Ibid., 453, 20–21.

38, 24–25: Ibid., 456, 7–8.

38, 25–27: Ibid., 453, 21–22.

38, 29: Ibid., 457, 11.

39, 1–2: Ibid., 19.

39, 2–3: Ibid., 21–22.

39, 27: Ibid., 479, 16.

39, 28–30—40, 1: Ibid., 18–21.

40, 2–3: Ibid., 24–25.

40, 8–10: Franz Kafka, *Briefe an Felice und andere Korrespondenz aus der Verlobungszeit* (Letters to Felice and other correspondence from the period of the engagement), ed. Erich Heller and Jürgen Born (Frankfurt: S. Fischer, 1967), 595.

40, 13–22: Franz Kafka, *Briefe 1913–1914* (Letters 1913–1914), ed. Hans-Gerd Koch, in *Kritische Ausgabe* (1999), 40, 23–31.

41, 4–5: Kafka, *Das Schloss*, 453, 19–20.

41, 7: Ibid., 23–24.

41, 12: Ibid., 479, 16.

41, 15: Ibid., 278, 14–15.

41, 17–19: Ibid., 308, 18–20.

41, 22–23: Ibid., 15.

42, 1: Ibid., 473, 5–6.

42, 3–7: Ibid., 15–19.

42, 8–9: Ibid., 472, 10.

42, 17–18: Ibid., 473, 22–23.

42, 19–20: Ibid., 24–25.

42, 21–22: Ibid., 474, 2–3.

III. "There's No Traffic Here"

43, 4–5: Franz Kafka, *Das Schloss* (The castle), ed. Malcolm Pasley, in *Kritische Ausgabe* (1982), 20, 24–25.

43, 6–7: Ibid., 21, 3–5.

44, 5–6: Ibid., 16, 8–10.

44, 7: Ibid., 19, 26–27.

44, 8–9: Ibid., 20, 12–13.

44, 9–10: Ibid., 24, 20–21.

44, 13: Ibid., 25, 9–10.

44, 13–14: Ibid., 23, 8.

44, 14–15: Ibid., 24, 1–2.

44, 17: Ibid., 23, 9.

44, 23–24: Ibid., 24, 27.

44, 27–28: Ibid., 24, 27–25, 1–2.

45, 28–29: Ibid., 174, 6.

47, 4: Ibid., 90, 22.

47, 7–8: Ibid., 215, 18.

48, 1–3: *Atharva Veda*, II, 4, 21.

49, 25–26: Maurice Blanchot, *De Kafka à Kafka* (From Kafka to Kafka) (Paris: Gallimard, 1981), 196.

50, 11–12: Kafka, *Das Schloss*, 494, 27–495, 1.

50, 22–23: Ibid., 8, 5–7.

51, 6–11: Ibid., 27, 21–27.

51, 17: Ibid., 92, 4.

51, 21–25: Ibid., 11–14.

51, 27: Ibid., 93, 2.

51, 27–28: Ibid., 5.

51, 28–29: Ibid., 8.

51, 29: Ibid., 6–7.

52, 6–8: Ibid., 92, 21–23.

52, 14: Ibid., 43, 2.

52, 17–18: Ibid., 92, 23–93, 1.

52, 23–24: Ibid., 93, 13–14.

52, 26: Ibid., 14.

52, 28–29: Ibid., 16–17.

53, 4–7: Ibid., 24–27.

53, 19: Ibid., 23.

53, 20: Ibid.

53, 23–27: Ibid., 94, 1–4.

54, 11–12: Ibid., 76, 6–7.

54, 13: Ibid., 89, 11.

54, 13–15: Ibid., 78, 26–27–79, 1.

54, 16: Ibid., 78, 9.

54, 16: Ibid., 11.

54, 17: Ibid., 23–24.

54, 26–27: Ibid., 90, 22–23.

54, 29–30: Ibid., 91, 22–23.

55, 2–3: Ibid., 21–24.

55, 11–18: Ibid., 94, 8–12.

56, 8–9: Ibid., 97, 9–10.

56, 10: Ibid., 11.

56, 21: Ibid., 102, 7.

56, 21–23: Ibid., 10–13.

56, 26: Ibid., 15.

56, 27: Ibid., 14.

57, 3–4: Ibid., 104, 25–26.

57, 8: Ibid., 105, 16.

57, 9: Ibid., 17–18.

57, 9–10: Ibid., 17.

57, 10–12: Ibid., 18–20.

57, 18: Ibid., 22–23.

57, 21–22: Ibid., 23–24.

57, 27: Ibid., 101, 6–7.

57, 28–29: Ibid., 10.

58, 1–2: Ibid., 8–9.

58, 6–7: Ibid., 106, 7–8.

58, 8–9: Ibid., 6–7.

58, 17–18: Ibid., 12–15.

58, 21–22: Ibid., 18.

58, 27–28: Ibid., 21–23.

59, 3: Ibid., 25.

59, 5–6: Ibid., 106, 27–107, 1.

59, 9–12: Ibid., 107, 2–6.

59, 17–20: Franz Kafka, *Briefe 1902–1924* (Letters 1902–1924), ed. Max Brod (Frankfurt: S. Fischer, 1958), 386.

59, 24–25: Kafka, *Das Schloss*, 96, 15.

59, 27–30: Ibid., 107, 7–10.

60, 6–7: Ibid., 13, 1–2.

60, 8: Ibid., 1.

60, 10–13: Kafka, *Das Schloss*, App, 126.

60, 16: Kafka, *Das Schloss*, 93, 15.

60, 23–24: Ibid., 12, 20–21.

60, 25–29: Ibid., 12, 27 – 13, 1–4.

61, 13: Ibid., 236, 26.

61, 18: Ibid., 196, 7.

61, 25–28: Ibid., 237, 14–16.

61, 29: Ibid., 24.

62, 1: Ibid., 22.

62, 4: Ibid., 20.

63, 8: Kafka, *Das Schloss*, App, 424.

63, 16: Kafka, *Das Schloss*, 94, 11–12.

63, 20–21: Ibid., 173, 25–26.

63, 22: Ibid., 172, 22.

63, 22: Ibid., 173, 26.

63, 26–27: Ibid., 172, 19–20.

64, 6: Ibid., 138, 10–11.

64, 21: Ibid., 187, 22–23.

64, 24–25: Ibid., 216, 1–2.

64, 26: Ibid., 221, 10.

65, 16–17: Ibid., 163, 17–19.

65, 24–25: Ibid., 26–27.

65, 27–30 – 66, 1–3: Ibid., 164, 10–15.

66, 5–8: Ibid., 17–20.

66, 13–14: Ibid., 24–25.

IV. The Way of Women

68, 3–4: Franz Kafka, *Das Schloss* (The castle), ed. Malcolm Pasley, in *Kritische Ausgabe* (1982), 257, 21–23.

69, 1: Ibid., 428, 8–9.

69, 2–4: Ibid., 428, 1–4.

69, 8: Ibid., 14.

69, 11–13: Ibid., 25–27.

69, 21: Ibid., 429, 7.

69, 28–29: Ibid., 386, 23–24.

70, 2: Ibid., 392, 14–15.

70, 7–13: Ibid., 429, 10–15.

70, 24–26: Ibid., 400, 20–22.

70, 29–30: Ibid., 398, 27 – 399, 1–2.

71, 4–6: Ibid., 399, 5–6.

71, 14–15: Franz Kafka, *Der Process* (The trial), ed. Malcolm Pasley, in *Kritische Ausgabe* (1990), 77, 27–78, 1.

71, 18: Ibid., 77, 26–27.

71, 21: Ibid., 78, 6.

71, 25–26: Kafka, *Das Schloss*, 474, 10.

72, 4–7: Kafka, *Der Process*, 83, 2–6.

72, 16: Ibid., 82, 22.

72, 16–17: Ibid., 27.

72, 17–18: Ibid., 86, 3.

72, 18–19: Ibid., 82, 19–21.

72, 21: Ibid., 84, 10.

72, 25–26: Ibid., 83, 25–27.

73, 2: Ibid., 81, 13–14.

73, 3–4: Ibid., 26–27 – 82, 1.

73, 5–6: Ibid., 82, 7–9.

73, 12–13: Ibid., 55, 6–7.

73, 18: Ibid., 70, 7–8.

73, 27: Ibid., 9–10.

73, 30–74, 1: Kafka, *Der Process*, App, 192.

74, 5: Kafka, *Der Process*, 77, 17.

74, 7: Ibid., 24.

74, 19: Ibid., 75, 18–19.

74, 19–20: Ibid., 20–21.

74, 25: Ibid., 99, 21–22.

74, 26: Ibid., 20.

74, 28: Ibid., 19.

75, 1: Ibid., 89, 26.

75, 11: Ibid., 90, 7–8.

75, 17: Ibid., 14.

75, 20: Ibid., 91, 8.

75, 27: Kafka, *Das Schloss*, 455, 17.

76, 1–2: Kafka, *Der Process*, 92, 2.

76, 9–10: Walter Benjamin, *Gesammelte Schriften*

(Collected writings), eds. Rolf Tiedemann and Hermann Schweppenhäuser (Frankfurt: Suhrkamp, 1977), vol. 2, part 3, 1225.

76, 14–15: Ibid., vol. 2, part 2, 413.

76, 15–16: Ibid., vol. 2, part 3, 1213.

76, 17: Ibid., 1224.

76, 23–24: Kafka, *Das Schloss*, 202, 14–15.

76, 25–30: Theodor W. Adorno, *Prismen* (Prisms), (Frankfurt: Suhrkamp, 1955), 324.

77, 2: Kafka, *Das Schloss*, 258, 18.

77, 16: Franz Kafka, *Tagebücher* (Diaries), eds. Hans-Gerd Müller and Malcolm Pasley, in *Kritische Ausgabe* (1990), 498, 11–12.

77, 27–28: Ibid., 495, 6–7.

77, 29–30: Ibid., 10–11.

78, 11–12: Ibid., 497, 7.

78, 14–16: Ibid., 498, 6–8.

78, 23–24: Ibid., 499, 19–20.

78, 25: Ibid., 20.

79, 1: Kafka, *Der Process*, 129, 14.

79, 3–4: Ibid., 20–21.

79, 11: Ibid., 143, 3–4.

79, 23: Ibid., 146, 8–9.

79, 25–26: Ibid., 144, 19–20.

80, 1–2: Ibid., 141, 3.

80, 4: Ibid., 143, 11.

80, 7: Ibid., 145, 14–15.

80, 8–9: Ibid., 24.

80, 10: Ibid., 22.

80, 14: Ibid., 146, 7.

80, 14–16: Ibid., 1–3.

80, 16–17: Ibid., 4–5.

80, 18–20: Ibid., 13–14.

80, 28–29: Kafka, *Das Schloss*, 157, 27–158, 1–2.

80, 30: Ibid., 159, 13–14.

81, 1–2: Ibid., 15–17.

81, 9–14: Kafka, *Das Schloss*, App, 240.

81, 15–16: Kafka, *Das Schloss*, 160, 5–6.

81, 19–20: Ibid., 7–9.

82, 19: Kafka, *Der Process*, 78, 6.

82, 19: Kafka, *Das Schloss*, 474, 10.

83, 4–6: Kafka, *Der Process*, 87, 15–18.

83, 9–10: Ibid., 86, 3–4.

83, 18: Kafka, *Das Schloss*, 389, 11–12.

83, 20–21: Ibid., 468, 21–22.

83, 25–26: Ibid., 390, 9.

84, 1–2: Ibid., 397, 8.

84, 7: Ibid., 401, 7.

84, 10: Ibid., 399, 5–6.

84, 15: Ibid., 402, 22.

84, 17: Ibid., 93, 2.

84, 24: Ibid., 395, 19–20.

84, 25–26: Ibid., 398, 12–13.

84, 29: Ibid., 366, 27.

84, 30–85–1: Ibid., 366, 25.

85, 1–2: Ibid., 367, 1–2.

85, 3: Ibid., 6.

85, 8: Ibid., 33, 12.

85, 10–11: Ibid., 399, 12–13.

85, 11–12: Ibid., 396, 23–24.

85, 15–16: Ibid., 99, 4.

85, 20: Ibid., 1.

85, 26: Ibid., 25.

85, 28–29: Ibid., 26.

85, 30–86, 1: Ibid., 390, 25–26.

86, 3–7: Ibid., 381, 3–7.

86, 9–10: Ibid., 396, 24–25.

86, 22–23: Ibid., 316, 4–5.

86, 23–27: Ibid., 279, 4–7.

87, 15–16: Ibid., 365, 8–9.

87, 21: Ibid., 264, 23–24.

87, 22–23: Ibid., 25–26.

87, 28–29: Ibid., 53, 6–7.

87, 29—88, 1: Ibid., 55, 5.

88, 2–4: Ibid., 264, 27–265, 1.

88, 29—89, 1: Franz Kafka, *Nachgelassene Schriften und Fragmente* (Posthumous writings and fragments, vol. 2), ed. Jost Schillemeit, in *Kritische Ausgabe* (1992), 134, 17.

89, 21–22: Kafka, *Das Schloss,* 388, 21.

89, 23–24: Ibid., 22.

89, 24–25: Ibid., 349, 1–2.

89, 27–28: Ibid., 390, 11–12.

90, 78: Ibid., 448, 15–16.

90, 11–12: Ibid., 21–22.

90, 13: Ibid., 449, 19.

90, 17–18: Ibid., 23–24.

90, 29–30: Ibid., 296, 24–25.

91, 5: Ibid., 297, 4.

91, 6–7: Ibid., 6–7.

91, 7–11: Ibid., 264, 13–17.

91, 12: Ibid., 17.

91, 13–14: Ibid., 19–20.

91, 21: Ibid., 296, 3–4.

91, 23–24: Ibid., 7–9.

91, 25–27: Ibid., 325, 17–19.

91, 29: Ibid., 27.

93, 6: Ibid., 269, 8–9.

93, 14–17: Ibid., 311, 2–5.

93, 17–18: Ibid., 312, 10.

94, 2: Ibid., 327, 22–23.

94, 10: Ibid., 299, 16.

94, 15–17: Ibid., 327, 11–14.

94, 23–25: Ibid., 336, 21–22.

94, 25–28: Ibid., 336, 26–27—337, 1.

95, 12–14: Karl Kraus, *Die dritte Walpurgisnacht* (The third Walpurgis night), (Munich: Kösel, 1952), 122.

95, 28–30: Kafka, *Das Schloss,* 270, 17–20.

96, 9–13: Ibid., 269, 2–7.

96, 16–20: Ibid., 269, 7–11.

96, 29–30: Ibid., 331, 21.

97, 3: Ibid., 323, 8–9.

97, 5–9: Ibid., 268, 22–25.

97, 12–13: Ibid., 270, 15–16.

97, 16: Ibid., 269, 11.

98, 2–7: Ibid., 323, 14–21.

98, 9–12: Ibid., 324, 21–23.

98, 14–15: Ibid., 323, 12.

98, 17–20: Ibid., 22–25.

98, 24–99, 1: Ibid., 26–27—324, 1–7.

99, 11–12: Ibid., 450, 18–19.

99, 21–22: Ibid., 492, 17.

99, 23: Ibid., 494, 1–2.

99, 29–30—100, 1: Ibid., 493, 5–7.

100, 2–3: Ibid., 7–8.

100, 8–10: Ibid., 447, 24–26.

100, 10–11: Ibid., 26–27.

100, 16–18: Ibid., 493, 24–27.

100, 19–21: Ibid., 493, 27—494, 1–2.

100, 22: Ibid., 494, 2–3.

100, 28–29: Ibid., 3–5.

101, 6–8: Kafka, *Das Schloss,* App, 485.

101, 21: Kafka, *Das Schloss,* 247, 19–20.

102, 25–28: Ibid., 186, 11–13.

103, 3: Ibid., 377, 13–14.

103, 26: Ibid., 377, 27–378, 1.

103, 28–29—104: Ibid., 378, 3–5.

104, 10–12: Ibid., 9–11.

104, 14–15: Ibid., 13–14.

104, 18–19: Ibid., 16–17.

105, 4–5: Ibid., 408, 3–4.

105, 6: Ibid., 407, 22.

105, 7–8: Ibid., 408, 5.

105, 8: Ibid., 6.

105, 9–10: Ibid., 411, 5–6.

105, 19: Ibid., 379, 10.
105, 25–27: Ibid., 382, 21–23.
106, 19: Ibid., 492, 11.
106, 20: Ibid., 17.
106, 21–22: Ibid., 57, 21–22.
106, 24–25: Ibid., 492, 9–10.
107, 5–6: Ibid., 445, 13–14.
107, 8: Ibid., 446, 23.
107, 9–10: Ibid., 13.
107, 12: Ibid., 447, 1–2.
107, 16–17: Ibid., 417, 6.
107, 19–20: Ibid., 447, 3–4.

V. Powers

109, 9–10: Franz Kafka,
    Nachgelassene Schriften und
    Fragmente (Posthumous writ-
    ings and fragments), vol. 2, ed.
    Jost Schillemeit, in *Kritische*
    Ausgabe (1992), 40, 2–3.
109, 17: Ibid., 38, 11.
109, 18–19: Ibid., 38, 12.
110, 5: Ibid., 13.
110, 10, 11: Ibid., 17.
110, 14, 13: Ibid., 19.
111, 5: Ibid., 40, 23.
111, 13: Ibid., 16.
111, 19–20: Ibid., 17–18.
111, 25–26: Ibid., 41, 9–10.
111, 27–28: Ibid., 11.
112, 10–13: Ibid., 42, 1–4.
112, 30–113–1: Ibid., 38, 8.
113, 4–8: Franz Kafka,
    Tagebücher (Diaries), eds.
    Hans-Gerd Koch, Michael
    Müller, and Malcolm Pasley, in
    Kritische Ausgabe (1990), 562,
    6–10.
113, 28: Kafka, *Nachgelassene*
    Schriften, vol. 2, 38, 16.

114, 4–5: Franz Kafka, *Briefe*
    1902–1924 (Letters 1902–1924),
    ed. Max Brod (Frankfurt:
    S. Fischer, 1958), 382.
114, 7–15: Ibid.
114, 17: Malcolm Pasley, ed.,
    Max Brod, Franz Kafka: Eine
    freundschaft (II): Briefwechsel
    (Max Brod, Franz Kafka:
    A friendship (II): Correspon-
    dence) (Frankfurt: S. Fischer,
    1989), 377.
114, 23–30 — 115, 1–22: Ibid.,
    377–78.
116, 4–15: Ibid., 379.
116, 20: Ibid.
116, 29–31 — 117, 1–3: Ibid.
117, 9–13: Ibid., 380.
117, 20: Franz Kafka, *Briefe*
    1913–1914 (Letters 1913–1914),
    ed. Hans-Gerd Koch, in
    Kritische Ausgabe (1999),
    261, 27–28.
117, 22: Ibid., 26–27.
117, 23–24: Ibid., 28–29.
117, 28–30: Ibid., 268, 11–13.
118, 12–14: Kafka, *Briefe*
    1902–1924, 161.
118, 15–20: Kafka, *Tagebücher*,
    831, 5–10.
118, 26–31 — 119, 1–4: Franz
    Kafka, *Briefe an Milena*
    (Letters to Milena), eds.
    J. Born and M. Müller (Frank-
    furt: S. Fischer, 1986), 7.
119, 14: Franz Kafka, *Briefe*
    an Felice und andere
    Korrespondenz aus der
    Verlobungszeit (Letters to
    Felice and other corres-
    pondence from the period of
    the engagement), eds.

Erich Heller and Jürgen Born (Frankfurt: S. Fischer, 1967), 564.

119, 16: Kafka, *Tagebücher*, 9, 1.

120, 12: Ibid., 899, 11.

120, 17–31: Kafka, *Briefe 1902–1924*, 372.

121, 9–12: Kafka, *Briefe an Milena*, 183.

121, 15–18: Kafka, *Tagebücher*, 878, 12–15.

121, 19–20: Ibid., 13–14.

121, 21–22: Ibid., 7–8.

121, 26–29 — 122, 1: Ibid., 1–5.

122, 1–4: Ibid., 7–10.

122, 6–9: Ibid., 10–13.

122, 10–11: Ibid., 14–16.

122, 13–14: Ibid., 22.

122, 14: Ibid., 16.

122, 17: Ibid., 878, 6.

122, 25–27: Ibid., 8–11.

123, 7–8: Ibid., 12.

123, 13–18: Ibid., 877, 17–21.

123, 27: Ibid., 874, 1.

123, 29–30 — 124, 1–2: Ibid., 2–5.

124, 12–19: Ibid., 892, 12–20.

124, 20–21: Kafka, *Nachgelassene Schriften*, vol. 2, 119, 16.

124, 23–24: Franz Kafka, *Das Schloss* (The castle), ed. Malcolm Pasley, in *Kritische Ausgabe* (1982), 425, 22–23.

125, 15–17: Kafka, *Tagebücher*, 892, 12–13.

125, 17–21: Ibid., 893, 1–5.

125, 23–24: Ibid., 520, 11–12.

125, 29–30 — 126, 1–4: Ibid., 12–18.

126, 19: Ibid., 902, 4.

126, 22–25: Ibid., 4–8.

127, 2: Ibid., 926, 5.

127, 4–7: Ibid., 5–8.

127, 9: Ibid., 8–9.

127, 10–11: Ibid., 925, 17–18.

127, 14–19: Elias Canetti, *Der andere Prozess* (The other trial), (Munich: Hanser, 1969), 36.

127, 21–25: Kafka, *Tagebücher*, 865, 19–21 — 866, 1–2.

VI. On the Waters of the Dead

128, 1–2: Franz Kafka, *Nachgelassene Schriften und Fragmente* (Posthumous writings and fragments), vol. 1, ed. Malcolm Pasley, in *Kritische Ausgabe* (1993), 306, 1–2.

128, 3–4: Ibid., 307, 24.

128, 14–15: Ibid., 309, 12–13.

128, 16–17: Ibid., 311, 18–19.

129, 1–2: Ibid., 310, 6–7.

129, 19–24: Ibid., 7–11.

129, 27–30: Ibid., 312, 10–13.

129, 30: Ibid., 312, 15.

130, 12: Ibid., 382, 1.

130, 14–15: Ibid., 382, 3–4.

130, 18–19: Ibid., 383, 5–7.

130, 27–28: Ibid., 26–27.

131, 15–16: Ibid., 309, 23.

131, 20: Ibid., 383, 26.

131, 21: Ibid., 382, 13–14.

131, 25–26: Ibid., 310, 10–11.

131, 29: Ibid., 382, 1.

132, 4–6: Ibid., 383, 3–4.

VII. A Photograph

133, 3–4: Franz Kafka, *Tagebücher* (Diaries), eds. Hans-Gerd Koch, Michael Müller, and Malcolm Pasley, in *Kritische Ausgabe* (1990), 491, 5–6.

134, 22: Franz Kafka, *Drucke zu Lebzeiten* (Texts published in his lifetime), eds. Wolf Kittler, Hans-Gerd Koch, and Gerhard Neumann, in *Kritische Ausgabe* (1994), 57, 4.

134, 23–24: Ibid., 60, 19–20.

134, 24–25: Ibid., 21.

134, 26–27: Ibid., 61, 9–10.

135, 5–6: Kafka, *Tagebücher*, 491, 6–7.

135, 18–19: Ibid., 492, 6–7.

135, 23–30 — 136, 1–2: Kafka, *Drucke*, 57, 4–13.

136, 12–19: Franz Kafka, *Nachgelassene Schriften und Fragmente* (Posthumous writings and fragments), vol. 2, ed. Jost Schillemeit, in *Kritische Ausgabe* (1992), 205, 12–19.

136, 22–23: Ibid., 19–21.

137, 2: Ibid., 22.

137, 6–7: Kafka, *Tagebücher*, 491, 2–3.

137, 11–12: Ibid., 8–9.

137, 13–16: Ibid., 10–13.

137, 18: Ibid., 13.

137, 20–21: Ibid., 14–15.

137, 23–25: Ibid., 18–20.

137, 25–27: Ibid., 492, 2–4.

138, 5–6: Ibid., 6–7.

138, 6–7: Ibid., 5–6.

138, 7–8: Ibid., 8.

138, 21: Kafka, *Drucke*, 49, 18–19.

138, 26–27: Ibid., 50, 13–14.

139, 17–19: Kafka, *Tagebücher*, 460, 18–20.

139, 22–22: Ibid., 22–24.

139, 25–27: Kafka, *Drucke*, 52, 4–5.

139, 28–29: Ibid., 17–18.

140, 10: Ibid., 26.

140, 15–17: Ibid., 53, 21–23.

140, 23–24: Ibid., 54, 12–13.

140, 27: Ibid., 22–23.

141, 1–2: Ibid., 55, 2–3.

141, 7: Ibid., 9.

141, 17–18: Ibid., 56, 4–5.

141, 21–23: Ibid., 8–10.

141, 25: Ibid., 15.

141, 27: Ibid., 21.

141, 29–30: Ibid., 23.

142, 1–2: Ibid., 25–26.

142, 4–5: Ibid., 57, 4–6.

142, 6: Ibid., 7–8.

142, 10: Ibid., 58, 1.

142, 11–12: Ibid., 10–11.

142, 16–17: Ibid., 16–17.

142, 17–18: Ibid., 25.

142, 23: Ibid., 60, 12.

142, 25–26: Ibid., 19–20.

143, 3–4: Ibid., 61, 4–6.

143, 12–13: Kafka, *Tagebücher*, 547, 18.

143, 13–14: Ibid., 742, 17–18.

143, 17: Kafka, *Drucke*, 60, 20.

144, 2: Kafka, *Tagebücher*, 461, 6.

144, 3–5: Ibid., 463, 4–7.

144, 7: Ibid., 461, 18–19.

144, 18–19: Ibid., 17, 9–10.

144, 21–22: Ibid., 18, 1–2.

144, 24–26: Ibid., 19–20.

144, 28–32: Ibid., 20, 8–11.

145, 1–4: Ibid., 23, 7–10.

145, 6–11: Ibid., 27, 14–18.

146, 4–14: Ibid., 18, 3–12.

146, 16–33: Ibid., 18, 21–26 — 19, 1–10.

147, 1–12: Ibid., 20, 11–22.

147, 14–33 — 148–1–2: Ibid., 26, 21–27 — 27, 1–13.

148, 15–18: Franz Kafka, *Briefe en Milena* (Letters to Milena), eds. J. Born and M. Müller (Frankfurt: S. Fischer, 1986), 71.

149, 21–22: Kafka, *Tagebücher*, 870, 4–5.

149, 22–24: Ibid., 7–8.

149, 26–27: Ibid., 13.

149, 30: Ibid., 15–16.

150, 7–8: Ibid., 871, 12–13.

150, 10–17: Ibid., 13–21.

150, 28–30 — 151, 1: Ibid., 870, 23 — 871, 1–3.

151, 2–3: Ibid., 869, 12.

151, 3–4: Ibid., 9–10.

151, 4–5: Ibid., 10.

151, 5–6: Ibid., 10–11.

151, 11–12: Ibid., 875, 7–9.

151, 14–15: Ibid., 6–7.

151, 25–30: Ibid., 9–15.

152, 11–15: Ibid., 876, 1–5.

153, 3: Ibid., 1041, 18–19.

153, 25–26: Ibid., 463, 16.

154, 1–8: Vladimir Nabokov, *Lectures on Literature* (London: Picador, 1983), 251.

154, 21–23: Kafka, *Tagebücher*, 288, 3–5.

VIII. The Blanket of Moss

156, 10–12: Franz Kafka, *Tagebücher* (Diaries), eds. Hans-Gerd Koch, Michael Müller, and Malcolm Pasley, in *Kritische Ausgabe* (1990), 859, 22.

156, 27: Franz Kafka, *Nachgelassene Schriften und Fragmente* (Posthumous writings and fragments), vol. 2, ed.

Jost Schillemeit in *Kritische Ausgabe*, (1992), 424, 21.

157, 5–6: Kafka, *Tagebücher*, 870, 15–16.

157, 10: Kafka, *Nachgelassene Schriften*, vol. 2, 424, 21.

157, 16–31 — 158, 1–11: Kafka, *Tagebücher*, 889, 7–24 — 890, 1–5.

158, 19–20: Kafka, *Nachgelassene Schriften*, vol. 2, 600, 23.

158, 26–27: Ibid., 600, 23.

158, 30–31: Ibid., 596, 3–4.

159, 17–18: Ibid., 630, 4.

160, 1: Ibid., 612, 6–7.

160, 3–4: Ibid., 618, 18–19.

160, 6–12: Ibid., 625, 12–17.

160, 14–17: Ibid., 628, 22–26.

161, 6: Ibid., 600, 1–2.

161, 22–23: Franz Kafka, *Drucke zu Lebzeiten* (Texts published in his lifetime), ed. Wolf Kittler, Hans-Gerd Koch, and Gerhard Neumann, in *Kritische Ausgabe* (1994), 117, 11.

161, 29–30 — 162, 1: Ibid., 120, 17–19.

162, 7–8: Ibid., 17.

162, 13–14: Ibid., 128, 15–16.

162, 15: Ibid., 115, 13.

163, 10: Ibid., 177, 21–22.

163, 11: Ibid., 193, 7.

163, 19–22: Ibid., 172, 21–25.

163, 26–27: Kafka, *Tagebücher*, 871, 17.

163, 28: Ibid., 18.

163, 30 — 164, 1: Kafka, *Drucke*, 184, 24–25.

164, 4–5: Ibid., 185, 2–3.

164, 8–9: Ibid., 25–26.

164, 13–14: Ibid., 186, 5–6.

164, 20–21: Ibid., 20.

164, 21–22: Ibid., 21.

164, 23: Ibid., 300, 1.

164, 30–161, 1: Ibid., 12–13.

165, 4: Ibid., 189, 15–16.

165, 5–6: Ibid., 194, 20–21.

IX. Ladies' Handkerchiefs

166, 1: Franz Kafka, *Drucke zu Lebzeiten* (Texts published in his lifetime), eds. Wolf Kittler, Hans-Gerd Koch, and Gerhard Neumann, in *Kritische Ausgabe* (1994), 203, 1.

166, 4–5: Franz Kafka, *Tagebücher* (Diaries), eds. Hans-Gerd Koch, Michael Müller, and Malcolm Pasley, in *Kritische Ausgabe* (1990), 823, 15.

166, 10–11: Kafka, *Drucke*, 233, 22.

166, 12–13: Ibid., 204, 16.

166, 18–19: Ibid., 22–24.

167, 3: Ibid., 205, 10.

167, 10: Ibid., 209, 6.

167, 14: Ibid., 210, 11.

167, 16–17: Ibid., 13–15.

167, 26–27: Friedrich Hebbel, *Tagebücher* (Diaries), n. 5483, in *Werke* (Works), (Munich: Hanser, 1967), vol. 5, 214.

168, 11–12: Kafka, *Drucke*, 211, 12–13.

168, 16–24: Kafka, *Tagebücher*, 899, 11–20.

169, 15: Kafka, *Drucke*, 217, 27–218, 1.

169, 16: Ibid., 217, 25–26.

169, 20–21: Ibid., 220, 1.

169, 29–30: Ibid., 223, 17.

170, 4–5: Ibid., 233, 9–10.

170, 7–8: Ibid., 229, 17.

170, 9–10: Ibid., 222, 13–15.

170, 12: Ibid., 229, 16.

170, 16–17: Ibid., 234, 7.

171, 2: Ibid., 212, 15–16.

171, 5: Ibid., 215, 8–9.

171, 7: Ibid., 11.

171, 16–17: Ibid., 236, 24.

171, 20: Ibid., 238, 13.

171, 25–26: Ibid., 240, 5.

171, 26–27: Ibid., 7.

172, 27–28: Franz Kafka, *Briefe 1902–1924* (Letters 1902–1924), ed. Max Brod (Frankfurt: S. Fischer, 1958), 153.

173, 1: Ibid.

173, 3: *Franz Kafka: Kritik und Rezeption zu seinen Lebzeiten, 1912–1924* (Criticism and reception in his lifetime, 1912–1924), ed. Jürgen Born (Frankfurt: S. Fischer, 1979), 119.

X. Scuffles and Escapes

174, 9: Franz Kafka, *Der Verschollene* (The missing person), ed. Jost Schillemeit, in *Kritische Ausgabe* (1983), 7, 12.

174, 17–18: Ibid., 11, 25–26.

175, 22–23: Ibid., 156, 21–22.

176, 8–12: Robert Musil, *Gesammelte Werke* (Collected works), vol. 2 (Reinbeck bei Hamburg: Rowohlt, 1978), 1469.

176, 14–16: Ibid.

177, 9–12: Kafka, *Der Verschol-*
lene, 8, 10–14.

178, 3–4: Ibid., 20, 1–3.

178, 13: Franz Kafka, *Briefe*
1913–1914 (Letters 1913–1914),
ed. Hans-Gerd Koch, in
Kritische Ausgabe (1999), 196,
20–21.

178, 23–24: Ibid., 197, 4.

180, 7: Kafka, *Der Verschollene*,
55, 21.

180, 7: Ibid., 24.

180, 9–10: Ibid., 24–26.

180, 14: Ibid., 56, 15.

180, 20–21: Ibid., 60, 6–7.

180, 23–24: Ibid., 62, 2–3.

181, 1–5: Ibid., 60, 26–27—61,
1–3.

181, 8: Ibid., 22–23.

181, 15–16: Ibid., 88, 4–6.

181, 27–30: Ibid., 87, 20–22.

182, 6–9: Ibid., 89, 20–23.

182, 12–17: Ibid., 208, 18–24.

182, 26: Ibid., 85, 15–16.

182, 25: Franz Kafka,
Nachgelassene Schriften und
Fragmente (Posthumous writ-
ings and fragments), vol. 2, ed.
Jost Schillemeit, in *Kritische*
Ausgabe (1992), 114, 21.

183, 26: Ibid., 20.

183, 27–28: Ibid., 21–22.

184, 1–3: Kafka, *Der Verschollene*,
282, 1–3.

184, 10: Ibid., 144, 14.

184, 10–11: Ibid., 12–13.

184, 11–13: Ibid., 140, 18–22.

184, 23: Ibid., 222, 21–22.

184, 24–25: Robert Walser, *Jakob*
von Gunten, in *Das*
Gesamtwerk (Collected work),

vol. 4 (Genf und Hamburg: H.
Kossodo, 1967), 409.

184, 26: Ibid., 336.

185, 2–6: Ibid., 425.

185, 12–13: Kafka, *Der*
Verschollene, 184, 26–27.

185, 14–17: Ibid., 185, 1–4.

185, 30—186, 1: Ibid., 245, 17–18.

186, 11–12: Ibid., 247, 22–24.

186, 27: Ibid., 251, 12–13.

186, 29–30: Ibid., 14–15.

187, 17–18: Ibid., 289, 17.

187, 26: Ibid., 274, 25.

187, 28: Ibid., 211, 8.

187, 29: Ibid., 220, 16.

188, 8: Ibid., 339, 7.

188, 11: Ibid., 354, 6.

188, 13–14: Ibid., 303, 18.

188, 19–23: Ibid., 309, 4–9.

189, 78: Ibid., 352, 13–14.

189, 16: Ibid., 6.

189, 17–18: Ibid., 9.

189, 22–23: Ibid., 358, 22–23.

189, 30: Ibid., 357, 12.

190, 2: Ibid., 362, 11–12.

190, 7–8: Ibid., 359, 13.

190, 21–22: Ibid., 365, 23.

190, 28–29: Ibid., 368, 27–369, 1.

191, 2–3: Ibid., 369, 5.

191, 4–5: Ibid., 370, 24–25.

191, 6–7: Ibid., 371, 9–11.

191, 16–17: Ibid., 383, 24–25.

191, 23–24: Ibid., 384, 12.

191, 25: Ibid., 10.

191, 27–29: Ibid., 13–16.

192, 2–6: Ibid., 16–21.

192, 12–13: Ibid., 394, 3.

192, 13: Ibid., 12.

192, 16–18: Ibid., 396, 9–10.

193, 5: Ibid., 387, 17.

193, 7–8: Ibid., 4–5.

193, 10–11: Ibid., 7–8.

193, 12–13: Ibid., 12–13.

193, 14–15: Ibid., 13–14.

194, 1–21: Ibid., 389, 19–27—390, 1–11.

194, 32—195, 1–3: Franz Kafka, *Tagebücher* (Diaries), eds. Hans-Gerd Koch, Michael Müller, and Malcolm Pasley, in *Kritische Ausgabe* (1990), 757, 3–6.

XI. The Riskiest Moment

196, 1–9: Franz Kafka, *Der Process* (The trial), ed. Malcolm Pasley, in *Kritische Ausgabe* (1990), App, 168.

196, 14–19: Ibid.

197, 19–21: Kafka, *Der Process*, 170, 26—171, 1–3.

197, 28: Ibid., 251, 5.

198, 7–8: Ibid., 171, 2–3.

198, 12–13: Ibid., 30, 16–17.

198, 15: Max Brod, *Über Franz Kafka* (About Franz Kafka), (Frankfurt: S. Fischer, 1974), 104.

198, 20–21: Ibid.

198, 22: Ibid.

199, 5: Ibid.

201, 5–7: Kafka, *Der Process*, 13, 9–11.

201, 13–15: Ibid., 10, 15–16.

201, 28–29: Ibid., 13, 26–27.

202, 3–5: Ibid., 11, 21–23.

202, 6–8: Ibid., 14–15.

202, 10–13: Ibid., 17, 10–13.

202, 14–18: Ibid., 14–17.

202, 19–20: Ibid., 14, 27.

203, 1: Ibid., 17, 17.

203, 26–28: Ibid., 17–19.

203, 30—204, 1–2: Ibid., 311, 23–25.

204, 6–7: Ibid., 15, 11–12.

204, 9–13: Ibid., 14, 18–23.

204, 20: Ibid., 167, 6.

204, 24: Ibid., 166, 21–22.

204, 28: Ibid., 69, 16.

204, 29: Ibid., 168, 6–7.

205, 2: Ibid., 11–12.

205, 3–4: Ibid., 5–6.

205, 13–14: Ibid., 169, 10.

205, 14: Ibid., 312, 24.

205, 23–28: Ibid., 169, 4–6.

206, 1: Ibid., 8.

206, 5: Ibid., 170, 7.

206, 9–22: Ibid., 9–22.

207, 5–8: Ibid., 22–25.

207, 12–14: Ibid., 186, 22–24.

207, 17: Ibid., 187, 7.

207, 26–27: Ibid., 179, 14–15.

208, 5: Ibid., 187, 17.

208, 9–10: Ibid., 10–11.

208, 20: Ibid., 173, 15–16.

209, 1–7: Ibid., 174, 5–11.

209, 13–17: Ibid., 12–15.

209, 30: Ibid., 20.

210, 2–4: Ibid., 18–19.

210, 17–18: Ibid., 15.

210, 19–22: Ibid., 175, 8–9.

210, 29: Ibid., 23.

211, 7: Ibid., 174, 14.

211, 10–12: Franz Kafka, *Nachgelassene Schriften und Fragmente* (Posthumous writings and fragments), vol. 2, ed. Jost Schillemeit, in *Kritische Ausgabe* (1992), 7, 1–3.

211, 13–15: Ibid., 3–5.

211, 21–24: Ibid., 6–9.

212, 1–2: Ibid., 10.

212, 4: Ibid., 20–21.

212, 5–6: Ibid., 11–12.

212, 7–9: Ibid., 19–20.

212, 10: Ibid., 8, 11.

212, 12: Ibid., 3–4.

212, 13–14: Ibid., 9, 8.

212, 16–19: Ibid., 9–12.

212, 25–28: Ibid., 14–17.

213, 3–4: Ibid., 20–21.

213, 6–8: Ibid., 11, 9–11.

213, 16–23: Ibid., 14–21.

214, 5–7: Ibid., 12, 8–10.

214, 13–14: Kafka, *Der Process*, 168, 22–23.

214, 15–21: Ibid., 168, 23–27–169, 1–3.

214, 28–30–215, 1: Ibid., 143, 23–26.

215, 21–22: Ibid., 289, 25–27.

216, 25–27: Ibid., 108, 16–18.

216, 28: Ibid., 111, 4–5.

217, 5–6: Ibid., 103, 15.

217, 11–13: Ibid., 116, 18–20.

217, 18–19: Ibid., 117, 1–2.

217, 23–24: Ibid., 14–15.

218, 10: Franz Kafka, *Tagebücher* (Diaries), eds. Hans-Gerd Koch, Michael Müller, and Malcolm Pasley, in *Kritische Ausgabe* (1990), 253, 6.

218, 14–15: Ibid., 12–13.

218, 16–19: Ibid., 15–20.

219, 7–8: Kafka, *Der Process*, 67, 10.

219, 10: Ibid., 69, 16.

219, 13: Ibid., 22.

219, 13–14: Ibid., 12–13.

219, 15–16: Ibid., 13–14.

219, 17: Ibid., 14.

219, 21–22: Ibid., 72, 18–20.

220, 1–2: Ibid., 64, 18–19.

220, 4–7: Ibid., 15–19.

220, 9: Ibid., 20.

220, 21–22: Ibid., 70, 12.

220, 24–25: Ibid., 71, 22–24.

220, 30–221, 1–2: Ibid., 72, 23–25.

221, 5: Ibid., 98, 9.

221, 7: Ibid., 93, 5–6.

221, 8: Ibid., 8–9.

221, 17: Ibid., 95, 24–25.

221, 19: Ibid., 93, 23.

221, 20–21: Ibid., 95, 18–19.

221, 23–24: Ibid., 102, 22–23.

221, 27–28: Ibid., 102, 21.

221, 28–29: Ibid., 24.

221–30–222, 1: Ibid., 101, 9–10.

222, 3: Ibid., 103, 11.

222, 10–12: Ibid., 14–16.

222, 16–17: Ibid., 105, 18–19.

222, 21–23: Ibid., 8–10.

222, 24: Ibid., 25.

222, 25–27: Ibid., 106, 1–4.

222, 29–30–223, 1: Ibid., 102, 6–8.

223, 6–7: Ibid., 99, 12–13.

223, 20: Ibid., 22–23.

223, 22–24: Ibid., 8–10.

223, 24–26: Ibid., 16–18.

223, 29: Ibid., 33, 15.

223, 30: Ibid., 32, 8–9.

224, 1: Ibid., 33, 21.

224, 3–4: Ibid., 24–25.

224, 7–8: Ibid., 34, 3–4.

224, 9–16: Ibid., 4–12.

224, 18–19: Ibid., 32, 18.

225, 18–24: Ibid., 34, 12–15.

226, 4: Kafka, *Der Process*, App, 168.

227, 3–4: Kafka, *Der Process*, 278, 15.

227, 6: Ibid., 278, 20.

227, 13: Ibid., 270, 9–10.

227, 24–26: Kafka, *Tagebücher*, 220, 10–12.

227, 27–28: Kafka, *Der Process*, 312, 19–20.

228, 8: Ibid., 305, 5–6.

228, 9: Ibid., 10.

228, 9–10: Ibid., 12.

228, 10–11: Ibid., 13.

228, 13–14: Ibid., 306, 25.

228, 17–19: Ibid., 312, 12–15.

228, 24: Ibid., 311, 6.

228, 24: Ibid., 3.

228, 27: Ibid., 9–10.

228, 27–28: Ibid., 10–11.

229, 7–11: Ibid., 311, 27—312, 1–3.

229, 19–20: Ibid., 312, 4–5.

229, 27: Ibid., 2.

XII. The Stuff of Legends

231, 3–4: Franz Kafka, *Der Process* (The trial), ed. Malcolm Pasley, in *Kritische Ausgabe* (1990), 204, 11–12.

232, 10: Ibid., 199, 27–200, 1.

232, 12–13: Ibid., 200, 2–4.

232, 20: Ibid., 201, 9–10.

232, 25: Ibid., 202, 11–12.

232, 26: Ibid., 15.

232, 28: Ibid., 14–15.

233, 2: Ibid., 203, 11.

233, 3: Ibid., 207, 19.

233, 5: Ibid., 206, 10.

233, 7–8: Ibid., 207, 21–22.

233, 22–23: Ibid., 181, 9.

233, 24: Ibid., 194, 15.

233, 27: Ibid., 208, 4.

234, 1–2: Ibid., 205, 21–22.

234, 3–4: Ibid., 207, 26–27.

234, 10–11: Ibid., 208, 2.

234, 13: Ibid., 9.

234, 14: Ibid., 8.

234, 16: Ibid., 6–7.

234, 18–19: Ibid., 12–13.

234, 25: Ibid., 14–15.

235, 12–13: Ibid., 23–24.

235, 16–17: Ibid., 208, 27–209, 1.

235, 18: Ibid., 209, 5.

235, 22: Ibid., 13–14.

235, 29—236, 1: Ibid., 6.

236, 7–8: Ibid., 208, 4.

236, 8–9: Ibid., 1–2.

236, 17–18: Ibid., 5–6.

237, 7: Ibid., 1–2.

237, 8: Ibid., 2.

237, 22: Ibid., 213, 10–12.

237, 23: Ibid., 9–10.

238, 2–5: Ibid., 213, 25–27—214, 1.

238, 12–13: Ibid., 13–14.

238, 15–16: Ibid., 15–16.

238, 27: Ibid., 214, 19.

238, 27–28: Ibid., 213, 18.

238, 29–30: Ibid., 19–20.

239, 2: Ibid., 214, 6.

239, 4–6: Ibid., 9–11.

239, 8–9: Ibid., 207, 21–22.

239, 10: Ibid., 20.

239, 11–12: Ibid., 201, 5–6.

240, 18: Ibid., 214, 15–16.

240, 27–28: Ibid., 6.

240, 29–30: Ibid., 216, 13–14.

241, 4: Ibid., 312, 23.

241, 6–7: Franz Kafka, *Das Schloss* (The castle), ed. Malcolm Pasley, in *Kritische Ausgabe* (1982), 426, 2–3.

241, 9: Kafka, *Der Process*, 202, 15.

241, 13: Ibid., 292, 9–10.

241, 18: Ibid., 160, 20.

241, 19–20: Ibid., 22–23.

241, 22–24: Ibid., 303, 1–2.

241, 26–27: Ibid., 3.

242, 17–30—243, 1–8: Franz Kafka, *Nachgelessene Schriften und Fragmente*

(Posthumous writings and fragments), vol. 2, ed. Jost Schillemeit, in *Kritische Ausgabe*, 16, 13–25 — 17, 1–7.

XIII. Lawyer Visits

244, 2–3: Franz Kafka, *Der Process* (The trial), ed. Malcolm Pasley, in *Kritische Ausgabe* (1990), 253, 25–26.

244, 4–8: Ibid., 254, 16–18.

245, 15–16: Ibid., 250, 14–15.

245, 19: Ibid., 16.

245, 21: Ibid., 18–19.

245, 23: Ibid., 129, 14.

245, 25: Ibid., 21.

246, 2–4: Ibid., 165, 10–12.

246, 5: Ibid., 259, 2–3.

246, 8: Franz Kafka, *Das Schloss* (The castle), ed. Malcolm Pasley, in *Kritische Ausgabe* (1982), 471, 8.

246, 14: Kafka, *Der Process*, 165, 8.

246, 19: Ibid., 255, 3.

246, 24–25: Ibid., 258, 19.

246, 29: Ibid., 201, 22.

246, 30–247, 1: Ibid., 239, 1.

247, 2: Ibid., 3.

247, 5: Ibid., 251, 11.

247, 11–12: Ibid., 237, 1–3.

247, 13: Ibid., 6.

247, 15: Ibid., 5.

247, 16: Ibid., 4–5.

247, 17: Charles Baudelaire, "Mon cœur mis à nu" (My heart laid bare), in *Œuvres complètes* (Complete works), vol. 1 (Paris: Gallimard, 1975), 678.

248, 11: Kafka, *Der Process*, 251, 5.

248, 15–17: Ibid., 5–7.

248, 24–26: Ibid., 10–12.

248, 26–27: Ibid., 14.

248, 29–30 — 249, 1: Ibid., 236, 22–24.

249, 21–22: Ibid., 151, 26–27 — 152, 1.

250, 3–4: Ibid., 152, 2–3.

250, 6: Ibid., 6–7.

250, 16–17: Ibid., 1–3.

251, 1–2: Ibid., 157, 17–18.

251, 3: Ibid., 20.

251, 3–4: Ibid., 18–19.

251, 7–8: Ibid., 156, 26–27.

251, 12: Ibid., 157, 7–8.

251, 13–14: Ibid., 6–7.

251, 22–24: Ibid., 22–24.

252, 1: Ibid., 25–26.

252, 2–5: Ibid., 158, 1–4.

252, 9–10: Ibid., 160, 20.

252, 12–13: Ibid., 16–17.

252, 15–19: Ibid., 20–25.

252, 27: Ibid., 4.

253, 9–10: Ibid., 13–14.

253, 13: Ibid., 158, 18.

254, 2–3: Ibid., 160, 25–26.

254, 6: Ibid., 233, 4–5.

254, 8–9: Ibid., 17–18.

254, 10–11: Ibid., 18–20.

255, 4–5: Ibid., 260, 6–7.

255, 5: Ibid., 4.

255, 8–9: Ibid., 263, 4–5.

255, 19: Ibid., 238, 26.

255, 20–21: Ibid., 248, 6–7.

255, 24–25: Ibid., 5–6.

256, 2–3: Franz Kafka, *Briefe an Milena* (Letters to Milena), eds. J. Born and M. Müller (Frankfurt: S. Fischer, 1986), 24.

256, 6–17: Ibid., 26.

256, 22–25: Kafka, *Der Process*, 247, 22–25.

256, 31: Ibid., 264, 23.

257, 2–3: Ibid., 9–10.

257, 9–11: Ibid., 261, 2–5.

257, 13–14: Ibid., 263, 10.

257, 19–20: Ibid., 264, 7–8.

257, 23–26: Ibid., 10–13.

258, 5: Ibid., 251, 14.

258, 5–6: Ibid., 264, 13.

258, 8: Ibid., 18–19.

258, 9: Ibid., 265, 5.

258, 11–13: Ibid., 5–8.

258, 17–20: Ibid., 17–19.

258, 23–26: Ibid., 19–22.

258, 29: Ibid., 23–24.

258, 30 – 239, 1: Ibid., 266, 1–2.

259, 6–7: Ibid., 2–4.

259, 11–13: Ibid., 15.

259, 13–14: Ibid., 16–17.

259, 15: Ibid., 244, 17.

259, 20–21: Ibid., 266, 22–23.

259, 22: Ibid., 20.

259, 23–28: Ibid., 266, 25–27 – 267, 1.

260, 3–5: Ibid., 267, 15–17.

260, 7–8: Ibid., 19.

260, 10–12: Ibid., 21–23.

260, 15–17: Ibid., 268, 7–10.

260, 18–21: Ibid., 14–16.

260, 23–24: Ibid., 16–17.

260, 27: Ibid., 19.

261, 5: Ibid., 18.

261, 8–10: Ibid., 21–23.

261, 11: Ibid., 269, 4.

261, 15–16: Ibid., 11–12.

261, 30 – 262, 1–3: Ibid., 261, 21–24.

262, 7: Ibid., 260, 6–7.

262, 15–16: Ibid., 50, 14–16.

262, 25: Ibid., 235, 8–9.

262, 27–28: Ibid., 12–13.

262, 29: Ibid., 236, 3–4.

263, 3: Ibid., 239, 21.

263, 4: Ibid., 23.

263, 6–8: Ibid., 14–16.

263, 9: Ibid., 23–24.

263, 17: Ibid., 240, 13.

263, 21–22: Ibid., 244, 19–20.

263, 23–24: Ibid., 246, 24.

263, 25–26: Ibid., 244, 16–18.

263, 29: Ibid., 7, 15.

264, 8–27: Franz Kafka, *Tagebücher* (Diaries), eds. Hans-Gerd Koch, Michael Müller, and Malcolm Pasley, in *Kritische Ausgabe* (1990), 868, 7–24 – 869, 1–2.

XIV. Nighttime Interrogations

266, 9–10: Franz Kafka, *Das Schloss* (The castle), ed. Malcolm Pasley, in *Kritische Ausgabe* (1982), 424, 23.

266, 12–13: Ibid., 25.

266, 14–16: Kafka, *Das Schloss*, App, 437–38.

267, 19–26: Kafka, *Das Schloss*, 425, 15–23.

268, 2: Ibid., 14.

268, 24–25: Franz Kafka, *Nachgelassene Schriften und Fragmente* (Posthumous writings and fragments), vol. 2, ed. Jost Schillemeit, in *Kritische Ausgabe* (1992), 119, 16.

268, 29: Kafka, *Das Schloss*, 417, 6.

268, 30 – 269, 1: Ibid., 419, 21–22.

269, 2: Ibid., 407, 4.

269, 4–5: Ibid., 421, 2–3.

269, 6: Ibid., 4.

269, 8–9: Ibid., 422, 11.

269, 9–11: Ibid., 424, 9.

269, 12–13: Ibid., 10–12.

269, 20–21: Ibid., 409, 26.

270, 14: Ibid., 425, 21–23.

271, 3–4: Ibid., 20–21.

271, 10–11: Franz Kafka, *Der Process* (The trial), ed. Malcolm Pasley, in *Kritische Ausgabe* (1990), 285, 14.

271, 11: Ibid., 286, 23–24.

271, 13–14: Ibid., 292, 11–12.

271, 16: Ibid., 304, 20.

271, 19–20: Ibid., 190, 14–15.

271, 20–21: Ibid., 202, 11–12.

271, 25: Ibid., 292, 16–17.

271, 26: Ibid., 295, 4.

271, 26–27: Ibid., 292, 17–18.

271, 29: Ibid., 18–19.

272, 6–8: Ibid., 301, 24–26.

272, 9–11: Ibid., 302, 4–6.

272, 12–13: Ibid., 295, 7–8.

272, 14–18: Ibid., 302, 27–303, 1–3.

272, 24–25: Ibid., 303, 13–14.

272, 28: Ibid., 4.

272, 30: Ibid., 290, 24.

273, 15–16: Kafka, *Das Schloss*, 425, 20–21.

273, 17–18: Ibid., 22–23.

273, 26: Kafka, *Der Process*, 303, 5–6.

273, 27–28: Ibid., 6–7.

274, 1–2: Ibid., 289, 14–16.

274, 2–5: Ibid., 290, 7–10.

275, 10: Kafka, *Das Schloss*, 410, 4.

275, 15: Ibid., 409, 5.

275, 15–16: Ibid., 20.

275, 21–22: Ibid., 410, 24–25.

275, 24: Ibid., 411, 18.

275, 28: Ibid., 412, 17.

275, 29–30: Ibid., 21–22.

276, 12–13: Ibid., 414, 17–18.

276, 15: Ibid., 415, 4.

276, 18–19: Ibid., 412, 24–25.

276, 20–21: Ibid., 415, 6–7.

276, 25–26: Ibid., 410, 8–10.

276, 27–28: Ibid., 13.

276, 30: Ibid., 410, 6.

277, 1–2: Ibid., 408, 17–18.

277, 3–4: Ibid., 14.

277, 5–6: Ibid., 25–27.

277, 11–16: Ibid., 414, 3–7.

277, 17: Ibid., 8–9.

277, 19–20: Ibid., 9–12.

277, 22–23: Ibid., 12.

277, 24–25: Ibid., 15.

277, 30–278, 1: Ibid., 411, 13–14.

278, 6: Ibid., 412, 17.

278, 6–8: Ibid., 12–13.

278, 14–16: Ibid., 413, 19–21.

278, 25–29: Ibid., 443, 5–9.

279, 4: Ibid., 16–17.

279, 9–10: Ibid., 412, 5–7.

279, 12–13: Ibid., 443, 9–10.

279, 15–16: Ibid., 11–12.

279, 20: Ibid., 445, 1.

279, 20–21: Ibid., 444, 24.

279, 21–23: Ibid., 15–17.

280, 8–9: Kafka, *Der Process*, 189, 20.

280, 10: Ibid., 202, 20–22.

280, 15–17: Kafka, *Das Schloss*, 415, 8–9.

280, 17–18: Ibid., 415, 10.

280, 20–21: Ibid., 17–18.

280, 23: Ibid., 24.

280, 25–26: Ibid., 24–25.

280, 30–281, 1: Ibid., 416, 8–9.

281, 10–12: Franz Kafka, *Tagebücher* (Diaries), eds. Hans-Gerd Koch, Michael Müller, and Malcolm Pasley, in *Kritische Ausgabe* (1990), 868, 4–6.

281-25: Kafka, *Das Schloss*, 416, 23–24.

281, 25–26: Ibid., 26.

281, 26–27: Ibid., 24–25.

281, 28–29: Ibid., 416, 26–27 – 417, 1.

282, 1–2: Ibid., 417, 1–2.

282, 13–14: Ibid., 419, 2.

282, 15–16: Ibid., 5.

282, 16–17: Ibid., 417, 6–7.

282, 20–21: Ibid., 419, 9.

282, 28: Ibid., 422, 2–3.

283, 5–12: Ibid., 423, 18–25.

283, 24: Ibid., 27.

283, 25–26: Ibid., 26.

283, 26: Ibid., 423, 27–424, 1.

283, 30 – 284, 1–2: Ibid., 422, 23–25.

284, 3–4: Ibid., 424, 16–17.

284, 6–7: Ibid., 423, 27.

284, 10–11: Ibid., 156, 10.

284, 12–13: Ibid., 12–13.

284, 15–22: Ibid., 14–22.

284, 27–28: Ibid., 164, 19–20.

285, 12–13: Ibid., 421, 2–3.

285, 14: Ibid., 4.

285, 18–21: Ibid., 4–7.

285, 26: Ibid., 17.

285, 27–29: Ibid., 22–23.

286, 7–21: Ibid., 422, 3–16.

286, 27–28: Ibid., 23–24.

287, 2–4: Ibid., 423, 7–9.

287, 5–6: Ibid., 16.

287, 11: Ibid., 25.

287, 12–13: Ibid., 22–23.

287, 17: Ibid., 27.

287, 20–21: Ibid., 424, 2–3.

287, 24: Ibid., 9.

287, 25–26: Ibid., 10–11.

287, 27: Ibid., 11–12.

287, 28: Ibid., 14–15.

288, 5: Ibid., 15.

288, 6: Ibid., 12–13.

288, 7–8: Ibid., 12.

XV. Veiled Splendor

289, 7–8: Franz Kafka, *Briefe 1902–1924* (Letters 1902–1924), ed. Max Brod (Frankfurt: S. Fischer, 1958), 180.

289, 16–17: Malcolm Pasley, ed., *Max Brod, Franz Kafka: Eine Freundschaft* (Max Brod, Franz Kafka: A friendship), vol. 2, *Briefwechsel* (Correspondence) (Frankfurt: S. Fischer, 1989), 160.

290, 6–7: Kafka, *Briefe 1902–1924*, 181.

290, 27–31 – 291, 1–8: Franz Kafka, *Nachgelassene Schriften und Fragmente* (Posthumous writings and fragments), vol. 2, ed. Jost Schillemeit, in *Kritische Ausgabe* (1993), 127, 20–24 – 128, 1–8.

291, 15: Pasley, *Max Brod, Franz Kafka*, 199.

291, 16–18: Kafka, *Briefe 1902–1924*, 202.

291, 21–27: Ibid.

291, 29–30: Ibid.

292, 9–27: Ibid., 197–98.

293, 2–3: Pasley, *Max Brod, Franz Kafka*, 202.

293, 6–7: Kafka, *Nachgelassene Schriften*, vol. 2, 606, 8–10.

293, 17–26: Kafka, *Briefe 1902–1924*, 203–4.

294, 6–8: Pasley, *Max Brod, Franz Kafka*, 190.

294, 12–15: Ibid., 195.

294, 19–20: Ibid.

294, 23–24: Franz Kafka, *Tagebücher* (Diaries), eds. Hans-Gerd Koch, Michael Müller, and Malcolm Pasley, in *Kritische Ausgabe* (1990), 831, 1–3.

294, 29–30 — 295, 1–10: Franz Kafka, *Briefe en Milena* (Letters to Milena), eds. J. Born and M. Müller (Frankfurt: S. Fischer, 1986), 36.

295, 14–15: Kafka, *Nachgelassene Schriften*, vol. 2, 35, 5–6.

297, 18–19: Pasley, *Max Brod, Franz Kafka*, 245.

297, 25–26: Kafka, *Nachgelassene Schriften*, vol. 2, 113, 11–12.

298, 2: Maurice Blanchot, *De Kafka à Kafka* (From Kafka to Kafka), (Paris: Gallimard, 1981), 64.

298, 12–13: Kafka, *Nachgelassene Schriften*, vol. 2, 115, 2–3.

299, 2–3: Pasley, *Max Brod, Franz Kafka*, 302.

299, 4–10: Ibid., 312.

299, 16–17: Kafka, *Nachgelassene Schriften*, vol. 2, 124, 3.

299, 17: Ibid., 124, 5.

299, 21–22: Kafka, *Tagebücher*, 863, 16.

299, 24–29 — 300, 1–3: Ibid., Komm, 204.

300, 21–31 — 301, 1–16: Pasley, *Max Brod, Franz Kafka*, 282–83.

301, 10–20: Ibid.

301, 21–23: Kafka, *Nachgelassene Schriften*, vol. 2, 128, 16–18.

302, 6: Ibid., 17.

302, 10–14: Ibid., 124, 5–7.

302, 15–16: Ibid., 2–3.

302, 27–30: Ibid., 129, 12–15.

303, 17–18: Ibid., 132, 8–9.

303, 19–20: Ibid., 11–12.

303, 22: Ibid., 15.

303, 26–27: Ibid., 21–22.

303, 27: Ibid., 16.

304, 8: Ibid., 127, 12–13.

304, 10: Ibid., 12.

304, 12: Ibid., 119, 16.

304, 15: Ibid., 127, 15.

304, 16–19: Ibid., 15–18.

304, 22–23: Ibid., 131, 18.

305, 4–9: Kafka, *Tagebücher*, 866, 12–18.

305, 18–21: Ibid., 831, 11–13.

I would like to express my gratitude to Timothy Rogers, who facilitated my consultation of the Kafka manuscripts housed in the Bodleian Library at Oxford, and to Maddalena Buri, who followed the final stages of this book with a wise and watchful eye.

A Note About the Author

Born in Florence, Roberto Calasso lives in Milan, where he is publisher of Adelphi. He is the author of *The Ruin of Kasch*, *The Marriage of Cadmus and Harmony*, which was the winner of the Prix Veillon and the Prix du Meilleur Livre Etranger, and *Ka*.

A Note About the Translator

Geoffrey Brock received the PEN Center USA Translation Award and the MLA's Lois Roth Award for his translation of Cesare Pavese's *Disaffections: Complete Poems 1930–1950*.